RIDING
IN THE
RUMBLE SEAT
A MEMOIR
E. ANNE POUNDS

RIDING IN THE RUMBLE SEAT by Anne Pounds

copyright©2024 by Anne Pounds

Print Book ISBN: 9798991053105

eBook ISBN: 9798991053112

LCCN: 2024913402

Cover and interior designed by Ellie Searl, Publishista

Muskrat Creek Press
Chadds Ford, PA

DEDICATION

O F COURSE, I DEDICATE THIS book to my dear and zany mother, Dorothy Elizabeth Wise Field Fech, who dug deep to make life beautiful for us in unexpected ways, and to my four dear siblings, who were along for the ride.

The rumble seat ride is a wild one, with the wind blowing in your face; but it's a ride I doubt any of us would have traded for a sedate one with seat belts buckled. I for one have always been so glad to be along for the ride.

Acknowledgments

I AM FOREVER INDEBTED TO my dear sisters Linda and Nancy for sharing their clear memories of events my mind had sealed off from the "bad periods" it was safer to forget, and I extend my empathy to my younger brother Danny for enduring many "bad periods" in which he was too often ignored for all the wrong reasons.

I am grateful to my late and taciturn big brother J. G. when, on several *rare* occasions, he poured out the contents of his heart in what began as casual conversations, knocking me off my chair with deep revelations of his seldom revealed interior thoughts on his experience with my mother and in our family.

I thank my friend Ellie Searl, who has been my loyal writing partner after we met at the Brandywine Writers Group in West Chester, PA, and whose insights, writing skills, professional formatting, graphic design and editing knowledge she has shared with me as we've written together — she is a multi-talented genius. I was lucky to learn that she has helped many authors bring their books forth through her Publishista.com business, and now she's helped me.

I thank my friends and family beta readers, who took the time to read the manuscript and help make it a better piece of writing: Ellie Searl and Bob Pounds (who also served informally as editors), Judith Lee, Eileen Sizer, and Rich and Edie Janik. Each contributed thoughtfully and with great heart.

I thank my beloved husband, Bob, who has never done anything but encourage and champion and care for and about me in every possible way. We have been business and marriage partners since we decided life together was too much fun to work apart from each other, and for several decades we've continued the crazy fun as sailing partners.

Since I am my mother's daughter, I caught the zany gene, and when I found Bob, I knew immediately it would be a wild ride through life with him—and so it has been.

Contents

CONTENTS

THIS WAS NOT THE BOOK I planned to write. Rather, it was the one I was compelled to write, as I struggled to decipher my mother's other life revealed through her scribbled letter drafts. It started as a lark, to see if I could find something funny she had written. I rediscovered her humor, but so much more I hadn't guessed.

The letters were rough to get through, even with a lighted magnifying glass, but as the tales unfolded, I found myself alone in my room laughing so hard the tears flowed, again and again. I thought I had heard all her good stories. How wrong I was—I simply had no idea she had this other life, one which was insanely funny and so touched with passion—and then so heartbreakingly sad. I've edited the letters when I couldn't decipher words, or to remove the side trips of the side trips of a compulsive storyteller to help the reader follow her story lines. I've changed some names to protect the innocent.

I have told her story with as much honesty and remembrance as I can. It's fair to say that it is both our stories. I include pieces of my story to reflect how she dealt with life's situations. As an undiagnosed ADD person, she often found herself barely keeping her head above water. When the water got up to her nose, humor was her breath of life, that breath which kept her alive.

Dorothy had the imagination and curiosity of a child, while she juggled the realities of being a suddenly single mother of three—

building a business out of thin air, making life with an abusive husband a hell of a lot of fun, raising a second crop of children, and creating a world of wonderful distraction.

To those who never heard of a rumble seat, the very last one was produced in 1940 by Chevrolet. A rough description of it is a seat which opened out on a hinge arrangement at the very back of a roadster, similar to a jump seat in a sports car, but totally separate and apart from the other seating in a car. It may have often been used for luggage, and it was considered a good "double date" car. Why that name? See if the story tells you the answer.

"TWO SILLY FADS PREVALENT NEAR the beginning of World War I were directly responsible for the pitiful condition in which I arrived in this world. The first was the fad for brides to weigh not more than 100 lbs.—just ask any small, but pleasingly plump lady from the age of 65 to 70 if she was always plump—she will proudly smile and say,

'Why bless your heart, I weighed an even 100 pounds when I married Jim.'

I am convinced that medical science should investigate this phenomenon— undoubtedly the rupturing of the hymen triggers off some hormonal change that leads to the life-long problem of obesity.

The second ridiculous custom was that of the 'secret pregnancy:' the first child arrived during the first or second year of marriage to the utter amazement of all who knew the young couple. This secret is known only to the pair biologically responsible, the lady's doctor, and her mother—if she lives nearby and is nosy.

Now this custom was carried out to a ridiculous conclusion in my case. My father, Dan Wise, had just returned from a very rugged expedition in Africa. He traveled up the Congo River and through the jungles in the most primitive way in a dugout canoe, often living on native food. At one point his canoe overturned, and he lost his food and all the gold with which he would pay for supplies for the next six months. He was as hard as nails, and quite stately from his pictures. And of course, not only longing for the woman he loved, but also for plenty of good home cooking.

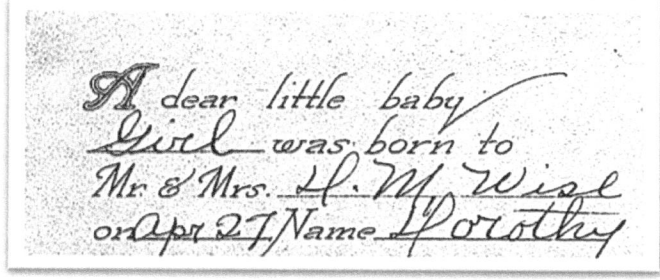

My mother, Lydia (nee Cranmer), was always slender; and she, too, had been working hard, teaching school, writing letters and learning to cook as a new bride. After the wedding in August the happy couple set up housekeeping in a nice apartment in Washington near where Dan worked. In satisfying his long-standing hungers for both aforementioned above, two things happened: I was conceived, and they both began to fatten up. Both parents come from South Williamsport, Pa; and in each family besides both parents, were eight children.

Well, they'd all come to visit the couple—and the Capitol—in twos and threes, with friends, so all reports were glowing about how both were blooming, but not a hint about the "little stranger" on the way: me.

My tiny mother switched successfully from apron to muff, so the lumpy mass of rapidly multiplying cells destined to be me escaped notice by all.

The hot water bottles borrowed from each apartment owner who lived close by worked: One hairless, nail-less, very underripe *[weighing two pounds]* female child arrived, in spite of Dan's desire for a robust son. Each time my head appeared during the birth process, he would mutter, 'It'll never live.' But 'it' did—although I certainly wasn't easy. I feel I must add that I was fed malt in a medicine dropper; and the chiropractic doctor, a lady who lived on the floor above, gave me a treatment every day.

I've often wondered if any of those borrowed hot water bottles helped my small spark of life to be guarded. I'll bet a few other sparks got started in the surrounding apartments, because by New Year's nearly every apartment had a new baby.

It gradually became apparent that I might make it. My nails materialized; hair began to sprout properly. My rib cage disappeared under a new layer of baby fat. In short, I got with it. My dad, satisfied that my mother could now be trusted to carry on, took off for some pretty harrowing adventures on the Amazon this time.

My life moved up a few notches. Mother took me to her parents' home in South Williamsport to wait out my father's return.

Now I had progressed from a tiny frame of opaque bones surrounded by pulsating protoplasm encased in incredibly thin blue-white skin to a plump little baby, beginning my life.

MY MOTHER WAS UP IN her bed again, the place to which she retreated when things got bad. After my father left, our house became very quiet, with my new baby sister and older brother now gone too. My family seemed to have disappeared. My mother spent

most of her days in her morning glory-flowered bedroom reading or sleeping. That Saturday morning when the doorbell started ringing, she was up there again, reclining like Blanche DuBois, asleep with her book open and face-down on the rumpled bed covers. She was younger than Blanche at thirty-one, but she had three children Blanche didn't have, and she was now wondering how to support them with her man having skipped.

Grandparents Lydia Cranmer-Wise and Daniel Wise with baby Dorothy

First came the milkman, with the Bond bread man right behind him. They always showed up on Saturday mornings to collect. The milkman delivered the milk and butter early in the morning but circled back later to collect. The Bond bread man sweetened his collection work by lugging in his giant tray of baked goods. At four years old, I remember welcoming the opportunity to make some thoughtful selections while my mother slept on in her deep depression. She was not shopping for groceries or doing much else either.

"She needs the powdered and the cinnamon donuts, some raisin bread with the icing on it."

With the two men still there hoping my mother would appear soon, the third man arrived in a business suit and carrying a briefcase, finding his way in behind the other two. "Is your mother home?" asked the man, who called himself Mr. Wilson.

I left Mr. Wilson and the other two standing in our downstairs hallway and went upstairs to fetch her. "Mommy, the milkman and bread man are here again, and another man who wants to see you." She reluctantly came downstairs in her wraparound flowered robe. She must have been embarrassed at not having enough money to settle her bills, and possibly to have been greeting a strange caller in a robe, but those days she hardly ever got dressed.

That day Mr. Wilson came, our lives changed. Strange men coming to the door was a regular event in the late 1940s, salesmen still a holdover of the Great Depression, and some who were suddenly unemployed returning soldiers, hungry for opportunity. They often brought interesting items, much of which my mother was later to sell as a door-to-door salesperson herself: shoes, dresses and jewelry, kitchen cutlery and pots and pans, windows and siding, clocks, Bibles and encyclopedias, Fuller Brush, produce, butter and eggs—even vacuum cleaners and evaporated milk. Saturday mornings the lucky salesman might also find the man of the house home.

So there stood Mr. Wilson, smiling just like Willie the Worm, from an early children's TV character which I only thought of later, since we did not have television in 1947.

Mr. Wilson waited patiently while she dispersed the two other men with small sums, after which he benevolently launched into telling her about a wonderful way to experience health and make sure she got the nutrients she needed in her diet. Mommy listened politely, chuckling. "Fascinating . . . ", she said. I found out much later that when she said that word, she was really saying to herself, "Bullshit!"

She encouraged him to go on, with the first grin I had seen from her in a long time. Her sense of humor had seemingly disappeared overnight after my father left. I don't know what she was thinking, but maybe she was smiling because he was an unusual looking character. She wasn't quite laughing at him, but maybe she was conjuring a good story about him to be retold later.

Mr. Wilson dove right into his elaborate pitch. He explained how difficult it was to get the essential vitamins and minerals—little things called Essential Food Factors—just from eating ordinary food now grown in chemically fertilized soils since the discovery of ammonia as a useful fertilizer ingredient.

"If it isn't in the soil, it isn't in the plant; and if it isn't in the plant, it isn't in the food. We're growing food with chemicals now, containing just three elements, nitrogen, phosphorous and potash, but we need all the other elements which are now missing. Our foods need to be supplemented," he gently informed her.

The next part I remember vividly. He brought out a gold-rimmed plate with a sheaf of wheat in the center and laid out little piles of actual grains of whole wheat, then the bran, the chaff, the farina and the wheat germ; and he said each time, with sad emphasis, "This is fed to cattle."

"Fascinating," Mommy said, looking interested. Maybe she meant it this time.

At the very last, he got down to the one lone component of wheat, white flour. "This is gassed to extend shelf life." Then he said with great emphasis: "Even rats won't eat this, but it makes up to forty percent of our diets today. If it's white, get it out of your sight." He smiled the benevolent smile.

Mommy finally seemed aware that she was still in her flowered cotton robe, as she pulled the shawl collar across her chest so her ample bosom wasn't quite so forthcoming. She had been leaning into the presentation and spilling out somewhat. My young mind felt a twinge of guilt: everything I had selected from our Bond Bread man's tray seemed white except for the raisins.

From there, on a second plate, Mr. Wilson performed a similar ritual with sugar cane. No nutrients left there either. By now my mother had come alive. She sat up straight, clenching her jaw in thought, gazing in a concentrated way out of the side of her half-closed eyes. I felt a palpable change happening.

He finished up with a flourish. "The crowning glory of the Nutrilite formula," he revealed, "is the Nutrilite Concentrate, which supplies the EFFs." He spoke of it as one might of the Holy Grail.

In the postwar era few people had heard of or thought much about food supplements, a radical idea. My mother and her contemporaries were all busy thinking about how to use Jell-O, Betty Crocker cake mixes and Campbell's soups for inventive casseroles. Alphabet soup casserole was a miracle in itself — canned soup added to hamburger — what could be easier? Everyone was entranced with the idea of squishing the yellow color capsule in the margarine ". . .so much healthier than butter," people said. Health concerns seemed to be overridden by convenience, interesting packaging and novelty.

When Mr. Wilson came back several days later, Mommy had a lot of questions. She sparked up for the first time in months — a touch of her old self, and my own first sense of assurance in a while, too.

Of course, I don't know what she was thinking. If I could guess from my adult vantage point, it might go something like this, but I don't know for sure:

Could I finally free myself. . .find a way out of this endless housewife prison I've been in? A new beginning? A way to keep my family, my house? Maybe I'm glad he left.

AFTER A FEW MONTHS, I would guess, it seemed my father was gone for good, taking off with Marie, one from his stable of women he tried on for size before making his final selection. It wasn't until decades later that we discovered he had married her.

Now Mommy needed to find her financial and emotional bearings. She had three little children and was alone. Possibly to enable her to start this new venture, she made a decision of which I was unaware at the time. Two of us three children, Linda and several months later, J. G., were sent to her Aunt Esther to be cared for, in Williamsport, PA, five hours away. Aunt Esther was a registered nurse and was looked up to for advice in child rearing. Linda, still an infant, was too young to be my companion; my only sense was that she wasn't around. It might have become clear to the adults in the family that my mother

*Our glamorous mother
Dorothy Wise Field
in about 1941, age 25*

couldn't care for an infant with a brace on both feet connected by a bar in the middle to alleviate her club foot, while finding a way to

support herself and her little family. Linda had to be carried everywhere till about age three. Sometime later, J. G. was also sent to Williamsport. Linda later told me she lived in Williamsport for about a year. I am not sure about J.G.

Both of Mommy's parents had died suddenly and recently, within six months of each other. My grandmother had a congenital heart illness, and my grandfather contracted meningitis which started with a severe earache and ended his life about one or two days later.

Beautiful French Aunt Janette

Our uncles enchanted with new nephew J.G.'s first steps

We lived in a pretty Cape Cod house on the corner with a bay window on one side and a pretty side porch with French doors into the living room on the other side. We had a big side yard. There were big old trees and fieldstone steps and walls leading to our back yard with a yellow rose climbing over a lattice fence and arbor, where

my mother hoped I'd be married. Purchased with a small inheritance from Mommy's father, this home was where she and

Grant started their married life. Now her quest was figuring out how to save her family and our home.

Over a span of time I was too young to identify, several of Mommy's siblings and their spouses alternately moved in to help Mommy stay afloat—who wasn't floating at all but was sinking.

With their family home now gone, our home was available, and Mommy needed the help. I'm sure her siblings also worried how she was going to survive on her own. With no real business training, she turned back to some of her former hobbies, attempting to convert them into paying enterprises. When my father left in 1947, almost every woman who was married stayed at home and raised a family, as she had vainly tried to do. She was no good at the wifely role. Hobby projects and volunteer work were what women did, in addition to church and club activities. She had had a checkered "career" of artsy hobbies as a housewife and mother, but none were for profit. All started but not finished, one after another seemed to always be "temporarily" set aside for another new interest. Later, as I matured, I observed these activities allowed her a pattern of regularly escaping the boredom of housewifery. She was always one who sought the side road to see what she might find. She was a random number, a wandering generality, to which no probability theory applied.

The Field grandparents we never saw again

"Don't anybody touch these pieces in the china closet; they're not glazed or fired yet, and they're very delicate," she would instruct. Her delicate hand-built pottery pieces were beautiful and almost museum quality. Unglazed and unfired, they were finally broken during our tea parties— as she moved on to the next project which interested her.

That next project happened to be designing unique hats. In the late 1940s, both men and women wore hats when they went out, especially to special events and church. Men took their hats off when entering a building, but women did not. Women's hats usually had some netting, maybe a few feathers, or artificial flowers or fruit.

Mommy was crazy about fabric and trim. If she found a bargain or a beautiful pattern, she tended to buy the whole bolt. Our family cedar chest still contains some of those fine fabrics; for instance, cashmere of an uninteresting pale beige—but so soft and hard to find. Surely the right project would reveal itself at some point. Batik print to turn into a luau outfit…black taffeta for an elaborate Halloween witch's costume…silk organza for my wedding dress. "Look at this beautiful fabric I found," she'd say. Eyes half-closed, her face a study of intense focus, she would wrap the fabric around me and envision a dress, a jacket, a bathing suit.

Her hats were of her own novel design, and clearly something no one had thought of before! She could corner the market, and her ship would come sailing in.

"Here. Put this on and hold still."

Mommy had a definitive way of telling you what you needed to do here and now. Her commands indicated that, at least for the moment, I had her attention, which happened infrequently. "Anne: Come here. Try this on."

"Nobody will wear one of these except you," I thought it best to inform her. Before or after he returned from Williamsport, J.G. and I may have at our young ages realized she was going "off the track" again and tried to discourage her from launching yet another unlikely project. We were getting used to being hungry, and hope was fading.

The hats were structured in colorful felt as elasticized square bags to be pulled onto the head, which could be contorted into an infinite number of styles. She would shape these things on her little models endlessly, making elaborate folds and pleats and swirls. She would circle slowly like Coco Chanel would, thinking deeply, then tucking, folding, and rearranging. As she tucked the fabric, she would tuck her chin in abruptly, which indicated deep thought. Maybe she'd add a hat pin for a decorative touch. I still remember J.G. shifting from one foot to the other with one of these hats on his head.

The felt hats were relegated to our cedar trunk, along with her fabrics and my grandmother's delicate silk trousseau lingerie. The silk unmentionables had a blood stain at the crotch, which made for proof of her virginity and were as fine as gossamer, imported from the Philippines by my grandfather. That the blood was never washed out of the garments speaks of times going back to Queen Victoria herself!

These intricately hand-stitched garments held a world of exoticism for us — that this reportedly stern and humorless man would have ordered such intimate garments for his bride in Victorian times reflected a passion never expressed in his many diaries during his explorations abroad or in family stories told about him. Many of the trousseau items are still there, in the same cedar chest, now holding a lamp in my living room.

In 1932, the year my mother graduated from Palmyra, N.J. high school, The Great Depression made college for most young women of the middle class not possible. In the buildup to the crash, my grandfather had been entrusted with friends' and family members' investment funds, now all lost. He had no funds for his children's college as he struggled to pay his trustees back.

Women were to find a good man to marry and settle down to raising a family and housewifery. School beyond high school was often "finishing school" for young ladies of the upper class, where they learned manners and dancing skills, I believe. As young women with their dictatorial father foretelling their futures, Mommy's sister Harriett went to secretarial school. Mommy attended Mrs. Eldridge's (or Mrs.

Somebody's) Dress Designing School in Philadelphia. She proved to be a skilled seamstress and designer, always sketching ideas for clothing. No real work of this type ever materialized, however. Once she married it was no longer necessary—or even practical— to think about working.

These attempts to convert her creative skills to income production happened in a few desperate bursts of activity shortly after Grant left. In between "projects," Mommy seemed to continue spiraling down. I had never seen her like this, hours at a time in bed reading. As a little person, I only felt a growing sense of unease. Mommy's children seemed to have become an afterthought, a state we would learn over time was not totally temporary. In between her escape bouts she was desperately trying to assemble her new reality.

Mr. Wilson and his nutritional supplements brought the change. While she began to focus after that experience, I was still struggling. In the fall after Grant left—we always called my father by his middle name, I don't know why—I began kindergarten, which should have been wonderful. Miss Early's classroom had a larger-than-life wooden giraffe, little mats on which we could lie down while we rested, and a cozy area where we sat cross-legged on the floor while our buck-toothed spinster teacher read stories to us. Snack time featured tiny glass bottles of pulpy orange juice and waxed-paper packages of graham crackers, neither of which I was getting at home, but which now didn't interest me at all.

I was miserable and only wanted Mommy. I could not stay— what if she, the only one of my family left, disappeared too? Each morning I assessed the situation and saw that I needed to get home quickly. But I had to be accounted for first. I developed a regular strategy which sometimes worked. After roll call I would sidle into the cloakroom and hide behind a coat, waiting for my moment to exit the room, like a burglar. After I assessed activities had begun, I would dash the two blocks to home to make sure she was still there. "Step on a crack, break your mother's back," I would repeat to myself, being oh-so careful to avoid those cracks as I ran home the several blocks now free of the sanctimonious safeties with the Sam Brown belts and the crossing guard in her cape. I needed my mother so badly, and preferably without a broken back.

There were other times Miss Early noticed I was not in the group. How I dreaded her entering the cloak room and poking around the coats and jackets to discover me.

"Anne, come on out and join us for story time, won't you?, Miss Early would coax me. "You are not allowed to go home on your own, and you need to stay in school. I didn't see a need to respond to her, just that urgent need to get home quickly.

Only recently my sister and brother unveiled to me their separation periods. Linda as a tiny baby was sent to Aunt Esther first, then apparently about six months later, J. G. was sent too. Linda stayed the first year of her life, and J.G. stayed about six months. Over time and as I grew up, my brain had gently erased my memory of the reasons for that stark period of loneliness. Then images began floating in: me sitting in a corner of the living room all alone playing with little rubber dolls, nuts for those little rubber babies who became my replacement companions. Under our big pine tree, I had my rich fantasy world, recreating it the way it should be. I dug roads and tunnels and brought my babies to life. Under that tree and in the corner of the living room, I tried to erase my sadness; they and I had perfectly normal happy lives where all was in order. My strongest memory is that of feeling terribly alone.

Dear Mrs. Field: Anne is having difficulty in our classroom and her anxiety is causing a problem. I cannot keep checking to see if she is gone, and she cries if I don't let her stay in the cloakroom. Can you please talk to her and tell her she must stay in the classroom when school begins? If you need to discuss this, please call at your earliest opportunity after the school day between 3:30 and 4:30 p.m. Thank you, Miss Early

First grade brought no improvements in me, except I finally understood I was not to leave. I simply took to putting my head down on the desk and sleeping. Doctors checked me for rheumatic fever or scarlet fever. I became skinnier and skinnier. I allowed no one to touch me or try to comb my knotted long hair. I used the hair to hide, and the messier it was, the less I felt like a person — which perhaps was my goal. I was lucky because my first grade teacher was Miss Yerger, who stuck with me through second grade. I didn't show much improvement or increased interest in either grade, but she was tolerant and patient.

I knew my mother was worried, but no one really knew what was wrong. Looking back, I can guess that I , too was deeply depressed at the terrible turn both her and my life had taken. And I still didn't know why my siblings were gone.

I NEVER SAW MY MOTHER cry the day our father left. In fact, I never knew she ever cried — until decades later when I found her letters. She was not the type to show her emotions — unless it was tears of laughter from one of her own funny stories or jokes. But on that day, she wasn't laughing.

It might have been about six months or a year after Grant left when we entered the Delaware County Courthouse and took stairs to the second-floor hallway. I was thrilled to spy my father across the hall standing next to a large pillar. His head jerked sharply toward us when we entered the hall. I was sure he saw us, but he turned away. He was in deep conversation

My father Grant, holding his first-born, J. G. on our stone steps

with a man dressed in a dark suit and felt hat. The man carried a fat briefcase. The shiny floors reflected images of unhappy people.

Mommy held tightly to my hand and would not let go. I felt her tension run through me like electricity. My big brother, two years older, seemed to know not to run to him.

I didn't understand. I was so happy to see him again. Why didn't our father come over to us? Why didn't he pick me up and swing me around, calling me Daddy's Little Princess? He had been away for so long! Today we seemed invisible to him.

My father still wouldn't look at us as we all entered the courtroom for what I learned later was a divorce hearing. Mommy, gripping my hand, turned toward the right side and got us seated, one of us on either side of her and my baby sister Linda in her carriage. Grant sat apart from us with his lawyer on the other side. I yearned for him and felt sick about this new distance.

The father I loved had turned our lives upside down. A few weeks after the divorce hearing, my mother had taken us again to his lawyer's office in Media. The lawyer simply shrugged his shoulders, palms turned outward and shoulders hunched, and told her he didn't know where Grant was or how to find him. Still she didn't cry, but I could tell she was tired, discouraged or angry. Fear was overwhelming me. She trudged the half mile home from the Shadeland Avenue trolley stop, dragging us and pushing Linda's carriage.

Her low mood turned to rage in an instant as we arrived home. "Stop!" She screamed. "Stop!" You can't do this!" She ran toward my father and began hitting him. I had never seen her or my father doing anything like this. Very much later in 1976 I learned through a lame and untruthful letter he wrote me, that he had "gone on the lam," as he put it, because my mother was suing him for child support. He and Marie took off with a small house trailer and "laid low" in Arizona.

On that day our father stopped for just a moment, taking the blows wordlessly. He was holding a heavy piece of furniture he and another man were loading into a big truck. Our front door was open. The truck was nearly full of what had been our home furnishings.

Defeated, she watched him throw the ramp into the truck and hoist up the tailgate. She shouted as he climbed into the truck, "You're not going to get away with this!" She had quickly gotten control of outrage as she realized the falsity of her utterance.

I knew the other man. He worked at my father's gas station. The man got into the truck and started it up. Grant climbed into the other side. He looked forward, keeping his window rolled up. I somehow knew he wouldn't be saying goodbye.

My brother, as their first-born son, had been given Grant's name. We called him J. G. after "John Grant."

J. G. told me recently what he remembered that almost-last day Grant was in our lives—aside from one brief appearance twenty-two years later. J. G. had stopped up the street to play with a friend as we walked home from the trolley stop. As the truck drove up our street, our father had his friend stop the truck when he saw J. G. He rolled down the window and called over his namesake.

"Son, I'm going to be away for a while, and I'm going to miss you. I'll be writing you, and we'll see you around." The letters never arrived. Nor did anything else until fourteen years later when he mailed a package containing a football to J. G. at the orphanage where J.G. lived at the time—the football, a request of him our mother had made.

Many times after that day, J.G. and I pondered over our father's disappearance. Had we done something wrong? Did he miss us? Would he call? Would he ever come back? Would he write? Would he send Christmas gifts? Birthday cards?

We couldn't ask our mother. I believe that day was the last time my mother ever spoke of our father to us. I don't remember her even saying my father's name again. Somehow, without words, she made it clear to us youngsters that this topic was not open for discussion. Today I can imagine her bitterness, but then it was a part of the mystery. We never saw our paternal grandparents or aunts, uncles or cousins again until we found each other decades later. At age 27, she was on her own — except for their three little children. It was what our father would later call "a clean break."

When my father left with the furniture, Mommy went to the priest at St. Andrew's, where she had gone through the pre-marital steps of converting so she could marry a Catholic. Now she was desperate for help. Later she told us what the priest's advice was: "You made your bed, now lie in it." When my mother told him how dire her situation was, he summed it up: "Well, now, that's your problem, Mrs. Field, isn't it?" Women who've lived through the 1960s or earlier have heard this stock answer to any of those messy dilemmas, which seemed only to apply to a woman: bad marriage, spousal and child abuse, cheating, gambling or alcoholic husband, out-of-wedlock pregnancy — even a baby IN wedlock arriving before the critical nine months. But worst of all, a mortal sin and sin against the Church: d-i-v-o-r-c-e. We became Lutherans again, rushing back to our home church just a half block away from the Catholic church.

Chapter 4 – A Clean Break

ABOUT TWENTY YEARS LATER, WHEN Grant accepted an invitation to my brother's wedding, we saw him again. It was a festive time with the wedding happening the next day, but he requested to take us three out to lunch so we could "get reacquainted." We were so apprehensive about meeting him again that I remember literally shaking with fear—or was it anger? Strangely, it felt to me like being on a first date with somebody you already know you are madly in love with but strangely knew ahead of time it wouldn't turn out well. I couldn't have said why I felt anticipation—I should have hated him by then.

My father Grant as I remember him

He used those words he felt so comfortable with: a "clean-break kind of guy." That day before the wedding we were having lunch in a favorite place of his, the Media Town House, where we had never been. We had hardly been in any restaurant, ever—we grew up poor.

We met him there. He drove up in a white Cadillac with red and white Florida plates. The genteel Black man who greeted guests at the door addressed Grant personally. "Well, well, well, Mr. Field, how nice to see you again," he gushed. Grant greeted him with great warmth. We stood quietly by trying to puzzle this one out, but it got stranger yet. Grant ushered us three offspring upstairs—as if we were having a perfectly normal pre-nuptial celebrative meal—to a private room with a reserved table and pointed out with a grin the chair engraved with his name, where he sat down. This was a puzzle. His own engraved chair? Wasn't he an out-of-towner? Those questions got deduced as the afternoon wore on.

The bigger unanswered question loomed large in each of our minds. We had rehearsed many questions, going over them several times with each other, as we wondered what we should tell him about us, or even what he would want to know. He hadn't indicated in any way that he needed to know anything at all about us for several decades.

That big question was why did you leave? Whatever had caused it was our big mystery. We'd never heard his side of the story—nor any story at all from our mother. So now was our chance to ask.

My brother J. G. and dog Laddie

"It was my lawyer's advice: leave the state and make a clean break." The unfinished rest of the sentence we had finished in our collective minds over the years went something like this: " ... if I didn't want it to get awfully expensive in support payments, college tuition, medical bills—all those things which get in the way of a good time."

He presented his legitimate "excuse," such as it was.

"I could never get a clean ironed shirt out of her, or a regular meal. She just wasn't able to give me what I needed." That part made sense to us; neither could we. But somehow it didn't seem enough.

For some reason he strangely went on to describe to us almost as a confessional the following: "I had relations with some of our neighbors and friends.

"Do you remember Mrs. Powell on the opposite corner, from us? Well, her. And Dottie Duck; she and I carried on for awhile. There were a few others, and gradually things fell apart."

Linda and I excused ourselves to the restroom, where we both tried to get over our nausea. Here, finally, was our father, the man we had longed for all our lives.

Over the years growing up without him, there had been certain tidbits passed on to us children, mostly from my mother's sister, Aunt Harriett, who didn't think much of Grant. She'd told us that she had heard, as part of his "getaway plan," that he had secretly sold his service station business in East Lansdowne, part of which he had borrowed from Mommy's Aunt Esther in Williamsport, and used the money to start another married life in southern Florida with his new woman, whose name was Marie. He also put a mortgage on our house. They'd added a new daughter named Susan—she was ten years old when we briefly met her the next day at my brother's wedding. He introduced her proudly to us before the wedding in the vestibule. "Kids, this is my daughter Susan. I thought it was time for her to meet her brother and sisters."

She didn't look like us at all. I don't remember any conversation between any of us and her. But I will never forget how sick I felt, even then as an adult, as I saw him put his arm around her fondly during the wedding, a proud father.

I had always been pretty sure Mommy had believed he had left the state. Most of those years he was only ten miles away. Maybe she knew, or maybe she didn't. I found his Kennett Square address in a small address book among her letters years after she died.

After lunch he drove us out to the tiny historic district of Hamorton on the edge of Kennett Square in Chester County to show us his authentic Chester County fieldstone home built in 1865.

"See that, kids? That's a real antique working windmill, and it's been around as long as the house has been here. Over here is where we had the garden for vegetables, and I don't know if you remember, but we used to have rabbits, and I kept rabbits here too."

He was working at impressing us with his success. It fell short, as I remembered the lump in my throat when the steam shovel began tearing up what was our big yard and ripping out the barberry hedges with its teeth. He told us he had created a successful business selling real estate and eventually building beautiful custom homes in Chester County while he enjoyed his new little family. Later he retired to Florida, he told us, where he played a lot of golf. The restaurant we were lunching in was a favorite spot he often frequented during his Chester County years; thus, the engraved name on the chair and the staff's familiar greeting.

Grant generously paid the tab. We were stunned. So close, and we never knew. But now we didn't care, either.

My shadowy memory from when he was still with us is that of us as a happy family. My father had been the star of the football team in high school, a handsome and tall man at six feet, five inches. Many decades later, he sent me every yellowed newspaper clipping with his name underlined wherever it was mentioned in the sports coverage (as if to validate himself as our hero). Included was his handwritten letter describing how he had NEVER missed a support payment, how my mother had had him thrown "in the pokey" for six months till Marie came with money and bailed him out, and how tough it had been on him for those years—we knew otherwise. He made a few mistakes in his web of lies, and he thought he could get away with his attempt to redeem his name, waiting till six years after she died.

My mother was also tall, a glamorous blonde who had done some modeling in her late teens, against her stern parents' wishes. Both my parents were gregarious, and friends often came to our home. When Grant came home from the service station, I remember having fun with him. He'd let us tousle his dark curly hair, which he groomed with his "bear grease," actually Vaseline. He'd growl and pretend he was a bear, and we would ride on his back and grab onto his slippery hair and laugh and laugh. Pretty soon my mother would think about making dinner. At four years old, I adored him. My day began when he walked through the door, full of fun.

The new wife Marie wasn't so new to me. I never saw her again once he left, but she was one of the nice ladies he and I would happen to meet on Sunday outings to Woodside Amusement Park. Those occasional Sunday morning outings were a great treat for me, because they were an alternative to the long Latin mass at St. Andrew's. I must have known even as a child to keep my mouth shut about where we went instead of church. We were playing "hooky."

Mommy, with her staunch Lutheran tradition, was a reluctant convert to Catholicism and hardly approved of my father dragging me to Sunday Mass instead of Lutheran Sunday School. Our forays to the park were an education of a different kind, however. At the park we would meander along the pathway and just happen to find Marie (or another "old friend,") sitting on a park bench by herself, smoking a cigarette and enjoying her quiet amusement park Sunday morning.

"Honey, you remember Marie, don't you, our friend from a long time ago?"

Of course, I didn't. It was always a "happy surprise" to my father to come upon these women as we made our way to the kiddie rides. Instructed about keeping our hooky-playing a secret, I came to expect the next reward: a stop to my father's gas station where I got to pull a scratched greenish bottle of Coke from among the chunks of ice and water in the cooler. I see now that the stop to the business proved to be not only the perfect excuse for extending Sunday absences beyond church hours, but also an apt setting for some private time with his woman of the day.

"C'mon, little Miss Anne, I'll show you how I fix a tire over here." Or "sit yourself right up here on the fender while I take off this carburetor." I remember one of his employees would entertain me with all things interesting about cars and their internal workings. I didn't think about what occupied my dad while the hired help kept me busy.

MOMMY BEGAN TALKING ABOUT NUTRILITE to everyone she knew.

"Mr. Wilson is helping me learn how to sell Nutrilite. He says I simply distribute 25 of these brochures a day called "How to Get Well and Stay Well", then come back to answer questions and get people started on it on the other days. I feel wonderful, and I'm going to sell it. May I practice on you?" To herself, I believe she was thinking, "And I'll buy wholesale!"

I can't say how long after Grant left that Mr. Wilson knocked on our door, because it was a fog of sadness for her and me. But this I know: The sales presentation Mr. Wilson did that morning he came to save Mommy worked a charm on her. Mommy ordered a box containing two slim jars of gelatin capsules filled with the smelly stuff which was to change our lives. One was the miraculous Nutrilite Concentrate, and the other contained minerals and vitamins.

I don't know how she paid for her supply, because I remember not having much money to even buy food. The product was expensive, at $19.95 for a month's supply for one person! When she could, she got me taking some daily, too. When my siblings were eventually returned home from Williamsport, they too were given it. I remember opening the capsules and mixing it in applesauce to give to Linda in her highchair. She made a pucker face like the first time a baby tastes a lemon. But she got used to it. Mommy taught J.G. and me how to swallow the pills down with milk, (usually dried skim milk, reconstituted, a real money-saver) which we did three times a day most days. And Mommy ate it herself, of course. Mr. Wilson had carefully instructed her:

"You never say "take it," like an aspirin, but you "eat it," because it's food — and the most important item on your grocery list." It was just <u>like</u> taking an aspirin, but the bottles held a place of honor on the table — along with the rest of the *food.*

How many times I heard and said that in future years. And how many times I wished for some real food, like normal people. I know she did her best, but food preparation wasn't her strong point when she was struggling with so many difficulties.

Our lives began to improve dramatically, to my young mind. Hope is very important to a small child, and I was quick to notice that Mommy got out of bed and began appearing with clothes on. She resumed talking and being fun, cooking occasional meals again, and telling *everyone* about Nutrilite. Mr. Wilson kept coming back with more Nutrilite; things progressed. These signs were that spark of hope for me.

She had never sold a thing in her life nor even thought about it, but her confidence in the product grew every day. Actually, selling it would have been the only way she could keep all of us on the product and growing healthy. Besides, I now know we were her so-called guinea pigs, the confirmation she needed to launch herself. I would take a guess that Mr. Wilson was probably fronting her the product in order to get her to sell it, but I'll never know. I would also guess Mr. Wilson was sweet on Mommy, but I don't think he got very far with her. I don't know for sure, but perhaps Mr. Wilson was a widower. He had two adult sons, one of whom was a silent man who managed the inventory and stocked shelves with the few products, filled orders and shipped products and said very little to anyone. The other son was what would be called a lunatic at that time. He built rickety wooden steps covering the entire three-story Victorian house in Prospect Park, reaching every window and winding in every direction. He never spoke or was spoken of at all.

After being on Nutrilite for a while, I began feeling pretty wonderful myself! I got bouncy and happy, having recovered from my first grade's sleeping sickness and being promoted right on to second grade — this had seemed unlikely until Nutrilite showed up in our lives. I started participating in school activities. By the beginning of third grade I was a happy "A" student, though usually late and often having forgotten my spelling book. I loved school, fell in love with Tommy Rheimer, who looked like a squirrel and was about a foot shorter than I. All of it was a clear confirmation of the addition of Nutrilite — and hope — to our lives.

The would-be dress designer with no hope of pursuing her field in Drexel Hill, PA with three small children and no car, had found a light on the horizon!

Ah, yes . . . no car. She would have had to begin on foot, in our adjacent neighborhoods. And so she did. Then one day she uncovered a bonanza:

"Look what I found! Joannie Carr is throwing this thing out, and I'm going to resurrect it and expand my territory." Distributing her literature on foot proved to be quite limiting. Mommy had trash-picked the old iron bicycle from our neighbor across the street, a heavy monstrosity almost too weighty to hold upright. I remember that day she and I walked the bike the mile to Dietz's Bicycle Shop.

"You'll need new tires and inner tubes," Mr. Deitz said.

"Can you please put a basket on the handlebars, and do you have a hand pump to fit somewhere on the bike?" She was discussing the magic carpet to her future!

I still have that hand pump downstairs in our work room. We picked up the repaired bicycle about a week later, and it now allowed her to expand her canvassing beyond our middle-class neighborhood into the more upper-class parts, doing her drop-off and pick-up routine of the 25 "How to Get Well and Stay Well." It was soon evident that she was effective in relating her missionary zeal into making the sale. Of course, she was even more able to uncover the "live ones" than Mr. Wilson ever was, making every encounter a unique experience for her prospects and her. My mother had a depth of interest in everyone she encountered that was rare, and she lost herself in her mission to help them achieve the health she had found.

Everywhere she went she told the Nutrilite story, forsaking the bike and walking if she couldn't get a babysitter, with us two children and Linda, still wearing her brace, in the baby carriage. I have spent a good portion of my life hearing this presentation — or sitting in her car waiting for her, when she graduated to four wheels later. Once we had a car, we'd be on the way to the swimming pool, with us children waiting sometimes for hours for her to emerge from the house into which she had disappeared for a "quick delivery." We knew the drill and always had books to read.

The number of customers grew, and so did Mommy's territory. Soon she was getting regular help watching us and expanding her bicycle route to communities four and five miles away. Her "inventory" of the square green and white packages was stacked up in the linen closet of our only bathroom, usurping the towel space, the enema bag, diaphragm, and the raggedy "washrags," as we called them. We were all healthier, happier, and hopeful.

There were still periods of anxiety, I am sure. But even in her most difficult moments, Mommy didn't share her fears, anger or failures; there was a palpable resoluteness we saw in her far-off look through half-closed eyes and the Clench, where her bottom teeth would slightly overlap her top, and her lower lip would curve out just a bit. It wasn't anger; more dogged determination with resoluteness and a positive energy. It was the first time in her life she had found a purpose and a direction. She started calling the Double X boxes "gold bricks," and she never left the house without a few bricks, stopping and talking to everyone, everywhere. I can't begin to know what she was thinking, but if I had to guess, I'll bet it was something like this:

> **Ohboyohboyohboy, I'm on my way! I'm getting free! (now breaking into song as she leaps to one side and clicks her heels together) Whoopsie Doodle, I've lost my noodle. . .**

Yes, she expressed that kind of joy in odd moments. I observe now as an adult that she must have felt like she escaped prison: the prison of meeting the 1940's expectations of a housewife and mother and now building independence for herself and her family.

Her charisma charmed people, who listened, loved and bought. She poured herself into her sales work. Much of her charisma got used up in the marketing effort, but what she had left we scooped up in fragments, at our bedtime sessions. She would always be sure to tuck us in, say that prayer which certainly befuddles children, "Now I lay me down to sleep, I pray the Lord my soul to keep; If I should die before I wake, I pray the Lord my soul to take." I used to worry every night that I might not wake up and my soul would be gone.

And she'd sing to us in her off-key voice,

> **Oh, Mareseatoatsanddoeseatoats,**
> **and liddlelambseativy,**
> **akiddleeativytoowouldn't you?**

She read to us often from a vast collection of fairy tales, inherited from her literate family's library. We seemed to have every good story! First she read them to us, then later, in our bad times when she married again, we read these fairy tales to ourselves to distract from the reality. We had Aesop's Fables, Tales of Hans Christian Anderson, The Brothers Grimm—so many wonderful stories.

Ahh, those fairy tales and stories . . they gave us confidence, hope, inspiration and life lessons.

MOMMY WAS A VORACIOUS READER: but as her career in Nutrilite sales grew, she began veering away from novels and classics and turned to a new genre, eager to expand her knowledge of nutrition. She began by digesting Gaylord Hauser's LOOK YOUNGER, LIVE LONGER. She became one of what he called "My People." His "Wonder Foods," blackstrap molasses, wheat germ, yogurt, powdered skim milk, and brewer's yeast entered our lives in a big way. Our daily breakfast was blended in the *Osterizer*.

MOMMY'S PROTEIN SHAKE OF 1949

- Raw milk mixed with powdered milk for extra nutrition
- Nutrilite protein powder (the product line was growing)
- Corn oil (for smoothness and soft skin, digestive health)
- wheat germ
- brewer's yeast
- a raw egg (adds protein and a rich taste)
- sweetener of blackstrap molasses (Gaylord said it was loaded with nutrients)

The Concoction was usually shoved at us in a huge glass about five minutes *after* we should have been seated in the classroom, a ten-minute walk from home. We were perpetually late for school.

"Here! Drink this down," she would demand in her imperious way when she was impatient. This drink, the only breakfast we got, was swallowed down with an ever-increasing number of pills as her knowledge of nutrition increased. Some of the pills were chewable, so we would run to school with a mouthful of minty calcium tablets, which tasted like chewing blackboard chalk.

However, the results were in. We felt better and better, and so did she! Other aspects of her health program, such as her morning ablutions, expanded as well.

"Anne, bring me that bottle of corn oil from the kitchen," she'd request. She rubbed herself all over on an alternating daily basis with either corn oil or apple cider vinegar. Her ritual now seems ironic, as I now rub myself down after showers with my extra-virgin coconut oil and drink apple cider vinegar, both for immune function and energy increase.

Her next guru was Adelle Davis, whose four books Mommy acquired, pored over and annotated: *Let's Have Healthy Children,* *Eat Right to Keep Fit, Let's*

Several of our mother's new "Bibles" with her many annotations

Cook It Right (real life-ruiners for us, those books formed the basis for the Bad Food Era). Davis railed against white flour and white sugar, processed foods, pesticides and food additives. She promoted supplements and natural foods. Mommy fired the Bond bread man and began making her own delicious whole wheat bread. A slice of that with peanut butter and honey on it did a lot to help us recover from the loss of the white powdered sugar doughnuts.

Next was *Let's Get Well*, also by Adelle Davis, who was considered a food faddist and looked down upon by the American Medical Association and the Food and Drug Administration. I still have that well-used book, full of her notes in the margins as she studied and "prescribed" supplements to her customers. Much of it is so relevant today.

She claimed the medical industry was becoming wary of the impact of good nutrition on their future revenues. "The AMA doctors and the FDA are in cahoots. The doctors are getting worried that people won't be sick enough if they do all this health stuff," she pronounced. This new field of nutrition was catching the medical industry by surprise, and its missionaries like my mother were making wild claims and cures.

A psychiatrist might have described our mother at her lowest moment when Grant left as having gone through extreme depression. Maybe the same thing was happening to me. Adele Davis, on the other hand, might have pronounced:

"Dorothy is simply depleted of the anti-stress vitamins B-complex, especially B-5 and vitamin C. These vitamins are water-soluble and quickly depleted in times of stress. She can recover in a matter of days and should start immediately on my Anti-Stress Formula: 500 mg of vitamin C, 100 mg of pantothenic acid, and two mg each of vitamins B2 and B6 with each meal, between meals and every three hours during the night when awake. Additionally, half a teaspoon of inositol, five mg of folic acid, 50 mcg of biotin and 300 mg of PABA." Or something pretty close to that. And she would have started her on her Pep-Up drink and had her do it around the clock. A lot of her nostrums were around the clock, so you had to be waked up frequently for your dose.

But almost all of that good stuff was in the Double X, and it seemed to make miraculous changes as Mommy became a charged-up saleswoman whose confidence in her abilities and energies was increasing by the minute. Her good looks and designer clothes, which were rummage sale and thrift shop finds re-purposed by her designer skills, aided her ability to engage everyone she met. She looked interesting, and she was very interested in talking to anything that moved! The conversations invariably turned to health and nutrition — and Nutrilite Double X, and her missionary zeal would lead to the placement of yet another "gold brick" from the linen closet. Every gold brick sold would lead to increased monthly revenue from repeat customers who couldn't live without their Double X either. Gradually she developed a successful customer base.

As Mommy became a convert to Dr. Jarvis, author of *FOLK MEDICINE: A VERMONT DOCTOR'S GUIDE TO GOOD HEALTH*, she began having us drink apple cider vinegar, which was really only a teaspoon in a big glass of water. We refused the rubdown with corn oil and/or vinegar, because one didn't smell pleasant after a day or two; and we only had a bath weekly, if then.

Brewer's yeast began appearing in her luscious Gaylord Hauser whole wheat bread — our staff of life. Gradually it began to taste "polluted" to us. Something had gone wrong and we didn't know what. But when she started experimented with brewer's yeast in our homemade birthday cakes, she had trespassed on sacred ground. We let her know by boycotting her bread and the rare cakes. Not always attuned to fine details, she got up to sixteen uneaten loaves before she noticed we wouldn't eat it anymore.

Foot reflexology became a part of the repertoire, and since we got just the one goodnight hug and kiss per day at bedtime prayers, the massages on our feet were a sign of her love for us. She always found those sore spots — a sure diagnosis of whether our livers, kidneys and gall bladders were functioning. We were some of the rare children who even knew we had those organs. She would massage and poke till she found a hot spot. "OUCH!"

"Aha!" she would proclaim happily. "You need more *[insert corn oil, liver, calcium, etc.]*".

Adelle and Gaylord played a big role in expanding our daily supplement regimens as we chewed those hated calcium tablets, swallowed the whopping tablespoons of cod liver, castor and corn oils, and downed Nutrilite Juniors: a lesser version of the XX at a lesser price, but still containing the magic Concentrate.

Mommy had developed her marketing pitch to a fine point.

"The breadwinner of the family should always be the first one to get Double X if the budget only allows one person in the family to be on it," was the pitch. This was a wonderful guilt-inducing method to get everyone in the family going for the whole meatball, at least for an initial "health recovery period."

"When one first starts ingesting Nutrilite, there can be what we call "health reactions" as the body adjusts to this new zap of nutrients — sort of like a rebellion. You may get a cold, find yourself intolerant to foods you've loved, etc. And soon you will feel better than you've felt in ages." If customers had one of these health reactions, they got excited, because they knew good health was on its way — just as she had foretold.

And of course, the Nutrilite company began introducing additional individual supplements as new discoveries in nutrition were made at a dizzying pace. Strange as it seems now, it was not that many years before the late 40s that pellagra, rickets, beriberi and many other scourges were found to be "curable" and eliminated totally by the addition of certain vitamins and minerals.

Soon we were gulping 31 pills with the morning meal — which would be that protein milkshake — and lesser amounts at other meals (Her mantra was "start the day with a breakfast fit for a king." I imagined that somehow a king's mealtime was more interesting than this regimen.

Mommy began subscribing to a magazine called Prevention, and to read it was to think the authors were bordering on the edge of insanity — as it seemed Mommy was becoming, in our young estimation. It was one crazy radical article after another, and we used to read it aloud and hoot with laughter when the Prevention magazine arrived each month.

Today, all that "insanity" has long come home to roost and can be found in the whole foods movement: organic gardening, composting, sustainable agriculture, raising goats for digestible milk, chickens who ranged freely, and so much more. It was all there back then, in that seemingly wildly absurd magazine. The publisher and founder, J. I. Rodale, based a lot of his material on his own experimental work at the Rodale Organic Gardening Experimental Farm which he had begun in 1940 or so, and which we went to visit (of course). Mommy was no gardener, but she clearly believed that since Carl Rehnborg was on the west coast doing the same sort of experimental organic growing, using earthworm farming, composting and manure fertilization to raise the crops for Nutrilite products, she and we and her customers were getting all the benefits of an organic farm in those tablets we all swallowed three times a day The lessons were firmly ingrained:

"If it's not in the soil, it's not in the plant. If it's not in the plant, it's not in your food." My mother repeated this lesson regularly, as she strived to make us into healthy eaters.

That period of the early 1950s was the beginning of a long and continuing era of fake or ersatz foods, where convenience and the foundation of America's now-rampant addiction to salt, fat and sugar was being built by the food manufacturers. There are whole generations of children who won't eat anything that doesn't come in a package. I've seen parents peel a hot dog, so their child will eat it — and that's all they *will* eat, along with maybe the orange macaroni and cheese "food." Today many people talk about "eating clean," and eating "real food." Some people knew about it all along.

Somewhere in the early 1950s, just as she was getting into the rhythm of her new venture, my mother and her Nutrilite distributors confronted a threat. They believed The American Medical Association was trying to put the Nutrilite people out of business. The AMA was apparently able to get the Food & Drug Administration "feds" alarmed to the point that the FDA people began literally "crashing" Nutrilite meetings and stalking the salespeople to see if they could catch them doing what only doctors were licensed to do: "prescribe, diagnose and claim cures." This, of course, is exactly what they were rampantly doing in their "pitches," and the FDA seemed to be out to get them and put the whole company out of business. It was the Senator McCarthy communist witch hunt era, and that atmosphere prevailed. That is not to say "Nutriliters" weren't a wild bunch, as I remember it, their pitches running very close to that of faith healers. I still have a piece of their original literature, "How to Get Well and Stay Well."[1] The distributors' approach to selling the product closely rivaled religious evangelism.

----

[1] From Internet site www.Amquix.info:

"'How to Get Well and Stay Well,' which represented Nutrilite as [being] effective against almost every case" of allergies, asthma, mental depression, irregular heartbeat, tonsillitis, and some 20 other common ailments. The booklet, which contained testimonial letters, also implied that cancer, heart trouble, tuberculosis, arthritis and many other serious illnesses would respond to Nutrilite treatment.

After Mytinger and Casselberry, Inc. [the distribution organizing company and the first multi-level marketers in history], was asked by the government to show cause why a criminal proceeding for misbranding should not be started, the booklet was revised. A 'new language' was devised which referred to all diseases as 'a state of non-health' brought about by a 'chemical imbalance.' Nutrilite would cure nothing—the patient merely gets well through its use. Most direct curative claims were removed from the booklet, but illustrative case histories were added. Although continued governmental pressure led to removal of the case histories, the booklet remained grossly misleading.

After citing them and with the appearance of the new booklet the FDA began citing them right and left and made eleven product seizures. The FDA's plan was to make enough seizures to where they would have to either do something to correct the violation or go to trial. Mytinger and Casselberry filed suit against the FDA for the multiple seizures, and to enjoin the FDA from making seizures, claiming that Mytinger and Casselberry was proceeding in good faith and that the agency was harassing them and making these seizures to run them out of business before they could have any chance to make the necessary corrections.

In the end the whole issue was disposed of by a consent decree dated April 6, 1951. It ordered the corporation to refrain from distributing Nutrilite accompanied by specified articles, books, pamphlets and a motion picture, or matter which implied that it would be an effective cure for approximately fifty-four specified diseases or conditions, and from making other specific representations in writing, printing or graphic matter in promoting the sale of Nutrilite. The decree set forth certain allowable claims which might be made as to the need for or usefulness of Nutrilite and stated that petitioners could submit to the Food and Drug Administration for inspection and comment, written, printed or graphic matter to be used in the future merchandising of Nutrilite. The criminal and libel proceedings were terminated on stipulation."

DESPITE THE EXCITEMENT OF BECOMING a successful saleswoman on a bike, she and we children still struggled with poverty. While she had very good success in selling her product, she was not very interested in recruiting a team of wholesale distributors who did the same, which is how fortunes are made in multi-level marketing plans. Nutrilite was indeed the first multi-level plan in existence. She just loved to sell the product.

Our fatherless lives had become quite scaled down, with still not enough money for the basics, even with her good sales. Grant, the school football star from the "other side of the tracks" in East Lansdowne—aside from his good looks and likable

The family home my mother worked to keep

personality, didn't seem in retrospect to bring a lot to the union. After several years of not finding a good job, he borrowed against the house and bought that gas station back in East Lansdowne, either as a partner or sole owner. So she had his mortgage, the taxes, and the expenses of feeding and clothing three children.

Whether the business was a success, the marriage was not. While we were too young to notice such things, Dorothy apparently couldn't pay attention to the details of running a household, and Grant was apparently systematically working his way through many of the ladies in the neighborhood.

His strange confession to us those twenty years later was his tacit excuse for his sexual excesses. He was shopping around, I realized later. "I wanted dinner on the table at five o'clock, and I wanted a clean house and my shirts ironed and hanging in my closet." These concepts we had to admit were not in perfect alignment with several of her key traits.

In a never-sent "spoof" letter to the wife of the man Mommy later fell in love with, she writes:

> **. . . Of course, I know how you feel. I remember how I felt when my first husband asked me for a divorce Our third child was only three months old. My whole world was shattered. My bitterness at this woman for depriving my children of their father made me quite capable of murder. The miserable unhappiness the children and I lived through at that time I would never wish on anyone. But I found myself, and I became a stronger person because of it.. . .**

Mommy's attempt to get Grant to pay child support became a moot point after he made his mysterious escape. Welfare and government help were foreign concepts to our stubborn mother. "I'll scrub steps before I'll take welfare" stated her position clearly. She was not "cut out" to be a housewife and could have also used a nanny to mind the children—which she found eventually, on her own.

When I was born in July 1943, World War II was happening at a busy pace. Over the next several months the Allies invaded Mussolini's

Italy and systematically took back control of the country. The war wasn't officially over until May of 1945, when I was almost two years old. I believe that sometime in this period of several years, shortly after Grant left in 1947, there began the procession of family helpers, starting with her siblings who moved in to help with the groceries and mortgage. Our home also gave her siblings a temporary nest during the immediate post-war years. With both their parents suddenly and recently gone before I was born, ours became the new family home.

My baby sister Linda at age three with her braces removed

Each of her three siblings did a turn with us, starting with Uncle Dan, who had just come back from the last of World War II. He had been stationed in France for some time after the war ended, helping to stabilize Paris, which had been decimated, and he brought back his new French bride.

He had snagged her right out of the Paris Opera House where she and her sister were young prima ballerinas. Janette was beautiful and vivacious, and Uncle Dan was handsome, though not particularly tolerant of his somewhat squalid living conditions in our home, and Dot's little brats.

Aunt Janette spoke only French, but when she would learn an English word it was still French to us, her accent was so strong. We fell in love with her and absorbed through osmosis some of what she and Uncle Dan loved about her home province of Normandy: Calvados brandy from apples, cream, brie cheese, butter and red wine, none of which had graced our deprived and Prohibition-like household — my grandmother was in the Women's Christian Temperance Movement, and remnants of alcohol intolerance still lingered.

I remember what I think was Aunt Janette's first Thanksgiving in America. In wartime Normandy refrigerators and freezers didn't exist. Aunt Janette was impressed with our used Kelvinator fridge. Honestly, post-war consumers in the U. S. were just graduating from the iceman's delivery of the block of ice for their iceboxes, too.

In preparation for the big meal, Mommy pulled a tiny Cornish game hen out of the freezer, brought it into our huge bathtub, and with a great flourish, set it in the bottom of the tub to thaw overnight. Using many hand gestures and a little French, she explained that this was yet another great American invention:

"Zeez leetle tiny bird. . ." She adopted her French accent when speaking to Janette, thinking it would somehow make the English easier to understand. ". . .weel become a beeg turkey! Tomorrow morning you weel have a beeg surprise!"

Next morning there was a 25-lb turkey in the tub. Our extended family had all chipped in to get the biggest bird she could find. Mommy was busily stuffing this huge bird. For some reason she thought the bathtub a good place to do that. Aunt Janette was sent in to see if she could help. She almost fainted with excitement and disbelief as she gasped and ooh-la-la'd at the "Americahn miracle." Mommy just smiled and stuffed.

Aunt Janette didn't cook, but she and Uncle Dan knew how to live well. He had risen in the Army to captain in the quartermaster corps;

and as saviors to France, all good things flowed to those military "higher-ups' after the war ended. But it was hard for Captain Wise to enjoy whatever booty he had brought back in our household, with three hungry children hanging over his shoulder and our mother irregularly tuned in to cooking dinner. He had a way of excluding us from the aura of the good life he created for himself. It was only several years ago that he told me that the family vacations to which I was sometimes invited as a mother's helper only happened because, in his words, "your mother always stuck you with me."

Earlier Uncle Joe, my mother's younger brother by about eight years, spent time with our family. He came when he was thirteen, after his parents died in about 1940, under the guidance of his guardian, who probably thought his being with family would be helpful to him. His guardian removed him from our household when he was about seventeen, apparently about the time I was born and when the relationship between Grant and my mother began deteriorating. I only know this because Uncle Joe only recently told me his part in our family. He was, and still is an endearing and warm person who easily fit in.

Later, Aunt Harriett, Mommy's sister, and her husband Uncle Bob moved in. Aunt Harriett was as serious and sensible as my grandmother was reputed to be, and quite a contrast to my mother's never-ending sense of ridicule. Uncle Bob, a Florida cracker, as he called himself, was a good ol' boy-turned-steel-mill-builder who was a fun-loving jokester. He also loved The Good Life. Mommy and Uncle Bob were good partners in fun. Mommy was introduced to good wine, cocktail hour, salsa and tango dancing, and pate'. Uncle Bob fixed everything broken in the house and taught us that life was fun. Christmas brought the sounds of real reindeer and their jingling bells on our roof and Santa stomping off snow before climbing down our newly installed chimney and fireplace. I suspected it may have been Uncle Bob up there but only much later. Every day with him was a thrill. "Come on over here and give us a big ol' hug, darlin'," he'd say; and we would, with delight.

Uncle Bob was about to conquer the post-war world, being sent all over the globe possibly on the government's dime to design and build huge steel mills in Yugoslavia, France, post-war Germany, Pittsburgh, Iran, and yes, nearby in Phoenixville, Coatesville and Bethlehem. Many years later, his work took him and his young family to Peru, where our grandfather had worked earlier as a field research scientist.

Uncle Bob and Aunt Harriet and their two children eventually went on to settle and live in Peru for seventeen years, becoming more Spanish than American, with a full staff of household help (cooks, chauffeur, laundress, housekeeper), partying and entertaining dignitaries as if Uncle Bob was the U. S. ambassador to Peru. Likely funded by A.I.D., the Import-Export Bank, O.E.C.D., or other vast international sources of "walking-around money," they lived like royalty.

But before all that glory, he brought life to our house and lots of fun at the same time that Mommy was seriously pursuing her business-on-a-bike plan. She was fully engaged in saving her home and putting food on our table.

Before either her sister or brother came to live with us, we went through the most difficult period, when she was on her own and her two children who'd been sent away were now back home. It was tough going, but at least we were together.

Considering her almost non-existent food budget, it must have been hard for her to produce good meals. Mommy had a kind of deal going with the butcher at the A & P store about a mile away: she could have all the unsellable or unsold offal and organ meats she could haul away, free of charge. This offer proved irresistible—and of great interest—to her, so our meals were often scary, centered around liver, kidneys, heart, and sweetbreads—which I loved till I learned what they were, pancreas gland. I could just imagine my friends at school if they would ever have known what we ate for dinner, or if my mother made me a sweetbread sandwich, which she had actually done a time or two. Also on the menu were tongue, brains, tripe, marrow bones, tails, hooves and pigs' feet. Head cheese (which was a jiggly mess of simmered pig's head parts and the resulting gelatin from this cooking process) fit in there somewhere, sometimes with a pig's foot or tongue thrown in. Mommy loved this revolting selection, but no child wants to eat or be near it. We often had tongue sandwiches with Coleman's English hot mustard. Tongue was really good, like ham, till I noticed the cow's taste buds and learned it was a tongue I was eating. Some of this stuff was squishy and weird; but most of it was tough and overcooked, the result of Mommy's high level of distraction. To that natural tendency, we would also need to add her continuing anxiety about how to keep our boat floating and being constantly on the phone working to make another sale or appointment.

"Ewww! What is this stuff?" we'd ask.

"Steak!" she'd growl through gritted teeth. "Just eat it!"

Our family dog nearby, who was always wise enough to park himself under the table at mealtimes, often helped us out. Since we never purchased dog food, the dog got the plate scrapings and whatever else he could rustle up on his neighborhood rounds.

A rather lusty eater herself, Mommy seemed able and eager to eat all manner of odd foods. You could say she was an offal buff. She really was too busy to cook on a regular basis, so on a winter morning if she didn't feel inclined to make sales calls in the freezing weather, she'd distract herself by occasionally making up huge batches of unidentifiable concoctions which appealed only to her, with what scraps she could gather from our friendly butcher. Somewhere she had come across a find she couldn't resist: an ancient Chambers stove with five burners, a deep well for frying, and a griddle top. It was her prize possession, to say the least. In addition, at some rummage sale she had also picked up a massive commercial pressure cooker which was scary as hell with her distracted tendencies. She'd get busy talking to a customer on the phone, and that giant pressure cooker full of a platoon's worth of, say, oxtail stew, would start building up steam, whistling, snorting and rattling incessantly at an ever-increasing pitch. One time it just blew, and the pressure regulator on the top hit the ceiling and embedded itself right into the solid plaster. The stew was a little burnt on the bottom, and since the cooker pot was too big to fit into the Kelvinator refrigerator (which was already full of leftover and never-to-be-eaten brains and kidneys and hearts), the pot would sit out in the unheated lean-to shed, where it would remain at a slightly chilled temperature suitable to an overwintering fig tree but not a month's worth of stew. There it was, ready to serve at a moment's notice to any of us who proclaimed hunger.

"There's oxtail stew out in the shed," she'd sing out when we came home from school starving hungry. "Help yourself," and dish me up some, too, please."

She'd be so pleased with herself that she had the forethought to provide such a hearty dish for her children.

I did actually fish around in the mess once to see if I could really find a tail. Horrified, I did — I didn't think she was serious until then; thought "oxtail" was a euphemism for something edible. It was so dangerously close to that old nursery rhyme about what little boys eat: " . . . snips and snails and puppy dog tails . . . ". I know this little girl didn't mess with tails.

Mommy did have a few good specialty dishes, though: * she made homemade waffles in our huge waffle iron with the striped fabric cord and the big fat plug which sparked like crazy and took courage to plug into the solitary electrical outlet. We knew that with waffles went ice cream. The catch was that before one got to the ice cream course, one had to complete the first course, creamed chicken on waffles, which was really quite good, with peas and her own white sauce. I don't remember eating many additional vegetables; she probably figured they were in the vitamin pills!

Aside from hearts and gizzards, ice cream played big in Mommy's frame of reference. At least several times a summer she treated us to the Dairy Queen where we'd each get a butterscotch-dipped small cone. And if it ever hailed, with a great flurry of activity, we would gather up the hailstones and break out the hand-cranked ice cream freezer and rock salt and make a batch of banana or peach ice cream. We didn't question why it had to hail in order to make ice cream, and I'm not sure I know today. We just always hoped it would hail when a storm threatened.

When we did gather around the dinner table, we had a rollicking good time. Our meals were long, because Mommy insisted that we Fletcherize our food, which is to chew each bite 100 times. "The enzymes in the food mix with your saliva and stomach acids, creating a veritable *symphony* of digestion. All the vitamins--co-enzymes—in the food can then be fully utilized, and when you add in the Nutrilite XX (and all the other supplements we were now swallowing), *miracles* occur in your stomachs!" She really worked this theme.

In the words of Horace Fletcher, whose theory made him a wealthy man:

> **"Eat somewhat less but eat it more; Would you be hearty beyond fourscore.**
>
> **Eat not at all in worried mood or suffer harm from best of food. Don't gobble your food but "Fletcherize"**

I imagine Mommy's parents encouraged her to Fletcherize her food long before our time. I still eat my food slowly today.

Her bread, raw honey and butter saw us through the difficult Offal Period. The wonderful butter was delivered by the same guy who brought the Walker-Gordon Dairies Certified Raw Milk a couple times a week. Everybody had a milkman then. The bottles came with a pleated paper top cinched onto the rim, and a circle of cardboard popped into the top. The lucky one got to take the top off and lick the thick cream, thereby introducing pathogens into what Walker-Gordon Laboratories had worked so hard to avoid without pasteurizing, since 1891 ("Milk Untouched by Hand from Cow to Consumer"). Our milk was regularly touched by human tongue, every time.

As an adult I can look back and feel sorrow for her with the hardships she was going through, trying to feed her family on an almost non-existent budget. But as a child, it was easy to feel like her victim.

A S GRANT WANTED WHAT EVERY man felt he was entitled to back then — an orderly house and dinner on the table regularly — he didn't ever have a chance of getting those meager requests out of Mommy. As a '50s housewife whose sole responsibility had been to be a wife and mother as in *Ozzie and Harriett*, she was probably an unconcerned failure. She was a beautiful blonde-haired blue-eyed woman, well-spoken and with a wonderful wit — but she was a random number. Dorothy was a hell of a lot of fun, the life of every party, but nothing ever happened the same way twice, if at all. Or just nothing ever happened, period. She lost her keys and her glasses at least once a day. She was always busy doing something else.

She made a better saleswoman than a housekeeper. Hence, the passing parade of people, propping her up gently, who came and went in our home. During these "post-Grant years," with her status abruptly changed, she lost many of their friends who were still couples. Perhaps she knew of some of Grant's affairs, but I don't know. But now in her divorced state, my mother joined a sort of pariah class of women.

She had two good friends who stuck by her. Her close girlhood friend Bernice had gotten herself certified in the Good Housekeeping Course for housewives for her big accomplishment in life; and she would show up on occasion, coming from her perfect and sumptuous home in Brown's Mills, New Jersey to donate her time and skills to the task of saving the marriage and to propping her up afterwards before its demise. Her husband Bob was president of the R.C.A. Victor Company and occasionally donated to our cause ornate albums of 78 records of the world's great classical music: Strauss, Handel's Messiah, Bach, Mozart, which we played to death on our little kiddie record player.

Teams of Bernice and her friends would plan a day or a weekend to clean up and get her organized, gently coaching her on how to set up the broom closet, organize the kitchen cabinets, do creative things with Jell-O, and other useful techniques for household harmony. Bernice made everything look easy.

"Dot, let's make a Jell-O mold for your salad course tonight—I brought the cream cheese and fruit cocktail with me."

"Look how easy it is to find your colander and pressure cooker now that you're all organized." " . . . doesn't the breakfast room look darling with your yellow roses as the centerpiece, dear?"

" . . . I found some mint next to the house—have you ever put that in your iced tea, Dot?" Yes, she did, all the time, in her defense.

". . have you ever used Guardsman furniture polish? It's the best for your antiques."

"Look how these beautiful windows sparkle now, children. You can do that now, can't you?"

I honestly don't remember any responses or ensuing results from Mommy, because I think she just didn't care about any of this. She loved beautiful things, but she was more into admiring the little touches in *other* people's homes than creating them in hers. She did take an avid interest in creating beauty in clothing design, and she was darned good at redesigning her clothing she bought at rummage sales.

Her other friend, Shelly, was from the neighborhood and lived the next street over. There were possibly some similarities that formed their bond at the beginning, but I am not sure how the friendship happened. Maybe it was the children who brought them together through school or the swimming pool, where both families belonged. Shelly had about four children to Mommy's three, and she later had a crop of three more to Mommy's two more. Shelly and our mother were both fairly messy housekeepers, but Shelly could really cook! She loved creating food. One of her regulars was chocolate-covered frozen bananas. She was Jewish and made some wonderful stuff. Over time their friendship grew in importance. I was close friends with Karin, one of her daughters, and sometimes stayed overnight at their house. Karin's bedroom was in the unfinished attic, and she drew wonderful horses on the walls, full-size. She could also play the piano, compose, and write poetry. She had rheumatic fever and seemed to spend a whole year in bed, which was so difficult for a young child. She had an older brother who would do unusual things like hitchhike down to the jungles of Brazil and other wild places collecting exotic snakes, which he sold. Their house always had an assortment of boa constrictors and other exotics. I remember when the boa had babies that got away, all over the house. A sleepover was always a unique experience at their house

At early ages we children became Mommy's housekeepers. Part of it was sheer survival, such as setting the table in the hope she'd notice and maybe start cooking. Another part was just her utilizing a resource: us. We would shine shoes for church, where we always seemed to arrive about five minutes before Sunday school was over — which meant we'd arrive in our shined shoes to see the projects and drawings they'd done, the flannel board showing Jesus at the Well or Moses in the Reeds, the little pumpkin candle holders they'd made, the candy canes they'd gotten. And plum assignments for the pageant would already be assigned.

The Sunday School teachers were always quietly disappointed in us because they'd missed the opportunity to teach us an important Life Lesson on the damned flannel board, that constant rebuke of our failings. I remember several snowy Sundays when we were all pretty little, our mother pulled us three to church on our big toboggan sled to make sure we got our weekly dose of Lutheranism. We were getting our own Life Lessons through the dogged determination she showed. She was stubborn.

When the bathroom was satisfactorily inspected, we would be free to go and play with our friends. Play centered around digging, constructing, inventing, playing school and house, making and selling flower- decorated mud pies with flowers stolen from our neighbors' gardens — they never seemed to get the irony of that, nor did we — the theft provided raw materials for our product, mud pies, which enabled us to turn a small profit selling their flowers back to them. We did endless things with roller skates and orange crates, finding money in gutters, storm drains and pay phones, popping tar bubbles in the street with our bare feet, hide-and-seek, jumping rope, and the wide ranging "let's pretend," which could take you in any direction at all.

Swimming was the mainstay of summer activity. No matter how poor we were, Mommy always managed (sometimes not till well into July) to scrape together the money for our annual pool membership at the Aronimink Swim Club, where our family held a charter member bond. My pale green laminated membership card was my ticket to heaven. Since we didn't have a car for the first years after Grant left, and the pool was about two and a half miles away, sometimes we walked with my mother pushing that baby carriage piled up with towels, black inner tubes, toy boats, occasional packed lunches of sandwiches in tinfoil, and homemade lemonade — and a baby or two. On those days, she would stay and enjoy the pool with us.

On as many days as she could persuade him, Mommy got the boy across the street, Mark Burns, to drive us. He had an old coupe or roadster of some kind with a rumble seat, and we would use up every inch of space in that car. I was usually sitting all the way back in that rumble seat, piled high with the black inner tubes and towels. It was fun back there in the rumble seat, but it was always clear Mark really didn't love the assignment. Mommy's tendency to find ways to give us fun without engaging her own time or energies became a symbol for our lives back in her virtual rumble seat as she cruised through life.

Later, when she started driving her own car, it was easier, except that she often made deliveries or sales calls on the way to the pool, with us sitting among the towels and inner tubes, enduring the interminable waits— sometimes hours. After the second hour, we would honk that horn just once every fifteen minutes, breaking her rule of "NEVER honk the horn when I'm making a sale."

Since the pool lifeguards were her babysitter, we did have periods where she attempted to get us there in the morning at eight a.m. for swim team practice. Truthfully, it didn't happen often enough for us to remain on the team, and it was the only sport I ever remember participating in. She would find a way to pick us up sometime after everyone else's dinner hour, when we would be waiting in the parking lot with the whole collection of pool stuff, exhausted and

Our summer days were spent at the swim club.

hungry. I never thought of her as cruel, I just sensed she had to support us and was always pursuing a sale or making deliveries.

She had not intended to leave us there all day — she just often did. We would leave the pool and scour the local streets looking for discarded soda bottles, each of which yielded two cents, the big quart sizes a nickel. Quart bottles were rare, because soda bottle size was six ounces at that time, and a quart of soda would have been a rarer indulgence at a family dinner.

A bottle redeemed at the snack bar would yield a pretzel stick purchase AND all the free yellow mustard we could load onto it. We came to think of mustard as one of the four basic food groups. The rare quart bottle purchased a Moon Pie, which to this day equates to a trip to heaven.

Mommy was a former champion long-distance swimmer herself—we had seen her high school medal. She taught us each to swim at about age 2, by throwing us off the edge of the pool and jumping in, holding out her arms and saying gaily, "swim to me!" with a lilt in her voice. And we did, never getting any indication that we should be fearful of getting water up our noses, swallowing, coughing, going under three times. Everything that happened was good, all in the normal course of events, as we floundered our way to her smiling self. We all became human fish, as at home in the water as on land. Our days were spent swimming underwater holding our breath for as many laps in an Olympic-plus-size pool as we could challenge each other to do. We had swimming races, contests diving off the three diving boards, holding tea parties at the bottom of the pool, building boats by lacing rope through our black inner tubes and diving for treasure, touching bottom in the ten-foot area, and leaving the pool to wade in the nearby polluted rivulet of a creek, always looking for the bottles, driven by our hunger.

We were genuinely hungry most of the time. Mommy had no money to give us for food. Welfare, food stamps, church assistance— none of that was part of our lives. She was tough and proud—and we were, too. Maybe a couple of years into her Nutrilite career, after she acquired a driver's license and wheels, she would often arrive at day's end, with the picnic basket filled with tuna fish or egg salad or peanut butter and jelly sandwiches, a pitcher of Hawaiian Punch and the colorful spun aluminum tumblers. "How about a Hawaiian Punch?"

we would shout, as we giddily punched each other with joy at the arrival of food rations, repeating the advertising tagline. We were like piranha fish in a feeding frenzy. Ah, dinner . . . my God, we starved so much of the day! And the amount of calories we burned off in one day with the constant activity contributed to the hunger.

When we did eat at home after the pool closed for the season, dinner was in our beautiful "breakfast room," which was a charming English-ivy wallpapered room with dark green wainscoting and chair rail. What she put on the table was another story.

MOMMY WAS BORN ON APRIL 27, 1916, a month before she was expected to arrive, under the sign of Taurus the Bull, which in retrospect seemed prophetic. Possibly it was her father's declaration during her untimely birth, "It'll never live," that made her such a determined woman. She was as bullheaded as can be when she made up her mind about something, which often led her into great trouble.

Just before her first birthday, My grandmother Lydia, with her little baby Dorothy, was preparing to travel on the United Fruit Company's steamship to join my grandfather in Peru, where he was stationed on a long-term basis after having set up an experimental weather station near Cuzco in the Andes Mountains of Peru.

According to Mommy and her siblings, he was a rather dictatorial husband and father, instructing his wife in great detail in a letter to her on how to conduct herself and her new baby on the voyage.

As the voyage was about to begin, the United States joined the Great War, World War I. The war completely halted The Carnegie Institute's studies and funding; and Grandfather Wise was called back to Washington, D.C. where the Institute was headquartered. Apparently the job ended, and they moved to Williamsport where I think our grandmother's family was located. I don't know what he did or where they lived in Williamsport during those years when Mommy was a young child, but she was eventually joined by her three other siblings to make a very typical family group. I do know that a close family friend helped him secure a good position as an engineer with AT&T, where he spent the rest of his career. The opportunity may have taken them to Palmyra, New Jersey, and then eventually to Drexel Hill, where they bought a lovely home on Mason Avenue.

Mommy was thirteen in 1929 when the stock market crashed at the start of the Great Depression. My grandfather, like many breadwinners, was no longer employed. He began selling insurance door to door, a miserable time for a taciturn engineer to be attempting such a thing. He was working not only to feed his family and keep a roof over their heads, but to pay back those friends and family members who had entrusted their funds for him to invest in the flush of prosperity that preceded The Crash.

When she was eighteen, in 1934, money was still scarce; and college was not an option for female members of our family. As a student at the dress design school in Philadelphia, her experience there exposed her to occasional modeling opportunities. Her first big opportunity presented her with a chance to model on a real runway in the Atlantic City Convention Center, where the new Miss America Contest was held. The New Jersey seashore beckoned to her; the summer vacations in Avalon had now eluded her family since the Depression started. My grandfather was strict and unyielding, and no daughter of his would be permitted to go off on her own for such a lark. But she couldn't miss this chance to get back to the shore and maybe even get a swim in the ocean.

Her good friend Bernice covered for my mother, and the story she told went something like this:

"Father, Bernice has invited me to spend the weekend with her and go swimming with her family at Brown's Mills. I can catch the train, and her parents will pick me up at the station. May I go?"

At this time, they lived in Palmyra, New Jersey, so the train station was in her friend's neighborhood. Instead of stopping at the station near where Bernice lived, her real plan was to ride on to Atlantic City, stay one night in a boardwalk hotel, and fund the stay with the small sum she would be paid for the modeling job. And that's what happened--almost.

The plot thickened considerably once she arrived in Atlantic City. She learned just what the show was and what she would be modeling: women's lingerie: girdles, brassieres, corsets, camisoles, and other unmentionables! Her father and mother would have been aghast. Grandmother and grandfather were Victorian types--unthinkable that a daughter of theirs would expose herself in such a crude manner.

The thought of walking down that long runway was an image my mother could not let go of, so she did what she had been subtly taught to do by her own mother's example when dealing with her overbearing husband: she simply made different plans. It was a thrilling experience to see how long the runway was and to be cinched into a lacy corset beribboned to the teeth, with lacy bloomers underneath. The shoes were very fancy white satin high heels with pink ribbons on them, it was the first time she had ever put on such frippery. Backstage they got instructions on how to do "the Walk," which was not totally new from the few other jobs she had had— but the length of the runway and the scantiness of her outfit was new, with an audience of professional buyers on all sides. In the orchestra pit was a live orchestra, which would perform music as the models walked, did their turns and pranced their way back to change.

No one could ever guess at what motivated Dorothy Wise to do the things she did; but it was always clear that she could not resist a good joke once it occurred to her. As she began her graceful walk, she decided it would be fun to throw in a series of slightly obscene burlesque gyrations called "bumps and grinds." The crowd loved it, which spurred her on — she did love to dance, and her natural abilities came out in the best — or worst— way. The orchestra responded and changed up the music to what one might have heard at the burlesque house on Arch Street in Philadelphia, and the audience responded by clapping her down the runway as she moved into the music. Dorothy was the star of the show!

On her second walk, she had almost reached the end of the runway for her turn, which she had already decided would be a series of "bumps" through the turn, when someone in the audience caught her eye. It was her father, sitting there big as life, the only serious member of the audience (which is perhaps why he stood out so easily from the crowd, now wild with the fun of it all).

Thus ended the Great Atlantic City Caper. Dorothy was met by her father backstage, who embarrassed her into dressing and leaving by the back-stage door. It was a quiet ride home on the train, and maybe the end of her modeling career.

This pattern must have been passed onto many daughters from their mothers in a world that still prevails somewhat today where there is still the subtle belief, "wives should be subservient." Headstrong women did not handle this dictum well, and it's possible her mother had schooled her in passive-aggressive techniques. In any case, I doubt if my mother was contrite about her lark. She just needed to plan better.

CHAPTER 10 – FREE AS BIRDS

IF WE DIDN'T HAVE NORMAL food, nice clothes and an orderly life, we sure had our freedom. Much too busy to manage our lives and hers too, our mother was gaining confidence in making money. Her new business really took off when she found that ancient bicycle. As she improved her pitch, she moved the needle by combining that with gumption. As our poverty gradually began to ease up, we children had new-found hope and security. By about 1950 my little sister Linda grew out of her foot braces and into brown high-top corrective shoes; and at last she was mobile at age three. Her best friend and mine were sisters, but Linda and her friend Peggy Addison were good little girls; Peggy's big sister Janet and I were adventure seekers, which often led to trouble. They sewed and made cupcakes; we rambled and caught snakes in The Woods.

I speak with reverence of these woods, that vast open space of several miles, with Darby Creek running through it all the way to the next town, Clifton Heights, where it meandered through a park with a working spring. This is where our lives happened, just two blocks from home—this Laboratory of Life where we learned biology, history, geology, science, cooking, the facts of life (there was always a privacy-seeking couple to spy on) and camp craft. We built dams, ice skated and waded, and caught salamanders and crayfish,. The riches to be found there gave us adventures every kid dreams of: the historic Indian Rock Basin, our own cave, campfires with cans of soup and beans to cook over the fire, The Bad Dugan Boys to provide the villains, real horses at the Drexelbrook Stables, where, as we got older, we worked hard to scrabble some money to ride the horses there.

There was also up the hill between the woods and the houses, a field full of giant boulders where we played cowboys and Indians. Along the creek on the other side was the record factory where we could rummage through the throwaways and bring home music we played over and over—the entire discard pile was of the same song, "Grandma's Lye Soap" and the flip side, "What Shall We Do with the Lonesome Sailor."

We also had the resource of the Darby Creek. Everyone knew that submerging completely would be a sure route to polio, especially there, in the polio-water areas. Almost everyone knew someone who had polio and was perhaps in an iron lung. It was a scary time. The rough Clifton Heights kids (where no one cared about polio, apparently) jumped off the trolley trestle and swam freely in the creek while we watched in awe. I learned just a few years ago from my older brother that raw sewage was pumped directly into these scum-covered parts of the creek. We always found what we thought were balloons, which we would blow up, wondering why so many people would throw away a perfectly good balloon. J.G. let me know they weren't actually balloons.

"Didn't you ever figure out that the sewers emptied into the creek there, he asked me. It hadn't occurred to me. We just knew to stay out of the water because of the scum that caused polio.

Right along the creek was The Girl Scout Cabin, where our troop met for meetings. It was built in 1638 by Swedish immigrants in the New Sweden Colony, now fully restored and called The Lower Swedish Cabin— likely the oldest building still standing in Pennsylvania.

Home from school, all we had to do was change into our "play clothes," and shoes, head off into the woods, and be back around dark or when we got hungry. Most kids knew what time dinner was, but we knew Mommy didn't usually think along those lines till her hungry kids showed up.

Life was rich in the great outdoors, but there was that other side to our lives: we regularly came home to our realm of fear. One of the most worrisome indicators that things were going downhill was the yellow sheriff's sale signs nailed to the front door. The sign could be torn down, and sometimes we did that to spare Mommy, but the nail defaced our pretty front door. Maybe sometimes she removed the notice to spare us, but it didn't change the reality that the wolf was always lurking around the door.

I can feel the ball of fear in my chest at this moment as I remember those signs. For a period we lived life in continual states of fear, partially from the constant sense of loss and deprivation, but also from something that I would only be able to examine as an adult much later when I had gotten help to overcome what dysfunction does to a child.

Mommy was a big believer in her "ship coming in" philosophy, but a stronger undercurrent existed: that something would come along to ruin the ship's course toward her before long. We never had a sense of security or relaxation. She unknowingly taught us to believe that at some point it would all come unraveled again—and she surely never realized this belief gripped her. Maybe it was a leftover that many experienced from the Depression, but, as little children, it pervaded our belief systems, and with some of us it remains today. When you live with your limitations long enough, they become your best friends and keep you safe from risk and growth.

One afternoon we came home from school to find her in a meeting at our breakfast room table—the place where we ate our meals when provided and the only space regularly cleared of debris—with two men who seemed overly enthusiastic and focused; and there were long forms laid out on the table, which they were having her sign. Her heart seemed heavy. There were no explanations provided by her or them. It was the atmosphere that gave us the sense of something gone wrong.

Later we learned what had made her seem so heavy-hearted. The enthusiastic gentlemen turned out to be "tin men," specialists who talked innocent and desperate homeowners out of not only their money (of which Mommy had none) but also the bank's money with some slick moves many homeowners didn't understand.

They were experts at "helping" suckers like her to get not only enough from the bank to complete the aluminum siding and splendid new roof she didn't know she needed, but also a handy sum to settle any miscellaneous liens, such as those from that sheriff. These liens (and lienholders) were possibly easily discovered at the county courthouse — from whence all our troubles seemed to originate.

Before too much time had passed, the workers were there banging on a shoddy roof and ugly siding. I remember at my young age sensing that the roofing material was cheap, thin and ugly. We soon had a new look that gave our home (and many others in that era) a tawdry cover-up of what had been real and lovely — a hand-troweled stucco finish. Oh, and she got the money to settle the tax liens against the house and keep the sheriff from nailing up those notices for a while. Further down the road, when things piled up again, there would be someone else helping her with another scheme to help keep that wolf away.

But the next chapter of our lives was a happy one for her and us, when Annie came into our lives.

M AYBE IT WAS THIS TEMPORARY flush from the tin men loan that ushered Annie into our lives. Mommy's business seemed to be growing, and she now had recruited a few distributors "under her," but our circumstances were still what would be considered chaotic. My mother was not a long-term planner, and yet in this one instance she showed evidence of thinking ahead to create a semblance of order in our household.

I think I was in about third grade when I remember going with Mommy to "interview" Annie in her little row home on the other side of town. "Massas Fatch, won't you come in?" she asked in her strong Irish brogue. Probably easily in her mid-sixties, Annie was very gracious and very Irish; but husband Alfred was cold and unfriendly.

Like all ethnic groups, Irish people seem to come in several varieties. Two varieties are charmingly lovely or handsome, and another is downright painful to look at with red faces, rheumy eyes and bulbous noses. Annie was of the second variety. She wore a self-belted cotton house dress that had no visible indentation toward the middle, thick flesh-colored cotton stockings, sensible stout black oxfords with a thick heel, and bobby pins on either side of her crimped whitish-yellow hair. She had gaps in her teeth, that nose I mentioned; and her face was badly pock-marked. Her husband Alfred had very sharp features, looked disapproving, and over many years never once came into our home or uttered a word to any of us that we remember.

In our lives, he was simply her ride when he picked her up. My mother usually made friends with everyone who crossed her path, but I'm not sure she even tried to break down his barrier, whatever it was.

Annie agreed to come to work for my mother at the unheard-of rate of $20 per week, 9 to 5, five days a week — a pittance of a salary even at that time for a full-time housekeeper. It was maybe one of the best moves Mommy ever made, and I think Annie made her decision to take the job out of pure sympathy for her. They were a childless couple, and maybe we provided Annie some children to love and care for.

Annie seemed to bring a cohesiveness to our household we had never experienced before, and I believe we each felt for the first time ever a small sense of security and regularity. She was an absolute gift to us children, and she loved us dearly. Annie actually stayed with us through my mother's next husband, to whom she adapted herself nicely — although my mother certainly did not.

Annie was stern but loving. If we got too rambunctious, she'd clap her hands together and shout, "Less, noise, girls and boys!" And we knew to quiet down.

The meals started coming regularly now, and order entered our lives. Annie began arriving earlier than requested to make us a hearty non-Osterized, solid-food breakfast, and we walked home from school mid-day daily for her famous and unforgettable lunch: a bacon sandwich (just bacon and lots of it) on lavishly buttered white toast (yes, WHITE toast) and chocolate milk. It was so very Irish! Alternatively, it would be grilled American cheese with grape jelly — quite good, I thought.

Ooooh, life was so fine. Mommy's only food-related role now was that of purveyor, and she happily deviated a bit from the innards menu with her out there bringing in more bacon and Annie doing the cooking. Annie did things with hamburger (at 38 cents a pound) and chicken, and sometimes she could talk Mommy into getting a roast or stew meat. We might have Jell-O or pudding for dessert, and it was almost like eating a real meal at our friends' tables. (We each had a friend whom we could visit for those "regular" meals.)

Whether it was the cash influx, or the beginnings of genuine gradual success we'll never know, as we were too young. But we know we loved Annie and the order she brought to our home.

WITH HER SUCCESS IN SELLING, sporadic as it was, the better life was coming into full bloom for Mommy and her children. Yes, we still bought our clothes at rummage sales and thrift shops, but Annie's presence in our lives increased Mommy's selling success, and she was opening new vistas.

I would guess that around 1949 we had a momentous change in our lives. Mommy acquired her first automobile, a 1937 Plymouth 4-door sedan with a gearshift on the floor, purchased for $25. She learned to drive it with some help from Mr. Wilson, who wanted to help her to increase her marketing territory. I have no memory of her learning to drive it, only that she very capably and cheerily made the switch from the old iron bike to the old iron car.

The iron bike, at first the vehicle of our freedom. became one of the big disappointments of my life. It happened at Christmas, and it was the year J.G. and I got bikes for Christmas—what every kid dreams of finding under the tree. I should say that our Christmas tree was usually procured by us children at approximately 5 p.m. on Christmas Eve, when the Christmas tree sellers in the stores behind our house had grown weary and were ready to wrap it up. We would haul home the best one left, and we'd quickly decorate it in time for Santa to arrive. That year, Uncle Bob and Aunt Harriett had come to stay with us again, maybe between steel-plant building assignments; and they were there for Christmas. Uncle Bob loved to fix and build. That year he took some leftover paint he had from painting an old car of his and renovated the bike as a Christmas present for me. J.G. got a brand-new bike with the push-button horn, and I got Old Ironsides. I could barely hold it upright.

Once Mommy began acquiring cars (they were frequently replaced), the world opened to us. Suddenly we were going everywhere! To the pool, the Dairy Queen, the grocery store, and then farther afield. She took us on our first family vacation to meet our distant relatives in Williamsport and surrounding areas — an epic journey. I had never met her family there up until that point.

First we visited our family matriarch, Aunt Esther, and our great-great Aunt Clara, her mother (who was too old to be considered the matriarch anymore but who had nine cats, lots of kittens, and who spent most of her time in a rocking chair chuckling at us playing with the cats and kittens). And Aunt Esther's husband, Uncle Luther, who had no hair, eyebrows or eyelashes, because he had been "gassed" in the First World War with mustard gas — a substance later developed into chemotherapy treatments, with pretty much the same results — except that none of his hair *ever* grew back.

This pedestrian experience in our very old relatives' home was so novel to us I can remember today how everything just thrilled us: the jars of homemade jams and jellies Aunt Esther served with breakfast, clucking and scolding if we didn't eat the crusts of our glorious white toast. About every two minutes or less, Uncle Luther would nod approvingly for no reason we could observe and say, "Umh-humph . . . umh-hmph." Always twice. He approved of everything. They were childless, and he was enchanted to have children around him. He operated a thriving bakery right behind the big old house and garden where Aunt Esther grew and preserved and canned everything imaginable. And the cakes and doughnuts just flowed! We had all the white flour and white sugar we could have dreamed of! As much as we wanted, whenever we wanted! Cream doughnuts, jelly doughnuts, pastries, cupcakes stuffed with cream and topped with sugary icing! If we wanted more, we just went to Uncle Luther's shop; and we could have anything we pointed at. And our Health Nut Mommy partook happily, as she was on vacation, too. We and she just totally abandoned Mommy's regimens for the time. I still remember the incredibleness of those white boxes he filled with cinnamon buns and Danish pastries to send us on the return leg of our journey — delicious wonders we cradled with appreciation.

As a bonus, the West Branch of the Susquehanna River flowed right by their backyard, and as boring as it was right at that point, sort of like a big canal, it was all a thrill to us children. We were having a vacation on the water! After Aunt Esther's, we stayed overnight at Mommy's Uncle Sam's place on their farm, again people we had never met before. Uncle Sam's two sons were in their late teens or early twenties, and they were as enchanted with us as we were with them. And why? Because in our very separate worlds, life had held so little for them and for us, and we were easily entertained. They walked us about and introduced us to sinkholes, a wondrous natural phenomenon to us suburbanites. And then they taught us something big: how to shoot a shotgun. My shoulder was black and blue for two weeks, but I was so proud that I had shot a big gun.

But the real wonder was the breakfast on the farm table at 6 a.m.: platters of eggs, sunny-side up, another platter of thick-sliced bacon from their own pigs, big squares of cornbread with butter Aunt Sara had churned, giant glasses of milk from their cows, toast from home-made (also white) bread, and jars of home-made preserves, pickles, jams, applesauce and something called chow-chow — all for breakfast! We of the Osterized protein drink breakfast regimens were stunned at the bounty and variety. But best of all, and I am telling the truth on this, CAKE at breakfast! Their morning meal was a farm banquet. Gaylord Hauser and Adelle Davis had not descended upon this household, and we enjoyed every minute of our rebellion. If the health gurus had already been dead, they would have rolled over in their proverbial graves. We were delirious with joy at the food we were offered, and we couldn't get enough of it. We just didn't experience such a bounty in our lives.

That '37 Plymouth was changing our lives, and this tiny experience of entering our relatives' lives for a short time was turning us into vagabonds. We all (including Mommy) wanted to be everywhere but home. Home was where the fears, the problems, those yellow notices, and the ordinary were. We had wheels!

Our next adventure must have made Mommy very happy. She secured a tiny little shack along the causeway into Avalon, New Jersey, which had been her family's favorite coastal getaway when she was a child, and where she and Grant had vacationed with their friends. This opportunity had been missing from our lives since Grant left.

Our place was a pretty rundown little abode, with a rickety old dock out to the tidal flats and smelly mosquito-ridden marshes. There were no sewage provisions in these little shacks, so the stuff was pumped right into the bay; and it was the smell we always sucked in as we approached the causeway and said, "ah, the Jersey shore — we're here".

Due to its location, Mommy was probably able to rent it week-to-week cheaply. In my memory, two things sustained our ability to push on and stay a little longer: clams and Gold Bricks. Her friend The Old Clamdigger had a little clam shack across the causeway where he both lived and sold clams that he harvested out on the flats, He told her there were big surf clams to be found on the beach at low tide where she could dig for them herself.

At the beach, Mommy seemed to become one of those water

fairies she was always telling us about. Her water fairies lived at the beach and could be seen only at dawn just where the waves turned their last turn. The bits of foam in rainbow colors she'd present as evidence they'd been there that morning. While we were busy finding the clams and popping the bubbles in kelp, she would forage on the jetties, snatching up and eating raw mussels--yuck, we'd say, at the yellow slime she'd slurp down. With delight she would find the little baby coquina clams at the tide line and wolf them down too. In between, with J.G. watching us two younger ones, she'd swim and swim horizontally across the waves in her lazy slow crawl. And we did find some big surf clams; we'd dig for them in the hope that we could stay and sustain ourselves on her clam chowder.

Mommy found she could sell her Gold Bricks on the beach just about as well as anywhere else. She looked good in a bathing suit; and she was adept at starting conversations. Most people ended up talking with her. Coincidentally, right after the weather and surf conditions of the day were covered, it usually turned to the topic of nutrition, and then Nutrilite. And she always had a box in her beach bag.

As for the clam chowder, she just substituted her pot of oxtail stew with the unending pot of clam chowder. Manhattan style giant surf clam chowder, tough as old tires, which we'd chew and chew and chew just to get it down. It was like eating a bowl of rubber bands. And a plate of Jersey "tomadas," with Hellman's mayonnaise, never refrigerated.

What we never got—and what I craved heartily—were the flounder filet dinners, the crab cake platters, the shrimp in a basket at the roadside stand you could smell as you drove on by. I just wanted to taste that shrimp, and have that basket right in front of me, with the red plaid paper lining, just once. Pizza did not really exist yet. Really—there were no pizza shops then. The clam chowder extended our stay for several weeks many summers. We understood the tradeoff and got it down grudgingly.

The times we had on the beach were when we felt most that we had Mommy to ourselves. She had worked hard to get us there, I am sure saving up some money. During our shore time she didn't have any deliveries to run around to get done, and she loved the beach as much as we did. We stayed until the sun set most of the time, and she was so good at playing with us and teaching us to be brave in the waves.

CHAPTER 13 – COULD IT BE ROMANCE?

WHEN SHE BECAME DIVORCED, MOMMY moved into an uncomfortable role among her contemporaries. I don't know how close it was to the mythical scarlet letter "A" branded on a woman's forehead branding her as an adulteress, but apparently being divorced was almost in the same category. While she *was* warming up to her growing independence at a time when the Independent Woman was considered a small boat adrift at sea, pitied by some, feared by others, that their own man might be stolen away, she went blithely along seemingly unaffected by what others may have thought.

Except one time when I happened to be with her. A divorced woman could halt conversations when she walked into a room, and that's what happened. It was a ladies' garden party in the posh part of Drexel Hill, called "Drexel Park." The homes were big comfortable rambling mini estates (not by today's standards). I know exactly where this specific home is, and I could take you there today.

"Let's get dressed up and go to a garden party my garden club friends are having," she said to me. "We'll wear hats and gloves and have tea and little sandwiches and cookies, and we'll see some of my lady friends I haven't seen I a while.

Mommy had been a member of this fancy women's club, and it was their annual June event. I was all for it, and we both looked so pretty. I even let her brush my hair, which I avoided as often as possible. I can still see the bluestone patio with the quintessential stone fireplace with chimney and built-in grate. The outdoor fireplace was the height of patio fashion; there was even a built-in section in the stone for the stack of firewood — people didn't use charcoal then. This was her first return to the garden club, post-divorce. I sensed I was going as her shield. We showed up with our fancy hats and white gloves, and it was a pretty day.

As we entered the patio, I wouldn't have been surprised if all the ladies dropped their punch cups and stared at us. They did stare, then one of the ladies broke the ice.

"Well, Dorothy! How wonderful to see you again!" As if she had returned from her grave. I don't remember how my mother responded, because she didn't usually miss a beat, but I had this uncomfortable sense that her greeting was going to be the total of what anyone said to Mommy. The women covered their discomfort by turning away and continuing their chatter. No one was speaking to us or doing anything to make my mother feel like she fit in.

"C'mon, honey, let's have a cup of punch, she said as she pulled me along with her to the punch table. We put a few sandwiches on our plates, which I remember thinking I could eat twenty of them; and we drank our cups of punch, after which she and I made our quiet exit without her saying goodbye. We were probably there for a total of twenty uncomfortable minutes. It was the only time, other than that time in the courtroom, when I can remember my mother seeming ill at ease.

Young children don't spend a lot of time wondering about whether their single mothers will find a good man. What I did observe is that Mommy seemed to have no real romantic interests in her life, which suited me. She was not exactly straitlaced, but she had a Victorian air toward romance. She seemed immune. To me, this was normal and good. We wanted no distractions from our gradually improving family life. We all wanted what we could get of her, all to ourselves. It seemed to me that any men who got around her became interested in her (were it not for the three young appendages in her life). The man who installed our new masonry fireplace (post-Tin-Men-money infusion, perhaps) was madly in love with her and wanted to marry, three kids and all; but she couldn't warm up to the rather solidly built and shorter-by-a-foot stonemason.

She did have friendships with men, though. For instance, there was Paul Lindsay, the hapless husband of Mommy's dear friend and hopeless hoarder, Ruthann. Paul and Ruthann lived in a little stone house on the gravel road along Darby Creek. The couple were interesting conversationalists and thinkers, lovers of good food, musicians and avid readers. But Ruthann was a mess of a higher order than our mother. While our place was mostly messy in certain areas, you could hardly get into their home, it was so piled high with reading material. Paul looked like a rumpled Scarecrow from the Wizard of Oz, always unkempt and un-ironed. Ruthann, who was an accomplished cellist in the Philadelphia Orchestra, was rotund, often unbathed, and frowzy. And Mommy wasn't.

Paul was a scientist, an engineer of some kind. J.G. remembers Paul showing him an invention he was working on called fiber optic cable, and he showed J.G. how light can travel around a corner through the cable, which contained many strands of round glass rods that transmitted the light. It's astounding to think now of how brilliant he was and probably how unrewarded too, for his genius. J. G., my taciturn brother, never told me this until a year before he died.

Besides his work, Paul also owned rental properties in Drexel Hill that were close enough to their home for him ride his bike to maintain them, his only mode of transportation aside from public transport. He biked everywhere he went, with handyman type tools mounted in a wooden box on the back to fix his properties. I often saw him on my own forays and always enjoyed visiting with him.

One day I saw his bike parked outside one of his rentals, which was a converted house with two apartments, one up and one down. Paul had been working on the upstairs one recently, so I expected to find him there. I must have been five or six at that time.

As I bounced toward the steps, though, I spotted Mommy's bike tucked under the steps. (That was still how she got around at this time.) Curious, I started up the stairs, but then I stopped.

I heard my mother moaning. Scared, I feared something was wrong. My mother was not a moaner. She so rarely showed signs of despair, I felt something must be terribly wrong.

I listened. The moaning accelerated. The she kind of whooped. "Judas Priest!" she roared. It was her ultimate expression of surprise. Maybe other people said "Jesus Christ!" But Mommy hollered "Judas Priest!" Something had happened. Was she safe? She didn't sound scared.

When I heard chuckles from her and Paul, I allowed myself to take a breath. It didn't sound like she was in danger. I somehow knew not to knock on the door. I crept back down and hid under the steps and listened. More laughter and talk from them, then more serious talk about whether he would leave Ruthann.

"You cannot leave her, Paul. She could not survive without you!" I was beginning to feel that it was time for me to leave. I sneaked away quietly, hoping my steps wouldn't crunch on the gravel. I never told anyone about it for some reason; and I never mentioned it to her.

Just this year, I asked J. G. if he ever thought she had had any "affairs."

"Just Paul Lindsay," he said. That's all he had to say. This subject had never been discussed by any us siblings, ever! I was shocked, thinking it was my secret alone. J.G. must have been seven and apparently as observant as I of our mother's activities.

Found in her letters:

> **January 2, 1970** *[almost three decades after the possible affair]*
>
> **Dear Dorothy,**
>
> **Happy New Year!**
>
> **I didn't send you a Christmas card and find that a sad lack on my part because you have been such a good friend—and so much more. I have a treasure of memories of you that are marred by the fact that I couldn't give you as much as you gave me. There must be a purgatory for people like me in the netherworld.**
>
> **I am "happily" remarried as you probably know, not to Ruthann. . .**
>
> *[the letter continues with a discussion of his girls]*
>
> **Love, Paul**

A S LIFE GOT EASIER FOR her, we saw Mommy's zany personality more often. She was truly funny, and everybody who wasn't the butt of her jokes loved her. Some people have higher levels of serotonin than others, and she must have been of that variety, or else how could she have kept such an upbeat attitude through so many travails? She made everyone around her laugh, and one never knew what silly thing she would do next to catch some innocent admirer or overly pompous person off-guard — but more in a gentle way or a private joke for herself.

I had often watched her just "be" somewhere, maybe enjoying people watching. She would beam at someone who interested her. Before long, as if to a magnet, that person would feel a pull. They might grin and ask, "What?" And she would continue beaming and say something like, "I noticed you're wearing unusual shoes, like me. I had mine molded to my feet in New York City in 1955, and I'm going to be buried in them. What kind are yours?" And off to the races, a conversation that might last for hours had begun.

As a young woman, she attracted a number of "perfect guys" whom she could have married, which we remember was the key point of becoming a young woman at that time. One of them was Charles Hubbs, or "Hubbsey," a handsome and fun guy who came from a good family and who was quite in love with her — until she embarrassed him beyond repair.

"It was my second date with Hubbsey. We were on a double date, and the other couple, his friends, were real stiffs. I decided to give myself a haircut. I cut off about two inches of my hair, and I stapled two bunches together onto cardboards. We were in a soda shop sitting in a booth when I decided it was time. I was wearing a pale blue short-sleeved angora sweater, so pretty it was driving Hubbsey crazy. I had inserted the cardboards with my hair stapled to them into the sleeves of my sweater, and when Hubbs reached salivation point, I yawned and stretched, the long tufts of blonde hair flowing out from under my sleeves. The stuffy couple were repulsed and horrified, and that was just the reaction I wanted. But Hubbsey was just as shocked. I thought he would get a good laugh."

Hubbsey probably thought it was the better part of discretion not to marry her. But she was not cured of these irreverent jokes and pranks.

As I thought over the years about how she and Grant met—a discussion we never had with Mommy—I have often wondered how they met and fell in love. She did say at one point that she was really in love with Grant's brother Art. My memory of them as individuals is simply that they were both full of fun, but I never assessed how they were as a couple. I feel that that memory was wiped out by the trauma of his leaving.

WE HAD ONLY ONE BATHROOM and no shower—just that great big tub. It took gallons and gallons of hot water to fill it. There was no lock on the door, which often proved an annoyance. Baths had to be scheduled. As youngsters, our bath was a communal affair, the Saturday night pre-church ritual, when we sloshed around and had a great romp.

The bathroom was also where we dipped our toothbrushes into Dr. Lyons tooth powder to clean our teeth. Other kids got to use toothpaste, but we were stuck with the economical powder. It was also where we scrubbed our faces nightly with the Fuller complexion brush and brushed one hundred strokes with the Fuller natural bristle boar's-hair hairbrush. Yes, she sold Fuller Brush products for a short while. There was an old-fashioned iron radiator under the window, and the windowsill had a messy collection of various Fuller products: hairbrushes, a brush to clean the radiator, a metal brush to clean the hairbrushes that I still have, and a lot of dust holding it all together. The windowsill and radiator never got cleaned because there were too many things to move.

In addition to her inventory of gold bricks kept in the linen closet, there were various other personal items such as the girdles and brassieres she sold for a time, her diaphragm (a much-handled source of mystery to us) in its own blue flat box, Epsom salts and other nostrums, that motley collection of "washrags," and the damned enema bag. The bathroom was the place where enemas were too often given on a towel on the floor, always a horrible experience, but her Aunt Esther considered them a frequent answer to many problems — along with Vicks Vapo-rub applied on the chest, up the nose, on the bottom of feet, and down the throat.

The bathroom was a weird place, kind of our communal meeting place where we hung out, chatting with Mommy if she was bathing, or bathing kids together. The only time for privacy was when someone was sitting down and hollered out, "Don't come in!" then the trespasser would stand outside the door and say, "Are you done yet?"

As we children grew up, privacy became more important, and the bathroom was the only place where one could have an all-too-short respite of privacy as our household grew. As a teen, I found it a ritual and sanctuary of last resort where my privacy became a sacred rite. I would lay out my personally purchased shampoo and soap (Mommy made her own soap, an awful and smelly lard and lye concoction with zero lathering features and a high melt factor), fill the tub with steamy hot water, and prepare the clean towel, ready on the toilet seat. Even the clean towel was a luxury, because most of the time the clean towel cupboard, our linen closet, was bare of towels and used for her Nutrilite inventory.

The towels instead were piled up in a mountain of moldering laundry in front of the second-hand washer in the basement, purchased for $25. She really counted on us to move the laundry through. So it meant having to do at least one load of laundry just to get the clean towel.

Usually, if one actually wanted a hot bath rather than a tepid one, the bather needed to boil big pots of water and carry them carefully through the breakfast room to reheat the bath water if it had cooled during the gathering of supplies. The red rubber hose would be run from the sink over to the tub (the water pressure was poor so that, by the time the tub was filled up, it would get cold. So, in addition to the task of heating water on the stove, we had a supplementary method that involved snaking that long rubber hose into the tub to add whatever more hot water so the tub could be filled faster. If the external water supplemental hose was unattended, it would sometimes slip out of the tub and continue filling the bathroom floor instead of the tub.

A supreme effort to bring that bath into reality, all in all. Like many Herculean efforts people perform daily, this was all routine.

The joy and anticipation of using a bath product I had personally selected, carefully hidden and anticipated applying cannot be explained properly. Some of the early personal care products our mother sold, Nutritilite's Edith Rehnborg line, and then Amway's early attempts, left a lot to be desired. Mommy herself had her own ritual with her home-made soap, vinegar, egg whites for the facial, salt, and corn oil, none of which she could convince her children to use. Right this minute I can still feel that thrill of slapping on some of my secret stash of Jean Nate' After Bath Splash, kept hidden in the bottom of my bureau drawer.

Too often this was the scene in the bathroom: I'd enter the bathroom in extreme anticipation, after all my preparation, finally ready. And there she would be, lounging in *my* bath water, smiling dreamily and with no apparent guilt at her outright thievery. She would have her broiled grapefruit topped with the caramelized brown sugar perched on the rim of the tub.

Mommy's ritual belied how she could possibly usurp my space and still get all *her* pieces together — without my knowing her plan. She would either have a Japanese dish of fresh egg whites on the generous curved edge of the tub to be applied to her face, or she'd have her green Edith Rehnborg clay masque on, that contented smile beaming through it, looking like a one-off variety of blackface minstrel. Also balanced on the rim there would often be her gold and white demitasse cup and saucer from her mother's fine china collection, in which she'd have her espresso. Where was I when she got *her* ritual organized? Probably laundering my towel.

"I won't be long, and it'll still be nice and hot for you," she'd beam at me or another of her victims.

So we often were forced to bathe in her grey water. How could I not forgive her, for stealing this one little pinnacle of luxury we had in our home? She was my everything, when all was said and done.

THERE WAS THIS ONE HIGH point in my young life, when I was almost seven years old, which still brings me pleasure today. Mommy took me, and me alone, as I remember, to a shopping center on City Line Avenue to a special live event to see Roy Rogers and his horse Trigger, and Dale Evans and her horse Buttermilk. This was huge! Our heroes were as real as life, and at that time what we saw in the movies we believed with all our hearts — maybe more than in real life. It was almost magic to see these people and their creatures for real! They played such a starring role in our lives, existing only in the serials at the Waverly Saturday matinee. We knew personally (but actually only on screen) Roy, Dale and Trigger, or the other giant hero figures in our movie-going lives, The Lone Ranger and Tonto. That day I would meet Mr. And Mrs. Rogers and their horses live and in person.

I can't imagine how Mommy managed to get this onto her schedule, because it was quite extraordinary for her to do a totally kid-focused thing. And I believe I remember being the only kid with her, but that may have only been because I was so astounded at what happened.

I pulled the winning ticket in the big drawing! What wonderful luck in a crowd of over a thousand! My winnings: a twelve-place-setting set of Rogers Bros. (as in "Roy Rogers") silver plate in a mahogany box with tarnish-preventative fabric inside holding each group of utensils separately. I can still smell that tarnish-preventative fragrance right now. How many times did I open that mahogany box and inhale it, feeling so utterly RICH? It was the high point of my childhood, becoming endowed with silver!

My life changed that day. I had become a Person of Importance.

I saw this silver as an excellent start—maybe a turning point in my life; maybe a sign that I wouldn't always have nothing of substance. There lay that one thing now, at the bottom of my converted "hope chest," my mahogany box filled with glittering silver utensils.

I intended to preserve the silver cutlery—along with my virginity, which didn't work out quite the way I had planned it either—until I was married. It was, after all, a key to being marriageable, the American version of the dowry. Some young girls actually had parents who helped them pick out a Lane hope chest, long before they were even near marriageable age. Friends would be invited over to see their hope chests. Sometimes it was a graduation gift from high school, as in "get it? Go find yourself a rich man and get that engagement ring." Every gift laid lovingly in the hope chest brought more pressure on the girl to make the right moves. The hope chest could start being filled as soon as a girl was a teenager, as parents' friends endowed the girls with gifts, usually stuff they didn't need or want to care for anymore but which had been wedding gifts to them. Little girls were conditioned from an early age to plan for their hope chests and what to put in them.

Up until this point I held no hope for my hope chest. I had the modified chest: that cedar trunk my mother had inherited that held some of my grandfather's artifacts from his explorations in Africa and Peru, and my grandmother's gossamer silk undergarments from her trousseau, but I had nothing to add to it. I feel pretty sure I was the only one in my family who ever gave any thought to my need for a hope chest filled with items for my married future.

You already know what was in my hope chest before the Rogers Bros. silver arrived. My grandmother's hope and dreams, and those of my newly divorced mother, in the form of her bolts of fabric and her felt hats.

There was exactly one occasion, some years later, when I loaned my beloved silver to my close friend Gilda. She was a newly divorced woman with three children who had fled her crazy husband in the middle of the night from the cold country of Winnipeg, Canada. She was in her first apartment in Philadelphia on her own, with a new job as a secretary where I also began my first job; and she wanted to impress her family that she could "set a table." I bit the bullet and lent my set of silver to her with all good will.

When I went to retrieve my precious silver—plate, I should mention—there were ten pieces missing! She had absolutely no idea where they could have gotten to, and she was unconcerned. My greatest worldly asset, and now almost twenty percent of it gone before I even found my husband!

The next spring, I helped my friend dig her tiny vegetable garden on her tiny patch of land. While digging I turned up five of the ten missing pieces, mostly spoons, which she apparently had been using as gardening implements in lieu of a spade. Dismayed as I was, I didn't share my distress with her, because she wouldn't have understood what the silver meant to me. Her father was a furrier, and her casual attitude toward her small collection of furs put her in a different category than I. Worldly goods meant nothing to her—so how could she possibly have understood this loss, the breaking up of the complete set, my ticket to a better life?

MUCH OF MY MOTHER'S LIFE was itself a side trip, but on many occasions, we were lucky to be included. In fact, maybe we were her excuse, or perhaps partners in crime as she played hooky from revenue-producing work. It might be a day of swimming in the cedar water at Brown's Mills in New Jersey, or stops on the way to the shore to trek the woods looking for club moss, reindeer lichen, or the red-topped lichen she called "British soldier," and partridge berry and ground orchids. And of course, we'd be looking for turtle eggs, which my mother had no qualms about eating. Again, like the mussels, raw.

We had rollicking good times

One day on the way home from delivering to a Nutrilite customer, she and I detoured off the highway to drive along Crum Creek in Media to poke around the waterline. She found wild grapes, bunches of them. " Here, Anne, taste these, wild Concord grapes; taste how sweet they are, she said." We gathered them up in a newspaper we found.

That night we made grape jam, and the fragrance and taste are still with me. We poured paraffin wax on the top of each jar. I could hardly wait to open a jar of our creation! It seemed such fun to pop off the wax lid and find this wonderful sweet discovery underneath. I have never again found wild grapes like that.

I don't remember (but have been told) that she used to pile my younger siblings in the car and drive them to Lover's Lane behind the sewage treatment plan in Marple to see if they could spy on me there with my boyfriend—or if not me, anyone else who might look interesting.

Cars were really just beginning to enter the lives of many middle-income Americans, and new ones weren't even available during the war until Ford started manufacturing again in 1946. But we weren't middle-income, and Mommy bought cars that didn't last too long— not that she intended for that to happen. I don't know how long each lasted, but she regularly seemed to turn up with a different one. J. G., a real car guy, gave me the succession of cars she acquired: The '37 Plymouth was followed by a '39 Plymouth, then a 1947 DeSoto, all of which gave Mommy quite a return on her small investments, continuing usually in the $25 to $50 range.

One day she and I were coming home from the A & P store with two bags of groceries in the back of the '47 DeSoto, when the car caught fire under the hood. It had stalled, and when she tried to start it, the carburetor loaded up and shot out flames. The fire quickly got big. We (naturally) had no fire extinguisher, so she calmly got the groceries out, handed a bag to me, and said, "Let's go, Anne. "

She didn't seem alarmed to me and probably wasn't sure what she could do about the burning car, so we took our groceries and began walking the two blocks home, leaving the burning car there. I don't remember what happened to the car after that—she may have dispatched it somehow. We were used to living with catastrophes, so this was a minor one. There was no further discussion.

We always wandered onto the sand roads on the way to the shore to see if we could spy some "Pineys" in the back woods of the Pine Barrens. It was such a beautiful place to go exploring, with the cedar creeks like Winding River running through the Barrens. On another side road on the way home from the shore, she made a sudden turn off our course, saying, "Kids, you are now going to see the birth of the American glass industry, right here in South Jersey." When we found the Wheaton Glass Company in Millville, New Jersey, it was closed for the weekend. We found a fenced-in area with a sparkling mountain of colored glass behind it. She actually led us into the act of breaking through that fenced area to climb a mountain of discarded glass to find almost-perfect bottles and colored glass shards. It didn't seem awful to do this; it was a low-security area with a giant pile of culls, just beckoning to us, her team of crack trash pickers. There we found many treasures, all free. The bottles and chunks of colored glass decorated our windowsills for years.

I remember one summer when Linda was probably about eleven or twelve, she got to go away to summer camp at Sandy Cove in Maryland, through the Faith Chapel. While there she met a friend who lived in Reading; and she of course begged Mommy to take her and her other camp friends to Reading to visit her friend. On the day of the trip Mommy expanded the agenda to introduce them to the red pagoda, so famous in Reading, and another interesting little exploration to visit a funeral home.

"You're going to meet Stone Willie, children," she explained, telling them to be on their best and most polite behavior, since there might need to be some convincing done that children should attend the viewing of this rather ghoulish sight. The children were in shorts, but she was dressed only in a bathing suit—which was often the case in the event a good place to swim presented itself—she was always ready. Where she had learned that there was this perfectly embalmed man whom the funeral directors had preserved and kept for many years is beyond me, but I believe he was an indigent man who died in jail and who the funeral home got permission to use as an experiment to see how long an embalmed body could be preserved. So all the children and she marched into the Theodore C. Auman Funeral Home to see whether they could pull this off.

"Hello, may I speak to Mr. Theodore Auman, please?", she asked in her most dignified manner. How to be dignified while speaking to a funeral director while making an unorthodox request and doing so in a bathing suit and nothing else is something I have not mastered yet. Only my mother knew how to do that, and she did not pass on every one of her "people skills."

"We are on a summer field trip today; and I am giving my students an educational experience on funeral arts. I've read all about Stone Willie and wanted them to see the value of a good piece of embalming work," she explained, appealing to the ego of the master embalmer. Before long, Mr. Auman ushered them into Willie's chamber and left them, quietly backing out as he normally would when leaving a mourning family alone to say their last goodbyes before the casket is closed. Each of the children got to view Stone Willie and touch him, for an unforgettable introduction to the embalming arts. They described him as hard, brown, and not with fingernails and hair longer than would be expected. All in all, it was a typical day with my mother.

One of Mommy's other side roads played a very meaningful and long-term role in our lives. At some point she had been introduced through our Uncle Dan to a woman who became her friend, Lisette Golden. Lisette began to have a profound influence on Mommy in getting culture into her children. Lisette was "in the arts," meaning she dressed in fishnet stockings and danced in some city night club, but she played the theatrical role to the hilt. Lisette and her husband Dearie threw great parties, which we often attended and got to snitch the smoked oysters and caviar on crackers. Mommy often acted as her taxi to take her into the city for her nightclub act, since neither she nor Dearie drove. She could have been a stripper, for all I knew, dressed in her fishnet, black satin and feather boas. We were just along for the ride, there in the back seat.

"It's scandalous," Lisette told her, "that you're not exposing these children to the arts!" And with that, she began her crusade to make us cultured little ladies and gentlemen.

Our lessons began with our fabulous forays to the Robin Hood Dell in the Strawberry Mansion section of Fairmount Park. Mommy's 1947 De Soto (before it burned up) had a huge volume of space, and we would cram sometimes as many kids as we could fit in, with my mother at the wheel and Lisette and Mommy's neighborhood friend Shelly up front. Not a seat belt in sight, of course, giving us children the ability to sit on each other's laps, sometimes three-deep--there were three of us and about five of Shelly's children just in our two families, and usually another friend or two.

The Dell was the Philadelphia Orchestra's summer home, and they performed great family and children's orchestral music on Saturdays, conducted by Eugene Ormandy. This tradition had begun in 1930, when the Depression almost dissolved the orchestra, and from that period, they performed these concerts well into the 1950's for almost no money aside from an endowment fund, still totally free to poverty-stricken families like ours. We became very rich from the music to which we were exposed almost every Saturday.

When Lisette came along to supervise our musical education, she would sometimes have us meet the musicians and the conductor. Without our knowing it, she was teaching us to be comfortable meeting formidable personages. Mommy and Shelly would pack a picnic lunch with Mommy's homemade lemonade in a big jug and a large quantity of Shelly's tuna sandwiches.

Several years after Uncle Dan and Aunt Janette had moved out and established themselves in a center-city location, Uncle Dan began a film production business and was the first person to begin shooting film of the Eagles' games, which he did for decades and pioneered the video production that made the games so enjoyable as television quality improved. Aunt Janette, meanwhile, began working to build her ballet school in their Rittenhouse Square loft. It was probably Lisette who talked her into including me in her weekly lessons, at no charge, I believe. I was about seven years old at this point, and I was allowed to take the trolley and subway into the city to attend the school. I would call my mother the original free-range mother who seemed to trust the universe that this level of independence was right and good. I remember walking through Rittenhouse Square and feeling the exotic difference between the lives of these wealthy city dweller kids, sometimes with nannies, I believe, as I look back. I was struck by how at home they felt climbing on the bronze goat, rubbed shiny with wear, feeding pigeons, and playing different games than we played. We had The Woods, and they had just this one little square. But somehow I knew they were rich and comfortable in their skins.

I was invariably late, of course. I would sneak in to where the other little girls were already spinning their pirouettes across the floor one at a time, with Aunt Janettes's mother, Madam Maille, banging away Mozart on the piano. It was not fun being late to ballet class, and I felt like a giraffe in a roomful of gazelles, taller and ungainly, clearly not cut out *pour la dans*. Before long it became evident to my gentle teacher that this aspect of culture was lost on me.

Those ballet lessons, however long I survived them, enabled me to become adept at navigating public transportation by myself at a young age. This did not serve me well later.

The nature of her work introduced Mommy to many interesting people—or maybe it was just her nature to meet interesting people. One of her "customer clusters" was the in-residence actors at the historic Hedgerow Theater residence. The renowned theatrical director, Rose Shulman, was her Nutrilite customer, and Rose wanted every one of her actors to also eat Nutrilite. We sometimes got to engage with the odd collection of actors and learn about their lives. Mommy was always invited to their frequent parties, of course.

Later the side roads got longer and further away as she spun into almost-reality her imaginary character, Sadie Fletcher—her most grand hoax, which she kept going for years. Possibly it began when she needed to distract herself from her second marriage gone bad. We called this particular side road The Sadie Fletcher Caper, and it was a road she traveled down regularly over a period of years. The scheme gave her a continuous chain of storytelling fun and apparently gave her the ability to bounce back from the daily abuse of the second bad marital choice she made.

As inheritor of all her rough, hand-written-in-pencil drafts of letters from this period, I got interested in finding out what the letters were about many years after she was gone. I found that no one could make up stories like this—and yet she did, apparently regularly over years with +this prank. She ran this scheme while conducting a perfectly ordinary life, coming home to a difficult new husband, tending somewhat haphazardly to her now five children, still out there daily, selling and delivering her nutritional supplements, and starting other new businesses--all at the same time.

As crazy as she was, she taught me and my siblings to take that side trip, to wander down that woodland path, that turn in the road, to see what we might find. If that wandering off the path didn't catch the interest of the average person, she showed us the path away from average thinking: that by digging deeper we'd *find* something interesting. She taught me to explore people, to find out what might be interesting about them, to dig deeper until I found gold. There's always some gold there—she knew that, sure as anything.

In many ways, her life was a series of catastrophes, balanced by a series of adventures. Not much seemed to undo her that I remember. There were, however, a few critical points that fell into that category, which shall be revealed as the story unfolds.

CHAPTER 18 – A YOUNG CHILD'S DENTAL NIGHTMARES

OVER TIME, OUR LIVES SEEMED to be improving over where we had been—a little less despair and depression, longer periods of no sheriff's sale signs on the front door, but money was still tight. When it came to some of the necessities, such as getting our universally awful teeth fixed, we had no family dentist who cleaned our teeth every six months. We had to rely on charitable outfits like the Red Feather Agency on the corner of Broad and Sansom Streets, a dingy little place, for work on an as-needed basis by volunteer dentists who helped fill poor kids' cavities.

For me, the significant amount of work I needed to have done introduced an experience that was worse. I was probably seven or eight when I was assigned to the University of Pennsylvania Dental School. After Mommy got me set up by accompanying me on my first consultation there, I once again found myself traveling alone on the trolley and subway, depositing my gold PTC token in the turnstile and boarding that train to hell, sometimes twice a week after school.

Back then the school was a macabre den of terror filled with about 400 dental chairs, and a student for each chair who was using me or another victim to learn how to do their work. There were a very few professors who roamed the floor and checked on the students' efforts. To get one cavity done (I apparently had about twenty or so) sometimes took hours.

Here is how it went: Start with the rubber dam applied with big forceps around the tooth to be worked on, often blocking the nasal passages . . . then have the mouth loaded up with about ten cotton rolls and a big spit sucker hung over the corner of the mouth . . . next, the great big needle of Novocain, always administered clumsily in the wrong place the first two, three or four times . . . then waiting to see if I got numb.

"Can you feel this?" The student would tap my tooth with an instrument. Knowing if I said no, the big needle would return, I readily agreed that I had gotten numb, all right. But once the drilling started, it invariably turned out to be numb in the wrong place — not where the drilling was occurring.

I would then release a scream of terror, and as I was lifted out of my seat in agony the distressed student would drill my tongue or gum . . . then apply the gauze to stop the bleeding . . . more attempts at drilling, sometimes with the slow vibrate-your-teeth-out-of-your-head drill and sometimes with the new super high- speed one that sprayed water all over your face. Then interminable waiting till the roaming professor showed, checked the problem with the injection locations. Whereupon he or she would finally give up on the inept student and give me the shot. I remember how relieved I was when the female prof arrived, so fresh, fragrant and gentle.

Then there would be the medicated filling needed because the student had drilled down to China. Then came my reward---the fun part: the mercury filling. To distract me from the endless stream of tears rolling down my face, the student would give me a dime and some beads of mercury to apply to the dime to make it super shiny. I would do this while he requisitioned the triple order of mercury and silver needed to fill the crater. He'd mix it up on a thick piece of glass and pack it into the bottomless pit he had just created. Meanwhile, I was happily poisoning myself, it seems. And I got to keep the shiny dime.

Every time a student needed a piece of work to pass a test, I was his guinea pig, with fancy gold inlays and other exotic restorative processes—not always done well.

Traveling back on the subway/elevated PTC system, I would zone out, nightmare over for the moment. I would peer down onto Market Street and see the Jewish butcher, the fish market, the produce stands, the jivey-looking dark people in porkpie hats, their women in tight-fitting come-on outfits, and the black-kerchiefed and black-clothed Eastern European shoppers, all woven into a cloth quite different from our super-whitey world where I dwelled. The sights were curative and distracting.

When I stepped off the train, trauma receding, I'd re-enter the 69th Street Terminal, a world unto itself: four movie theaters within blocks of each other, one of which was the vaunted Tower Theater, still drawing famous musicians to the same place where Elvis first fell in love with me when I was thirteen. I was sitting in the second row, and he spotted me while crooning "Love Me Tender. In the terminal itself, there was the Terminal Market, the shoeshine stand, the news stand/smoke shop, and the high note of the Terminal, the Nedick's Donuts stand— where my wounds were salved. There was the friendly giant Black man, their baker, cranking out trays of wonderful glazed doughnuts, the finest medicine mankind ever invented.

I can see them now, on that stainless-steel rack, coming out of the glazing bin, glistening, still hot, and falling gently onto a tray from which my two were plucked, still warm, accompanied by a delicious and mysterious orange drink. The whole banquet took a quarter of my money, which was just what I had left, every time. My mouth was—of course—so numb I could not chew, close my teeth around the doughnut or properly suck the drink through the straw, but rolling that sweetness around in my mouth helped me regain my perspective and get on with life.

On those days before I left for an appointment, my mother had done everything she felt capable of to buoy me up: given me a double dose of calcium-magnesium tablets for pain and stress relief, the healthy blender breakfast drink, and the small sums of money for the trolley and subway. Then she went off and did what she had to do to keep her home and family together.

Linda and Nancy both suffered through their own experiences at Penn Dental School. We each got our braces there, another series of grueling experiences. Nancy recently told me that the first time she began seeing a "real" dentist as a young woman on her own and now determined to have regular checkups, she had a preliminary discussion with him.

"Look, I'm going to tell you once and one time only: You do *ONE THING* to hurt me—just one thing—and this arm is going to come up like this," as she exhibited a karate chop movement, "and knock you out of the way fast! There can be *NO* mistakes! I am warning you: this is an automatic reflex action, and I *WILL* protect myself," she warned again, as she repeated her rapid karate chop on his arm. She tells me her dentist has made good on his word for many years and has never hurt her.

"SELLING NUTRILITE IS LIKE BEING a missionary," Mommy often told us, making it clear that no matter how many other distractions she might have going on, she would never abandon her first commitment to help people with Nutrilite. This mission was clearly infused into her letters as I deciphered them, and the way she wove her mission into every encounter became one of my initial reasons for this story.

While some aspects of the business itself had become disappointing as the corporation made changes, she now had a regular customer base who were anything but disenchanted with the product. They contributed to any sense of security we had—that she could always "make a delivery" or get a new customer. "Hoop-La!" I just got another Nutrilite customer," she'd whoop. We knew it meant an addition to a revenue stream that might translate into better food, furniture, vehicle or fun.

There's a certain breed of people who are always scanning the outer fringes of the horizon to see who or what out there might interest them at the moment. Mommy was one of them. Maybe she had inherited the trait from our grandfather we never met, who somehow decided it would be a delightful experience—as a newly married man and father-to-be—to go crashing through the wild lands of Africa and Peru searching for the elusive magnetic southern pole. Mommy's explorations leaned more toward using her magnetic leanings pulling in exotic people, rather than places. While her main focus was always on selling the product, she had a small rag-tag "group" made up of under a half-dozen of what I'd call Outer Fringe people.

In a multi-level business, all comers are taken on without question, the idea being you never know who knows whom that might be your next star. When she sporadically focused on recruiting, some of those people she was drawn to joined to sell the product. I'm not sure why she didn't concentrate more on recruiting distributors, because it is a vital aspect of the MLM system. Maybe she felt it would slow down her selling ability. In any case, those in her group also became missionaries about Nutrilite, exhibiting a similar zeal that bubbled over always expressing excitement about who got "cured" over who made a sale. She and they would often be deep into research on their customers' health problems and what to prescribe for them, not thinking at that moment about improving their own lives.

For Mommy, beginning her career as a single mother of three youngsters, it was not workable to hold sales and training meetings in our home, as would be normal in a multi-level sales business. Later, in her disastrous second marriage, it became impossible with her new difficult husband present. So she usually got a sitter and went to her sponsor's meetings in those early years, where she could confer with her distributors.

Later, when I turned eleven and she had remarried and had two more children, I went from being "one of the kids" to being the person in charge of the younger kids. In a large family, which we had now become, the children kind of care for one another; and we could easily slip between being playmates to being team members getting our chores done so we could get back to playing. When we weren't doing either work or play, we could fight with and torture each other.

Before and after her second marriage, members of the troupe would often stop by to get "gold bricks" or sales literature, when we'd get to observe the show of the Outer Fringe group.

Ruth and Herb L'Oranger were two of her converts. Ruth was an impeccably dressed flamboyant woman with brilliant red lipstick and long black braids that she wore swirled atop her head. Herb always wore a suit and a bow tie. He had a mustache like Hitler (which never seemed like a good idea around that time). They presented as the types portrayed as extras in period movies of the 50s.

Then there was Alice Brant; everything she wore was purple or violet or some shade in between, as was everything in her home: the walls, the woodwork, the tile in the bathroom, all done by her. She had been a woman alone for years, perhaps as her ex-husband realized she was verging on incurably insane.

Alice usually showed up in a purple bucket hat with a bunch of silk violets pinned onto it. Her method of greeting was unusual. Some people just say hello; she would get right to business and take my poor unsuspecting face in her gentle hands, looking at me with melting eyes, tears running down her face in rapture. While caressing me, she would break into a stream of incomprehensible language, speaking "in tongues." Then she would interpret, telling me what God wanted for me. When Alice came around, we would either not answer the door if we were home when Mommy wasn't, or else hide in the closet if she was there.

Alice also did chiropractic manipulations (without a license) and always carried her ironing board with her so she could help people she thought needed it. She had an association—aka romantic liaison—with a chiropractor and had picked up a few manipulation tricks from him. In addition to selling Nutrilite, she also taught proper food combining, how to juice and eat raw fruits and vegetables, how to speak in tongues and how to have the complete Pentecostal experience right here and right now. She would pray over her subjects, both when she did the chiropractic and when she administered the first "meal" of Double X.

"Sweetheart, you may experience "health reactions" when you start eating Nutrilite. Your body might go into a kind of "shock" as it battles with the health pouring into your body, right NOW, as you eat your first meal of XX. Let's pray: Precious Lord Jesus, be with (insert names) as they begin a new path toward health and banish from their bodies the evils that have held them captive; Lord, lift them up and raise them to a new level of health and keep them safe. Hila-shalleka-luk-ateviana . . .".

Normally in a church setting there would be someone to interpret the tongues; but if no one was handy, she would do that herself immediately after. This cleansing ritual usually went on a lot longer, with some folks convinced they got that proverbial jolt from the battle "raging" inside them, as good and evil forces clashed when they swallowed their first dose. They were afraid to quit Nutrilite after that.

As big a role as Nutrilite products played in rescuing various aspects of their and our lives, after the FDA fiasco there was a kind of wounded feeling among the distributor network, as if the distributor organization were soldiers wounded in battle for the first time. I remember a subtle softening of that missionary zeal crept into Mommy's mind too. As a youngster, I felt a difference, but I didn't know what was causing it.

What I did know was that Mommy was opening some new horizons in her sales career. This marked the beginning of a new era, as she began adding on other products she got excited about, beginning with the "Slim- Gym." Recently I sat in a friend's "zero gravity" lounge chair and thought of my mother.

Slim Gym was a lawn-chair-type of device with a metal frame and canvas slings, but instead of settling comfortably into it like one would into a lounge chair, when you got into this contraption, it collapsed in half. Your job, as the person who wants to shape up and lose weight, was to get busy flexing up and down by pushing your feet down on the bottom edge and making the middle part flip UP! then DOWN! and UP! and DOWN!

Once you got momentum it didn't pay to stop; because then, not only would the contraption collapse in half, but the user would too. And that was the magic in it: it was hard to get started, and then she was afraid to quit. In that sense, it was just like Nutrilite XX. This Slim Gym addition to her offerings made sense: it added a physical component to what had been an incomplete health program until then. And I'm sure she had the motivation to slim down!

Almost everybody who was her nutrition customer had a Slim Gym bestowed upon them for a handsome price. We finally got our dreamed-of twelve-inch black and white TV with the extra money and unlimited potential this new gadget offered. I still marvel at the pleasure we got out of that tiny box of fun, after spending so many of our recreational hours on the floor in front of the giant Philco radio. I can see Mommy now, working her difficult middle part, giving it a complete exercise program while flipping about on the Slim Gym and hooting with laughter over her favorite comedians, Sid Caesar and Imogene Coco, Jackie Gleason and Audrey Meadows in The Honeymooners, and the George Gobel Show.

The World Book Encyclopedias, her next venture, became an addition that proved over time to be a wonderful enrichment to our own lives. We had finally graduated from that first little black and white TV with rabbit ears and the tri-colored screen across the front that made it a "color TV" to our next one, a big seventeen-inch number.

Enthralled with its gigantic size, we would watch incessantly, even with the limited programming available. We got Howdy Doody in the afternoon, and the wonderful series of cowboy movies, which we had only seen at Saturday matinees until then: Roy Rogers, Dale Evans and Trigger, The Lone Ranger and Tonto, Gene Autry, and

Hopalong Cassidy. Hopalong's name we didn't find at all amusing; we took him quite seriously and considered him a formidable model in our lives.

Then one day our lives changed. Mommy came home from (possibly unsuccessful) sales attempts of the Pennyrich bras. We wouldn't have known how her day went, because I don't remember her sharing her failures with us. It was nearly impossible to read her mood on the less successful days, because she stoically didn't show evidence if it wasn't good.

Whatever her results that day, we were all lying on the floor entranced, with our chins cupped in our hands watching Buffalo Bob and Howdy Doody interact with Princess Summer-Fall-Winter-Spring and marveling at her beauty. We hardly noticed Mommy's entrance. She walked in and quickly assessed the sad truth. None of our chores were done. We still didn't look up, hoping she'd go away. She may have asked which tasks had been done by whom, but I don't remember. What happened in the next two minutes overshadowed all else. I remember trying to appear casual while laden with guilt. Still, she said nothing, not a word.

"Oh, good," I quietly thought to myself, afraid to breathe or say anything, because she seemed kind of angry—which didn't happen very often. Still wordless, she walked over to the television and kicked in the screen!! BOOM! The glass shattered and made a big explosive sound as the tubes burst.

We were stunned. That bigger size TV was one of the most important signs of forward progress we'd ever had in our lives. I couldn't imagine life without Howdy Doody. We would be back to lying in front of the big Philco, listening to the serials and the "Teddy Bear's Picnic." She still said nothing; just headed for the kitchen to see about dinner.

And that was how we marked the entrance of World Book into our lives—and into her business model, such as it was. Was it a coincidence that it happened the same time she kicked in the TV? I don't think so. In fact, I think that is exactly what she had on her mind that day.

"How can I sell more books?" She may have been thinking that very thought. She may have decided books had a higher value than that television had, to boost her sales and play an important part in our lives. Conviction is an important aspect of successful selling, and she may have needed us as her demonstration tools. Yes, our family would become the beneficiary of her demonstration model set. A set of encyclopedias was a huge expenditure at that time, even with the ability to finance.

The pitch began. "Britannica's the top of the line, but it's exorbitantly overpriced and too complicated. It's absolutely not useful for children and most adults. Americana is middle of the line, but still too expensive. Ours is the most useful and best priced."

Still it was a price that set most families back when those door-to-door salespeople like our mother came calling. They longed for it, but more often than not, couldn't purchase it, even on the time payment plan with the little bank shaped like a book with a slot in the top, where you deposited your coins you saved by not buying coffee (which no one did back then — you used Nescafe or Maxwell HousE instant coffee, the cutting edge of modernity).

Our financed demonstration set was reverently displayed like the shrine to knowledge it became, on the old mahogany marble-topped dresser that served as our sideboard in the breakfast room — all twenty-two volumes at the ready for us to pore over after our meager evening meal — meager if Mommy were cooking, hearty if Annie performed.

Since we now had no other form of entertainment, every night after dinner we would each pick out a book and page through it, sharing our discoveries with each other and with Mommy. We would sit at the dinner table for hours. She glowed with pleasure, and I think it really helped her sales pitch to say that we wouldn't think of having a television in OUR home—we had the Books, the knowledge of the world at our fingertips. Truthfully, we loved those books. And we got smarter every day.

MOMMY HAD REGULARLY GAINED CONFIDENCE as a successful salesperson over time; but as her confidence in the Nutrilite management lessened, she continued exploring other income possibilities.

Sometime after she apparently had sold most of her regular customers the Slim Gym and discovered that sales of the World Book happened less frequently because of the high cost, she came home with another device, a bedwetting preventer pad, to which we had a hard time reconciling ourselves. I'm not sure how many of these items she sold, but she never made a sale to any of her children. This device seemed cruel and unusual punishment for the little bedwetter. If the poor unsuspecting child happened to have a little accident while sleeping, all holy hell would break loose in not only an audible alarm, but also a slight shock to the victim. "This device," the pitch went, "is child psychiatrist-approved and guaranteed not to hurt the child in any way—and also guaranteed to definitely modify behaviors. Let me demonstrate how you can stop having to get up in the middle of the night to change sheets and pajamas," she'd beam, as she poured just the tiniest bit of water on the pad. The loud buzzing sound of the alarm went off, and then she'd have the victim's parents touch the pad, so they could feel for themselves that the poor child would not be shocked into insensibility, but just a state of consciousness. She loved products she could demonstrate.

This behavior modification device has today evolved into a highly acceptable product used for pet control, employing the same technology to mildly shock dogs into staying within the confines of the designated space, often a yard. If the pet control device could be customized to teach the dog to hit the same area for the thousand or so times a day they seem to need to relieve themselves, I think my mother would rise out of her grave and start recruiting a team to get out there and tell the story.

This short-lived enterprise was followed some years later (after she had produced several more babies) to other lines of baby equipment that involved breaking down and converting highchairs into playpens or cribs or other nonsensical contraptions.

As Mommy oozed farther afield from what she had originally identified as her mission in life, she possibly overwhelmed herself looking for the way out of the maze and wondering where her ship was and when it was coming in.

As for our lives as her free-range children, we were already living somewhat self-sufficiently when she was out selling (a lot of which necessarily happened at night). We were used to independence and finding bits of nurturing and parenting here and there from our friends' parents, who gave us quite a lot. Each of us had our surrogate families who picked up pieces of our lives. Linda developed her own door-to-door route where she would regularly visit neighbors who fed her sweet snacks. The love they dispensed with the snacks they lavished on her filled some holes in her life. Through his years after Grant left, J. G. gradually got heavily into running traps on the Darby Creek and began forming friendships with other future "rugged outdoorsmen." His friends hunted and fished, and we often saw little of him. J. G. had his best friend's Jeff Lipton's parents, who took him in regularly and suited him well. Mr. Lipton was the sales manager of Penn Reels, and their two sons were also natural fishermen and hunters. Linda and I shared the Addisons, Janet's and Peggy's parents, as our quasi-parents. We regularly were invited to dinner at their table, along with their Scottish maiden aunts, Aunts Mamie and Evelyn.

"Jennet, yerr the limit," Aunt Mamie would screech at her. We would openly giggle at her criticisms. And Janet indeed was just that, the limit. I will never forget the opening day of Janet's brand new junior high school and her first day there also after she moved out to the country. In those lax times I was permitted to attend with her as her houseguest. Janet's mother stood at the door in her apron, waving goodbye. The school bus held a disparate collection of really rich landed-gentry horse-owner types and the other group, farm kids, who called out to her as the new kid, "Yo! Who's that lady?"

Janet blithely answered without missing a beat. "That's the maid." I could not have imagined saying anything so cruel about my mother. I adored her and considered her the most important person in my life—except for Janet.

The Addisons led very regular lives, which was so important to Linda and me, as it was in their household we learned how families live. Janet's father was a painting contractor who worked every day from 8 to 5 with his steady crew. Janet's mother would make grilled cheese sandwiches, creamed cheese and jelly sandwiches, and finnan haddie and Welsh rarebit for dinner. Their Scottish heritage was so exotic to me, eating such snacks as kipper snacks and saltines. Danish pudding was featured as a frequent dessert. At home we didn't have frequent desserts—or dinners, for that matter.

Janet's parents didn't curse. My mother didn't either, except to say, "Hot damn," or "Judas Priest!" Janet's mother, when exasperated beyond the breaking point, would exhort, "Cheese and crackers, young lady! You can just go sit in the corner with your face to the wall!" If it was really a serious transgression, which it often was, the expletive elevated to cheese and rice, a cleaned-up version of "Jesus Christ," I would guess. This happened often because Janet was a real exasperator. Once, she and I took ten little kids and "got lost" on an adventure walk that lasted well into the night and got us to the fringes of Philadelphia by flipping a coin at each intersection.

When we were finally found, the ultimate expletive came out.

"Cheese and rice! You can just stay in your room tomorrow morning!"

Once a week Mrs. Addison played daytime bridge with the ladies. On Friday nights Mr. Addison played poker with his men, and they drank whiskey sours, with us girls as wait staff and bartenders. As we sneaked some of each round, we'd get a little drunk. We loved the job.

We did not have such events in our home. Right after dinner and encyclopedia time when she was still a single divorcee, Mommy would hurry before it became too late to make her phone calls to sell whatever was current. Sometimes after she got some appointments set up, she used the bedtimes to read to us, and it was lovely. We never had alcohol in the house—just cooking sherry and Lydia T. Pinkham's tonic. After the remarriage, alcohol entered our lives, and our evenings became a long nightmare that started all over again each dinner hour.

The Addisons always included me in their family vacations at the shore. The bay across from the Stone Harbor Yacht Club where they rented a house was a different bay than we found at the shacks we stayed in with Mommy. Instead of rickety long piers leading out to the smelly mud flats teeming with mosquitos, their spot had a deep green bay at their back door. We'd dive with freedom right into that beautiful water, feeling the swell of the tide wanting to carry us away. We were both excellent swimmers from our Aronimink Swim Club experiences and Girl Scout live-saving courses.

Once or twice during the week Mr. And Mrs. Addison would include us on their fishing trip in their small rented outboard boat. The back bay then was awash with fish, and flounder were an easy catch. Mrs. Addison's culinary pinnacle to her usually bland menu, which was to me the height of normalcy, would be the fried flounder that night, the just-caught fish a heavenly experience, different from rubber band clam chowder. After dinner we'd all walk to Springer's for ice cream cones and sit on Springer's front porch licking contentedly.

It was heaven to be with the most normal family in the world and not have my little siblings to look after. Our unguarded freedom with Janet's parents was almost similar to Mommy's laissez-faire approach to parenthood. As pre-teens, Janet and I were free to go out looking for boys at night, walking up and down the main street of Stone Harbor decked out like little prostitutes looking for a John.

It was by chance years later that I happened to read the obituary of her father, whom I hadn't seen for a decade. He was the closest I had to a father. Neither of the Addison's had ever hugged me, but their love and acceptance were parental. The pain I felt at his loss was surprising and overwhelming.

MOMMY WAS GOOD AT DIGGING up or creating adventures out of thin air. Once we had wheels, she would take us on "field trips" to explore something new, making an ordinary day into something magical. We regularly drove to the airport to watch the planes arrive and take off and people-watch the hearty hellos and goodbyes. It was our vicarious experience of big travel, feeling their greetings.

One day after an airport visit, she drove us on rutted dirt roads nearby into what was then called The Tinicum Flats, now the John Heinz Wildlife Refuge. The Flats were a desolate stretch of dikes and mini causeways through flowing waters, part of an estuary system of the nearby Delaware River. It was wild and overgrown, but our road led to a run-down homestead where an old man came out to meet us. I don't remember the details of how she even knew of him, but I do remember that he spent hours teaching us about bees. We spent the good part of a day learning about beekeeping, hive management, and harvesting of the honeycombs. She was so good at engaging him and expressing honest interest in all aspects of beekeeping that we got the full treatment.

Before long he had us each try putting on a beekeeper outfit and holding the smoker to hypnotize the bees and having us hold a hive crawling with bees. He gently reached into a hive as the bees began to cover his clothing, his face, and the netted hat he wore. We looked on in fear for the bee stings we expected he'd get as he broke off some of their honeycomb and presented it to each of us. The bees didn't bother him—it was like they knew he was their friend. We all chewed on some of the honeycomb, enjoying the honey and finding the beeswax somewhat like the wax lips we bought at Dietz's candy store on movie Saturdays. The experience was a sort of miracle, which was often the nature of the discoveries my mother shared with us on her various "field trips." She had a lesson for us, too:

"If something doesn't interest you, DIG INTO IT DEEPER. You'll find there's something interesting there to learn, even in bees."

This field trip was actual research for her. It was part of my mother's Raw Honey Era when she was discovering the benefits of bee propolis and honeycomb and the raw honey itself for curing allergies and other things we didn't have (*no one* had allergies in those days). The application of raw honey to burns and wounds could heal truly serious injuries. Raw honey has anti-bacterial properties, so whenever any of us had any kind of an accident, before she brought out the mercurochrome, she'd get out the raw honey. She'd pour the honey right into open wounds and burns. I think she began hoping for wounds and burns to see the miraculous antibacterial results! We often felt more like her guinea pigs and less like her children. Interestingly enough, using honey for wound healing is cited today by the Centers for Disease Control at the National Institutes of Health; and Big Pharma has actually produced a bandage infused with honey, used for wound healing with diabetics. Ahead of the curve again by about twenty to thirty years, she was.

We came home that day with raw honey and honeycomb, our treasure, right from the hive!

Honey, of course, was added to her whizzed-up protein-drink-and-pills breakfasts. J.G., Linda and I invented something we loved, "honey-butter," a fifty-fifty mixture of those two ingredients, spread on her homemade bread. Since there was no white sugar in the house, this sweet treat sustained us through hunger periods when she forgot to cook. With her new addition, she developed her Peanut Butter and Honey Balls, our permissible candy, where the cupboard was often bare of other sustenance. Here is the recipe:

Dot's Peanut Butter Honey Balls

- *A quantity of crunchy natural peanut butter*
- *A quantity of honey*
- *Dried powdered milk*
- *Raisins*
- *Kretschmer Wheat germ*
- *(Sunflower seeds, coconut or other ingredients you think of may be added)*
- *Mix together and roll the first four ingredients into bite-sized balls, adding any extras that you want.*
- *Roll the balls in wheat germ (or alternatively, toasted sesame seeds or coconut), refrigerate and use for treats.*

These travel well, too, but the wheat germ is fragile and can go rancid, so shelf life in the refrigerator would be maybe two weeks. They never last that long.

Even with all her intent on creating a successful business, Mommy was always ready to distract herself from the Main Road to Success.

And yet she sure didn't allow herself to fall into a rut. Maybe it was the World Book, or maybe it was just her nature. But she found ways to make life interesting.

HOW OTTO ENTERED OUR LIVES was mostly a mystery to me. Mommy's letters revealed little more.

I was between six and seven years old when we began stopping after church to visit friends of Mommy's, the Breithopfs. They lived almost right next to our Grace Lutheran Church. They had a son called Junior who had lost an arm in the war, and I always think of him in his uniform with the empty sleeve pinned up or tucked neatly into his suit jacket, a fairly common sight in those postwar days.

Otto's family, just arrived from the Old World

Junior's father, Mr. Briethopf, was a jolly round man. On several occasions he took me all the way into Philadelphia on the trolley and the "el" subway. Once in Philadelphia, a real bonanza occurred for me, because it was lunch and sodas and a hot butterscotch sundae and chocolate candy at Schrafft's. Then the purchase of a little doll (I could pick *anyone*) dressed in a very decorative costume. It was bedazzling to have someone — especially a man — pay attention and shower me with gifts.

Looking back, I think I may have been removed from the scene so Junior's friend, Otto, could court Mommy without me hanging on to her. I have no idea where J.G. and Linda were dispersed to. The Breithopfs were featured prominently in the wedding pictures I found recently. I don't remember being able to single out my future stepfather during the courting stage, but I DO know that most her friends had begun urging her to find a man to marry, "for the children's sake."

In that era, it was common belief that a woman needed to be taken care of, and not by her own means. Care had to be

Otto and his fine Packard

dispensed by a man, so she needed to find one. And maybe they thought they had found one for her. One of her letters in particular revealed that she tried to back out of the marriage at the last minute but was deterred by her pastor and her friends.

> **. . . I do not love Otto. I married him for the sake of my kids. After I wanted to call off the wedding because of my doubts, but friends, relatives, our minister, all thought the match was right. I had understandable nervousness because of how my first marriage ended. I have only said the words "I love you" three times to him—only once since we've been married—and I would have given a lot if I could have been able to say it and mean it.**

She had never told any of her first batch of children this bit of information, and I am sure she wouldn't tell their next two children, products of Otto's and her union. In any case, one fine Spring day Crazy Otto, which became one of her nicknames for him, along with "Der Führer," came around to our house, with a great bag of candies, wearing a brown pin-striped double-breasted suit and showy brown and white spectator shoes. Otto was a veteran of the war also, a decorated hero with a Purple Heart and other medals. He'd taken shrapnel in the back of his head, which was repaired with a metal plate leaving a slick spot back there. As we got to know him, we wondered whether that metal plate was what caused him and us all those mental problems that began to surface.

He was the church organist and the choir director of a different Grace *Lutheran* church, not ours! Prophetic! Mommy was again a thoroughgoing Lutheran after my father left.

That big paper bag of candy gave us our first clue that he wasn't our type. As he prepared to dispense it to us candy-starved children, we stormed him, holding out our hands eagerly; and he smacked our hands while Mommy was absent from the room and yelped at us to behave ourselves.

So there we have it: a fine man, with a fine gleaming white Packard four-door touring car with side-mount spare tires and big running boards—very impressive to us of the $50 vintage junk cars. It was exquisite. But the car, the suit, the shoes didn't fool us! We let her know immediately that this man was not marriage material!

My mother designed and made her wedding dress.

We were so right—but she did marry him in 1950. I was seven years old, and I remember how beautiful she looked on her wedding day in her hand-made wedding dress, designed and sewn by her. It was made of fine silk organza, with a scalloped hem in between which its two layers were cut-out eyelet flowers with hand-sewn sequins holding them in place. She later made my wedding dress almost exactly like hers. Otto looked elegant in his double-breasted suit and boutonniere, and there was a champagne reception afterward at the Briethopf's, the perpetrators of this bad idea. It was again in their home, the opening scene of the crime.

Linda at age three was not at the wedding. J. G. and I of course were not present on their wedding night; but right then, she told us later, was the start of things falling apart. Otto, the choir director-teetotaler to that point, got very drunk and stayed drunk much of the rest of the marriage. I couldn't know now whether he had always been a drunk, or whether it was the grave disappointment he felt about his new situation that triggered the sudden change. I tend to suspect the former. Could my mother have been that wayward from the wedding night on? I doubt it, though she was for most of their marriage.

Otto next to his war-hero friend, Junior Briethopf.

Nancy shared her impressions recently with me, saying she didn't think he drank heavily from the beginning of the marriage, but that later he did. I can't be sure, and she didn't exist until two years into the marriage. But she remembers how much he loved music and would have his little Nancy standing on his feet to dance with him.

WE CHILDREN WERE WARY, AND soon he did another thing that made him suspect.

Our house was a Cape Cod design, with a center staircase and a roomy upstairs center hall with a window that looked onto our back yard. The hall led to two large rooms on either side with a long crawl space behind the hall connecting the two rooms, both sides of which had a small door into the crawl spaces. Inside each door, the eaves were crammed with piles of books my mother had probably inherited from her parents, a treasure trove of classic reading. Once Otto arrived, we three children made the cubby hole our secret refuge.

One day shortly after the wedding, in that center upstairs hallway, he had set up our old family cedar chest that was filled with my grandfather's artifacts from Africa and Peru.

Otto had draped the cedar chest in white sheets and set up big spotlights on either side. Each of us had to disrobe down to nothing but white underpants for this strange "photo shoot." We three each had to take our turn posing on top of the cedar chest in different poses, while he shot rolls and rolls of black and white film. He developed them himself, using Uncle Bob's darkroom in the basement.

I don't remember seeing the photos more than once and I don't know what happened to them. There was no repeat of this kind of thing. It scared me, and I didn't know what to be scared about, but it was an uncomfortable thing to do with a stranger we didn't trust who had now invaded our happy home. I imagine my mother might have had a talk with him about the event, but not sure. I was too young to even think of him as a pervert, but I remember feeling very ill at ease about the experience.

Our lives had been quite routine-free, every day different, disorganized, and carrying its own brand of freedom. We each did mostly what we wanted to do.

Otto worked in Philadelphia at the G.E. Switchgear Division. He never drove his chariot to work but took the Red Arrow trolley into 69th Street and then a P.T.C. trolley to the plant at 69th and Elmwood Avenues. He would leave in the very early morning with his big black lunchbox in hand.

Things deteriorated quickly; to my young mind it seemed that suddenly we were in prison. At the end of the day he would come lurching up the driveway, loaded up with shots and beers from O'Donnell's, the neighborhood corner bar, clutching two quarts of Schmidt's beer in the brown paper bag. He was not a happy drunk, so the moment he entered what had been OUR home, a pall settled over it. One of us would carry out his welcome-home ritual and pour him a beer, putting our finger on the top of the mug so the head was just perfect and not a drop spilled. He would then proceed from somewhat drunk to ugly. The demand was consistent: dinner on the table when he walked in the door. The table had to be set, children — who were to be seen and not heard — were called formally to the table, and he would launch into the evening grace before dinner. His state of drunkenness dictated how rambling the grace was. It usually started out, "Come Lord Jesus, be our guest, and with this food may Thee be blessed." The prayers would then become a vehement string of epithets against his new wife's wayward behavior, and he would forget about Jesus being a guest.

"Jeeeeezus Christ Almighty, God, help this woman to get the GODDAMN meal on the table on time, by Christ Almighty!" was how the rant would begin. It would go on, with him railing out to God what a wayward bitch she was, and what matters in particular "really burned his ass," and more. It was really a desperate plea to his God to get this god-damned woman straightened out—which we already knew by then was not going to happen. He began to know she was permanently crooked—we could have told him that.

If we dared to snicker or look up from our bowed-head positions during the protracted "grace," we could be smacked, flicked soundly with his middle finger on our cheeks, or just sent to bed without supper. Often it would be Mommy from whom emitted the first snort of laughter. Then another one of us. Naturally, it became hard not to explode with more laughter, bringing severe punishments for our transgressions.

We learned over time the pattern: that it was really *HER* transgressions that *WE* would pay for, which was his plan. She would sin, and we would do the penance. Mommy was often late getting home, because she had a broken clock in her brain and totally lost track of time. There was also the other matter of being the unbroken horse whom no man would ever get a harness onto, apparently. It just went against her grain to be "boxed in" by some man telling her what to do. She had earned her freedom and independence, recovering from a devastating loss when our father left suddenly. And she must have been well schooled by her mother before her to simply use passive-resistance techniques to go her own way and do what she wanted and felt she needed to do. Otto, on the other hand, was surely saying to himself, "This dog won't hunt." Result: the dog—or the unbroken horse, whatever she was—rarely gave or enjoyed a smooth ride for herself.

By this time, Mommy had established a reasonably successful nutrition supplement business, which had been supporting us, after a fashion, if not in fits and starts. Otto didn't seem to be bringing an influx of cash into the marriage. Most of his cash seemed to go to O'Donnell's, but that we don't know. Naturally, she wasn't about to even consider disbanding her business, which was probably what Otto expected.

There were several events that must have at least created a pause in her business for some period. She became pregnant shortly after the marriage, and she delivered son Daniel Gustav Fech in December of 1951. Thirteen months and twelve days later, Nancy Elaine Fech became the newest addition. Otto was so proud and happy, now that he had his *OWN* children. These two gave us a happy focus and a relief from his overbearing ways. We considered them *OUR* own children too, and they were welcomed into our family with real love. I can only guess that Mommy slowed down her business pace a bit to bring these two into the world. I am sure she found a way to get her Nutrilite deliveries done to keep her customers supplied. But during that period of baby production, she also launched a few new enterprises.

"This is The Baby Butler," she glowingly announced, introducing us with her practice pitch to a piece of baby furniture that converted from a highchair, to a play table with chalkboard, to a stroller. Maybe more. "It's the ONLY piece of baby furniture you'll need," she'd tell the parents-to-be, who were totally unschooled in what they would need. Newly pregnant first-time parents-to-be were her favorite prospects, because she was in top form with her two new babies, and she was able to educate them as a parent of now five of us.

Funny—just this minute for the first time I got the reference to "butler," referring to a person who makes life easy and smooth for you. As a pre-teen saddled with taking care of these babies—and now needing to spend a good part of my day converting the item into its next needed function, I didn't find it a butler-like at all—the item instead added to my workload.

The Baby Butler was like a Chinese puzzle that you could keep taking apart and turning it into something else, either directly after the child finished his or her meal, or when it was time to play, or go for a walk when a stroller was needed. I believe it also converted into a chalkboard as he/she got older. Anything that encouraged children toward artistic pursuits turned out to tie right into another enterprise she found, The Famous Artists Courses.

I can't really be sure when she launched this business, but it might have been after she had Nancy. This correspondence course began in the late 1940s, and by 1950 was selling for about $300 a course. I would guess she made maybe $100 out of the sale, which was a significant figure back then. As an artistic person herself, she became a spinner of dreams, which she did with real conviction. She was just a better salesperson than recruiter of a sales team.

The method of selling took a lot of persuasive phone calls and letter writing, which is why it might have worked better than door-to-door selling. The dream spinning began with little classified ads in the backs of magazines and on matchbook covers, and she would follow up generated leads. "Think you can draw?" the ads asked. "Think you can write?" There was a Famous Writers Course also. The little test the potential student needed to pass by calling the number or mailing in a form to determine their "aptitude" was one a trained clam could pass.

I don't remember if she was the person who studied the tentative sketches and essays people sent in to see if they could write or draw enough to qualify. I do know she would spend hours on the phone having sincere talks with the hopefuls, saying they had real talent and could possibly be accepted into the program. As she talked, she would always be doodling drawings herself. Then she'd set the appointment to "close the deal." So ultimately she did need to show up at their homes, but by appointment.

Quite regularly she'd come home, gloating, "Hot damn, I sold another one! My ship is finally coming in," she'd say. If she couldn't sell them one thing, she'd pivot to sell them another. Her ship was *always* coming in, just around the corner of her globe. In actuality, we began to think it had fallen off the edge and would never come in. We couldn't seem to get ahead, and Otto and his steady income didn't seem to have a great effect.

It turned out he wanted just what the first man wanted: a clean house, a well-cooked meal, and clean clothes. Add to that clean and quiet children and an obedient wife, none of which we were. It was a roll of the dice and a bad bet for him, taking on a wife and us three.

After Otto arrived, he took on creating order in the household. Shortly after the wedding, I was seven years old, when I was given the opportunity to stand on a little stepstool and wash the dinner dishes—and the whole day's dishes as well. My new dishwashing career was launched with a rare ice cream cone from Doc Raymond's pharmacy. We now also had regular chores, and lots of them. On Saturday mornings our friends would loiter outside our door till we finished sweeping, mopping, dusting and cleaning up the disorder as best we could, making neat piles of the many papers at Mommy's secretary desk, always covered with her scribbled notes, random phone numbers, word fragments, and drawings of fashionable women and clothing design ideas. Believe it or not, when we had finished our tasks, he actually put on white cotton gloves and checked for dust, something I assume his commanding officer had done in the barracks when he was in the Army. He tried so hard to make things go well.

Annie didn't clean or do laundry. She cooked and tended to us. Even though it was Annie who was now usually cooking the evening meal, it *had* to be Mommy serving it to him. Often Mommy would come gliding in the front door minutes before the E.T.A. of Otto; and each us would be hiding by a window on watch, ready to holler out his position: "Hurry, Mommy! He's halfway up the driveway!"

Annie would hold out and wave her apron like a toreador, urging her to quickly step into it, saying, "Harry, harry, Massas Fatch, hairrrr comes the Master!" My mother would glide into the apron as Annie tied it on her, Mommy grabbing a stirring spoon for effect; and Annie would dash out the front door where stolid husband Alfred sat waiting with the engine running in his black 1940 Ford coupe, ready to make a quick getaway. Mommy would serve a delicious home-cooked Irish comfort food dinner with great aplomb and that secret grin she had that allowed us all to share the triumph of the moment. Those were on the good nights.

T HE BAD NIGHTS GOT PROGRESSIVELY worse. We were never allowed to leave the table until we had asked "May I please be excused?" Often, we were not excused from the table till 8 p.m., not allowed to utter a word and prohibited from doing homework at the table or look at the World Books, depending on how much punishment he needed to extract for Mommy's sins of the day. We just had to sit quietly and suffer. I don't want our new life to sound exaggerated," but we three wild Indians were entering a new kind of life.

Sometimes on nights when she was home to serve dinner, she had evening Nutrilite meetings afterward to attend, and Mr. Wilson would pick her up. This would not be a good night. An important part of the Nutrilite business was built on meetings for recruiting new distributors and teaching sales. As much as the meetings were a key part of the business, Otto never wanted her out of the house at night and fought it bitterly every time. So what? She had responsibilities and people expecting her to bring products and help them with their people they'd recruited.

In my observation over the years, there was not a shred of romance between Mommy and Mr. Wilson, though he may have wished it otherwise. He was as colorless a person, always dressed in a tie and business suit, as I'd ever met. There was nothing romantic about Willie the Worm. No matter. Otto was jealous to the extreme and sure there was a hot romance going on.

In expression of his jealousy and desire to control her, Otto would go about locking the doors so she couldn't get out. We were always ready to aid her escape, covering for her and distracting him so she could go out a window or alternate door. If she did escape—and she usually did—he would shut off *all* the electricity, and we children would spend the night in darkness.

The dark nights happened frequently for other reasons also. If she failed to arrive home from her sales by dinner time, the lights would go out, and the doors would lock her *out* rather than in. She would have to go to each door and try to get in. Could we have expected otherwise from a mad switchgear man? Shutting the electricity down was his ultimate power.

It became a game and we were team-mates, and we developed into quite a team to help her escape on those nights. We'd do what we could, trying not to get ourselves in trouble but enjoying the game of outwitting him.

One night she sneaked out the back door while he was guarding the front door. She made it to Mr. Wilson's car. Otto stormed out the front door when he realized he'd been snookered, and he sat right down on the hood of the car. Mommy said to Mr. Wilson, "Drive on, Roy," in her calm voice; and Mr. Wilson pulled away slowly with Otto on the hood. When Otto realized the car wasn't going to stop, he kind of rolled off at about fifteen miles per hour and gave up—with us and all the neighbors watching. This sometimes made our neighbors wary of us as playmates for their children. We understood.

We went to bed with no supper and in darkness again. We began keeping flashlights and candles in our bedrooms so we could do our homework, carefully listening for his footsteps so we could feign sleep. I doubt we fooled him, but he was wise enough to avoid violence with us.

Sleep didn't come easily when we never knew what he would do to her in his rage and now increased state of drunkenness as we waited for her to come home . To distract ourselves we would crawl into the cubbyhole crawl space under the eaves with a flashlight to our treasure trove of children's classic books, and we would read, read, read those fairy tales as we tried to block out these days and the night to come. We hoped, and we prayed, too, that Otto would be asleep when she got home. He never was.

CHAPTER 26 – THE TASKMASTER

IN BETWEEN TIMES, WE HAD means of having as normal a routine as possible. We had the biggest yard on the whole street and one of the few single homes. This was one part of life where our resources were expansive, with stone steps, stone walls, access to the back side of all the stores, several great climbing trees, and plenty of secret places. Even so, our friends were scared to come into our home; and we were scared to invite them, never knowing what might happen. Usually Saturday mornings were a pretty good bet, but we had many chores to do before being released. While Mommy expected a semblance of order from her children; Otto considered himself a military drill sergeant. We literally had to clean the entire house including our bedrooms, bathroom and kitchen, polish the shoes for church, and mop the floors. I can see him now conducting his white-gloved critical inspection, sucking on his bad teeth and looking for flaws (he had never gone to the dentist during his reign with us or seemingly years before that). Meanwhile, our playmates lurked nearby, somehow attracted to his procedure. If one of us could escape for a minute, we'd update them on how we were progressing. Finally, if we passed, we were free for the rest of the day.

There were usually failures and more work to correct.

Early in the marriage, Otto had done something we came to appreciate. With pick and shovel, he had hacked down the basement

E. ANNE POUNDS

crawl space to be the same level as the other half of the unfinished basement, which essentially doubled its size. He'd had a concrete man come in and pour a floor over the tamped dirt. That was the solitary investment into our home I can remember his making, except for an indicator light on the hallway wall next to the basement door to indicate if someone had left on a light downstairs.

Every kid had roller skates then and never went anywhere without the skate key and skates. With the completion of the concreted area, we now had a full circuit we could skate around, impeded only by the cellar steps and two supporting brick pillars in the middle. "Pop," which is what we had to call him, would be at O'Donnell's by early Saturday afternoon, and we could skate the afternoon away, pretending we were at the Chez Vous Skating Rink in 69th Street. Our neighborhood attraction was the offsetting factor to life with our drunken father.

There was a basement entrance, so kids could sneak in and out the back door. If we heard him come in the kitchen door, our friends could scatter quickly out the basement door.

The basement held many good memories for us as our skating rink, but bad things happened there too.

WHILE HE DID NOT PHYSICALLY attack us children, Otto did sometimes brutalize Mommy. When she was pregnant with Danny in about her eighth month, he shoved her on the basement stairs when she was coming up from turning the circuit breaker back on to avoid another night of darkness, defying his punishment. Thwarting his highest power, she had just committed the ultimate sin with that act. It called for a higher form of punishment. He pushed her backward forcefully as she came upstairs. It was hard enough that she tumbled all the way down the stairs, and then he locked the door to the basement, where he thought he would keep her all night until she learned her lesson. It was a scary night. She didn't lose the baby, but we all saw what he would do when pushed. Her letters described that she sought a divorce then.

That night she pulled herself together and, in her stoic manner, went out the back door to our next-door neighbor Sissy and called the police. Otto spent the night in jail for drunk and disorderly conduct, which happened more than once. But she didn't press charges. At that time, the police never considered correcting "a woman getting out of hand" a serious misdemeanor.

In those days, the 1950s, women were still chattel—the meaning in the dictionary is defined as *"personal as opposed to real property; any tangible movable property (furniture or domestic animals or a car etc."*). I think many wives were considered chattel and viewed as wayward—by husbands as well as the policemen who "broke up" the fights.

Her way of interacting with husbands may have been her key mistake during the first marriage as well as the second. Mommy just couldn't conform or measure up on the housewife/mother/chattel score. She pursued her current tangent, attracted to what interested her at the moment and unconcerned about later consequences.

The basement stairs event was the experience that J. G. told me years later was when he decided he would kill our stepfather. He never voiced it; it was just a secret plan he wanted to accomplish.

When Uncle Bob and Aunt Harriett left, Mommy began thinking about taking in boarders, maybe to bring order and protection for her from Otto, and bring some cash into our home. "Taking in boarders" was a concept that had a healthy tradition in the previous century but might have been less popular after recovery from both the Great Depression and World War II. The 1950's by contrast were now "boom times." Yet few people owned cars; few families had a television yet. Compared to the Depression, though, Americans had arrived at the Good Life. The Field-Fech family had personally not landed there yet.

Soon we did acquire two boarders, well after Aunt Harriett and Uncle Bob made their graceful exit for the south of France. We had a "spare bedroom," just yawningly empty—I believe it was the new upstairs bedroom, which Otto had created by dividing one of the two large bedrooms into two rooms, one for Linda and me, and one for J. G. Otto and my mother moved into the first floor bedroom with the closet opening into the bathroom, which was a good place to eavesdrop on their bedroom scenes.

First, Scrappie arrived, so named because he apparently had a short temper and was always "getting into scraps," as he told us rather modestly with an embarrassed ducking of the head in a Southern way—he was from South Carolina. He was joined by his friend, Dick.

They added a lot to our household and filled in to babysit us, cook the meals, and help keep our house nicer than we were accustomed to. Dick fixed broken stuff and did laundry; and Scrappie, a short-order cook, often cooked. Mommy had a little extra money coming in from their board, Annie's workload lightened considerably, and Alfred didn't have the interminable waits in the car, seething, while we all waited for Mommy to appear so Annie could leave. Our stepfather seemed to be comfortable with the arrangement, as I remember it, probably because the evening meal was so regularly ready at a reasonable hour.

Scrappie was our equivalent of an angel arriving in the kitchen. He could do a mean hush puppies and fried chicken meal and other southern dishes. While Annie's cooking was solid Irish cooking, our dinners by Scrappie were Southern dreams. They were served around the time most people ate dinner. He got off shift about just the time Annie would need to leave for the evening.

Life was beautiful: we had what Grant had always wanted: an orderly house, meals on the table regularly, clean clothes and a sense of order in the home. We fell in love with "the boys," and Mommy was now able to keep herself busy pitching Gold Bricks.

How we actually acquired boarders I learned more about when I found the story in one of her letters, written to the man who became her lover about a decade after the boarders arrived. It seemed that it was to help her find the money for new furniture: twin beds to get some separation from the man she didn't love:

> **. . . One morning, after a horrible night—things were so bad (my daughter) Anne had to call in the Law—Irish Annie decided we had to do something about the situation.**
>
> **And that is how "Operation Twin Beds" became a plan. In spite of that, I failed to achieve Twin Bed**

Status in 1951. My beloved Irish Annie Master Minded the idea to help me achieve a little less togetherness in the bedroom. In spite of the effort, I bore a son to Otto; our dope addict boarder of whom I was very fond ended up back in prison; and my Irish Annie quit. I was only to get her back by bearing a 9-1/2-lb. son and asking her to be the most honorable Godmother to the splendid effort.

"After all these events I concluded that God may have been saying "no" to my Twin Bed Ambition, so I canceled the order at Lit Brothers— they were solid cherry early American; complete Mr. And Mrs. all the way. The cancellation of my order probably accounts for Nancy, for whom I have no regrets. She might be my best kid, so far. . .

(She went on to describe how Annie introduced the idea to her.)

. . . "Mrs. Fatch," she said, Yez should move out of the hupstairs Masterr Bedroom and teken hover the nursery—and rent oot that lovely beeg dining room to a coopla fine gentlemen. Thes would calm the Masterr down and you would be setting the rent mooney aside fer the purpose of obtainin' a new set of bedroom furniture—includin' the twen beds! Yaas, Life'll be aisier for ye!'

"And Annie, Mathilda (me mather-in law) and meself shines up the Masterr Bedroom and papers the closet with cedar paper, even. And I found meself two lovely gentlemen in shert order to provide me the mooney fer the twen beds fund.

[Mommy continues her letter, now describing Scrappy's sad story:]

He married the only daughter of a wealthy family who owned eleven factories throughout the South. Scrappy was studying at the University of Miami to be a lawyer when he received a phone call to come and work summers running a bulldozer for the father of the girl he was dating. As the situation presented itself, he married her, and his in-laws made him a vice president of the company; and he soon found himself wearing conservative ties and dark suits—a fake situation that wore him down. Gradually he took up drinking (possibly again).

Before long his wife has a very tiny C-section baby. Just as the baby is born, he faints, which deems him a failure of a man in his in-laws' eyes.

Next, since it was during the war, he was drafted into the Army. With relief on all sides, he goes off to war—quite confident he will be killed and die a heroic death and show his lousy in-laws that their daughter married a hero.

He gets stationed in Italy. Well, somewhere in Italy he spends two days and three nights in a foxhole with two dead buddies and is captured by the damned Nazis—which coops him up rather unheroically until the end of the war. When he comes home he sees that his in-laws don't want him around and have engineered a divorce. After the divorce is final, Scrap and his beautiful wife (who he loves but who is controlled by the family) and their little daughter spend their final night in their little house, with all furniture gone and just the wall-to-wall and drapes left. They swear to love each other always, in spite of her damned family.

Scrappy never saw her again and found she soon married a guy who looked and acted more like a V.P. Soon she has another baby, which Scrappy calculates is very likely his.

At this point Scrappy went off the deep end and somehow finds himself tangling with the nymphomaniac daughter of a small-town sheriff, who lured him to her daddy's hunting shack deep in the woods.. After a three-day orgy, her daddy hunts them down and sends in a couple of his boys to avenge her non-existent virtue. Cops come banging on the door of the cabin, and Scrappy (in a very weakened condition now) charges out and scuffles with the two big guys, who are holding revolvers on him. One of the cops drops his revolver in the scuffle; Scrap grabs it and shoots the poor cop.

Five days later the cop dies, leaving a wife and three kids. Scrap got sent to the state pen in Florida.

After seven or eight months in a chain gang, during which time he saw seven men beaten to death, he escaped through the swamp with bloodhounds chasing him..

He ended up in New York state and found his new friend Dick. Dick worked at some exclusive boys' summer camp in New York State as a cook. Dick was in love with Scrappy (he's a homo) and decided to dedicate all his resources to helping Scrap restart his life.

Scrappy is no homo himself but decides he needs to have some help. Scrappy has the dope habit by now, acquired during prison, but with Dick's help gets off the stuff and puts on a little weight and gets his nerves calmed down. Dick gets Scrap a job at Camp Dudley in Westport, N.Y. in the Adirondacks, no fingerprints required.

After the summer closed for the season, they somehow connected with my friends Ruthann and Paul, who introduced them to me; and they moved in as our boarders a week later. They both worked as short-order cooks at a bar and restaurant at 69th Street.

They thought Otto was a monster and took turns looking after me and the kids. They ran the vacuum, hung out clothes, and cooked the dinners. We had wonderful Southern fried chicken with hush puppies twice a week; and the boys provided a lot of the food from the restaurant."

"Well, I had never had it so good. —Scrappy even answered the phone and posed as my Japanese houseboy— it went over big with my high-class customers—until that one day he got carried away and told Annie "we" didn't need her anymore, and she got mad and quit. . .

We had some wonderful times with those two guys, and we all loved them dearly. We felt like a family again. Otto, of course, behaved much better with their presence at the dinner table and in our household.

Sadly, gentle Dick "came up queer" as I overheard in a murmured phone conversation. While I didn't know what it meant, and it wasn't something anyone felt needed to be explained to young children, Mommy probably didn't feel comfortable leaving her seven-year-old son to be babysat by Dick. Scrappie, it turned out, had that terrible secret of his own. In retrospect, it's possible that he began to have romantic feelings toward my mother. Late one night I overheard them having an earnest conversation in the breakfast room. I sneaked into the seldom- used dining room and listened at the door.

" . . . think I can just make a clean break and start over again if you'll help me, Dot . . . nobody saw me . . . got away clean . . . two years ago . . . we're good for each other, Dot."

"You have to do the right thing, Scrappie. You've got to turn yourself in. You can't live like this, hiding out here."

My mother seemed to be making a convincing case for something that had quite a bit of emotion and difficult decision making. She was firm. I remember his head was in her lap, and he was crying.

The next day Scrappie was gone. We wailed when Mommy told us they wouldn't be coming back—they were our saviors, our fun guys who cooked great stuff.

O TTO'S PARENTS LIVED IN BYWOOD, Upper Darby, and we would often go to see them on weekends or for a Sunday dinner. We children would even go by ourselves on the trolley, which had a stop close to their home. After all, they were the only grandparents we had, our relationships with our paternal grandparents cut off after Grant left and our maternal grandparents were both dead. Both Otto's parents were immigrants from Germany. Grandmom was a homemaker; and Grandpop was a fine cabinetmaker for Philco, making beautiful large radio and TV wooden cases, I imagine. Grandmom looked like a twinkly-eyed Mrs. Santa Claus, but we later learned she was someone to watch out for. She may have been the reason Otto was so nutty.

Our new Grandmom and Grandpop

She doted on Linda, the baby of the "step-family" at first. As a skilled dressmaker, she would make Linda the frilliest dresses imaginable. She made a few for me, but I was at that awkward age where I dressed sloppily and never brushed my hair.

We were her instant grandchildren until . . . the new babies arrived.

Every holiday, no matter how minor, Grandmom observed with candy from the confectioners on Garrett Road to celebrate the occasion. Washington's Birthday brought forth twin cherry hard candies on stems. Halloween brought candy corn and an assortment of pumpkin candies, and Christmas was a bonanza of ribbon, rock, and barley candy animals on a stick and those pastel butter mints. Easter—-words belie description; but it was where we first learned about the finer delicacies of Easter baskets, such as buttercream eggs with a YELLOW center, just like a real egg! Beyond that, she baked exquisite German pastries of every kind. Her brother, Uncle A (for Adolph), was a professional Austrian baker of the highest order. Since we had had only rare sweet treats till this point, we soaked up the experience—maybe they did, too.

Grandmom certainly did not approve of or like Mommy, who burdened her only son with baggage: us. And Mommy was not a good German wife, not even close to it. We got the perspective on why Otto had slapped our hands when we grabbed for the candy on his first visit. We attacked the candy he brought that day somewhat like wolves on a carcass they'd just taken down, and we learned she exhibited the same corrective procedures. "Att-dat-dat-dat!," she'd scold if we ever touched a piece of candy without asking permission. Table manners had to be impeccable: "Napkin on the lap, no elbows on the table, children do not speak unless spoken to. Say 'excuse me,' and wait until an adult answers before you speak." And don't even THINK of leaving the table without asking, "Excuse me? (pause) may I please be excused?" She must have thought us the equivalent of wild Indians.

Still, our visits to our very first grandparents were novel, even with the strict rules. We had a rather Gestapo- like life at home once Otto joined our household, so any change in routine was noteworthy.

But Otto, eager to legitimize the name "Pop," contributed to grandparent joy in the first several years with his two "real grandchildren" Danny and Nancy. Linda, J.G. and I then lost any status with Otto's parents. Grandmom devoted all her dressmaking skills and devotion to little Nancy and Danny, making them twin outfits and doting on them. I was relieved, and you can see in the photo how unsuited I was to wear these frothy concoctions.

I just wasn't the frilly dress type.

MOST OF OUR FUN ADVENTURES were ad hoc, occurring serendipitously as our mother wandered off the main highway to success onto a side road of distraction.

There was that day, however, when our mother rather uncharacteristically actually planned and executed a big family adventure at French Creek State Park. The park had everything we needed for a fun day: picnic tables, grills, a huge lake, and miles to wander and play. Today would be different—actually planned and anticipated, with a real cookout and swimming in the lake all day long. I remember her potato salad, which was an unusual occurrence. As great a place as our swim club was, spending all day, every day there got boring at times. The allure of more natural places to swim attracted: lakes, creeks, ponds, rivers, ocean and bay.

Otto was not coming that day, which always made it more fun. He didn't adapt well to these family fun occasions. He was rarely along on our excursions, because Saturday was his big bar day, with the usual consequences. I was in charge of the little ones. I was about eleven and had already accepted the yoke of childcare easily, since it happened so frequently. In fact, I began regularly babysitting as a commercial enterprise sometime around age eleven through a local babysitting agency a neighbor, Mrs. Gorman, had set up. I had a Girl Scout certification and earned fifty cents an hour after her cut. My experience with my three younger siblings made me quite in demand because I did the dishes and straightened up after getting them in bed.

Linda was seven and had graduated from being my charge to my sometimes helper. Danny was about three, and Nancy was two and full of such charm we called her Fancy Nancy. She made friends as easily as Mommy did.

And so it happened. Mommy was making friends with a family who got interested in Nutrilite, Danny was busy taunting my junior assistant Linda. I was both keeping an eye on Nancy playing at the lake's edge and enjoying the view of the novel charms of the lake in between being glued to my book.

Pretty soon I noticed that Nancy had slipped out of my view. I left the waterside to find her, grabbing Danny's and Linda's hands so we could search together. We didn't find her. And we didn't find her. And Mommy didn't find her. And the people around us who had seen us together didn't find her. And the park rangers and lifeguards didn't find her.

The afternoon wore on, desperation building as we faced the inevitability of the lake. It was hard to look in that direction. The land search became more frantic, with many people joining in as word spread. The guilt I felt sickened me. I hated that I had loved that water so much I forgot to love my little sister. She was gone. I still cannot imagine what guilt my mother must have felt, yet I felt the blame was mine. She had no words, no scolding, no angry looks. She just seemed to get methodical and distant as desperation built.

By 3 p.m. the park rangers gathered together the people who had given up their happy day to aid in the search. The rangers described how we would search the area of the lake near where Nancy had been playing by forming a human chain, holding hands and walking slowly into deeper water.

As men, women and children volunteers took each other's hands, spontaneous praying aloud began. But here was the problem: the words of the prayers were difficult to form, so they came out in stutters and stops. It can be hard to petition God to save a child while using your feet to find that child. Some people can pray at the drop of a hat and know exactly what God needs to hear to bring aid to the project. Not that day. No one wanted to ask out loud for help finding our Nancy's body. Unspoken prayers turned to wordless tears. This became infectious. I will never wipe from my memory the faces with tears streaming down. I prayed that I would not be the one to stumble over her. She was as much my baby as she was Mommy's.

Deductive reasoning drew me to accept (A) if the grownups were "dragging the lake," then (B) all other options had failed. Two other factors contributed. One was my mother's pattern of hoping for the best while not believing it would really happen or last long if it did. This belief pattern was now a part of each her children's mental processes as well. The additional presence of Otto in our lives had graphically conditioned us children to expect little and know it would soon become worse at any moment. The horror of knowing this loss was my fault washed over me with shame.

The solemn group of maybe 100 people slowly baby-stepped their way into the deeper part of the lake. We did not find her little body. The talk of kidnapping began, raising a different kind of alarm. A new search plan was mapped out.

At 4 p.m. a couple from the campground area of the park showed up at the office with a miracle: Nancy in tow. She had wandered almost a mile from our picnic site at the edge of the lake and, too young to tell them where she had come from, she had apparently enchanted them for several hours at their campsite until they decided somebody might be missing her.

I don't remember much of the reunion because my grief and guilt were still overwhelming me. I could hardly believe she was there, alive. I don't remember my mother's reaction. Nancy appeared like an apparition — like the green flash you get when you turn off a bright light. It was hard to accept that she was real, still alive. But there she was, Miss Fancy Nancy.

Mommy came home a few days later with a purchase and a plan. "Here. Put these on the kids," she said in her resolute voice. She had two harnesses and dog leashes, fresh from the Bazaar of All Nations Pet Store. It worked out perfectly. From then on, our two little charges wore them wherever we went. Someone always had to have hold of each leash, just as if they were little puppies. And they never got lost again until they got old enough to run away from home.

O NE THING FOR SURE, THE addition of a "breadwinner" who went to work every day didn't do much to change our lives monetarily. We still got our clothes from thrift shops and rummage sales, still got our dental work done through charity, and the only vacation I ever remember taking with Otto was a weekend in a rented room at the shore, all of us in one mildewed room. He didn't like the beach.

Rummage sales played a huge role in our lives, and it was truly where she got all our clothes and many household items, both before and after Otto arrived. This letter she wrote to Gil, her lover (yes, that happened), some years after that two-day vacation with our stepfather, describes well the thrill of the thrift shop hunt.

My Beloved Playboy (and Business Associate)

I have only to close my eyes to see my special portrait of you—it appears on the black velvet lining of my eyelids, the size of a Green Stamp in true and living color . . .

. . . Friday was a glorious Rummage day: one Methodist sale (I got three Nutrilite and one cosmetics lead), and one Episcopal, the Holy Redeemer. (Annie would say, ". . . and did youse get that from the Holy Redeemer?" I must stop and see her. I miss her daily.)

Well, as usual, Shelly (the ARTIST) went into the fray first. She grabs all the high-class stuff she can and looks it over after things calm down a bit, discarding what she doesn't want. I'm absolutely no good at this method. I'm too polite and end up handing wonderful merchandise to other determined grabbers. One time after the first twenty minutes, most ladies had bags full; and I was wandering around with an agate tea strainer in my hand—most of the ladies thought I was a helper, I guess. Meanwhile, Shelly had a complete trousseau, plus a nice lamp.

So now I approach the challenge in a different way: I arrive late (the grabbers are gone; and most, but by no means all, of the good stuff, too). And the Church Ladies are tired but happy (money in the till) and have, perhaps, had a cup of tea and a sandwich. I stroll in, well dressed, calm, hair combed, make-up fresh, white gloves on (if the costume calls for them) and wearing my Murray Space Shoes. I wear a tape measure around my shoulders. I look confused (which I am). The Ladies usually whisper about the M. Shoes and someone usually knows what they are and that they cost $90. Well, I soon have more high-class assistants than Grace Kelly-Rainier would get at Nan Duskin's. I have the chance to try on things, with advice; and I always pick nice ladies with big diamond rings for advice—they make the best sales prospects. Also, some rummage contributions arrive late—I got some real fine stuff on Friday in this happy way. Just for the heck of it, I'll list all I can remember of what I got for $23.00:

2 shirts (Danny), 2 pr. pajamas—boys his age wear out clothes, so very little

available

3 lovely blouses for Nancy

2 pr. Red wool knee sox for Nancy

1 scarf and one hat for Nancy (also one beautiful bouffant slip)

1 book on horses for Nancy, and 1 for Dan

For Linda: 1 brown suit (too small)

1 2-pc. Knit dress

3 blouses (OK)

4 blouses (too small)

Raincoat

Skirt

Lovely, lovely sweater

Bermuda shorts and 2 books

1 slip and 1 half-slip

1 nightie

Hat and gloves

For Anne: Nothing— she spends $5.00 on 1 BELT! I HAVE SOME THINGS

SHE WANTS, BUT SHE'LL HAVE TO PAY.

For Ott: 1 white sport shirt (new B.V.D.)

1 blue dress shirt (Arrow)

1 wild red (Florida type) shirt

(He didn't like any but wore 2 of them already)

Also: 5 prs. gloves (1 long black chiffon for witch costumes)

2 matching lampshades (look good)

2 crystal and silver salt shakers (don't match but nice)

1 yellow pottery teapot and small bowl

4 linen drapes, 2 wall hootenanny-things

2 guest towels (new)

Hatbox with dozen assorted roses and corsages (artificial)

14 hats

2 slips and 2 bras

For me:

1 red sweater (love it!)

1 gray jacket

1 navy dress (silk)

1 green wool dress

1 blue tucked jersey dress

3 skirts

1 pink eyelet dress

1 lavender dress (both summer)

1 blue wool suit (don't like it so I'll swap it)

1 pr. red stockings

Some belts and scarves

3 books: "Baruch (My Own Story), which I'm reading; The Devil's Advocate" and

"Crime and Punishment."

5 nice pocket books (Hardy Boys)

4 bureau scarves

Holy Hannah! Didn't realize what I was getting into when I started this!

BEST of all, a blue lame (silver thread) sexy, sexy dress I wouldn't be caught dead in. However, I saw Shelly looking at it several times with longing; but Joyce and Margaret said "NO! Absolutely NOT!" So I bought it in order to use it as bait to pry "my" dress out of her at the right moment—and, joy of joys, it worked!

Last summer we went to a sale (Jewish), and I stayed in the car while Shelly engaged in the

Rummage Scrimmage—at which, as I told you, I'm no good. Fortunately for me, Shelly loves the kind of clothes I look good in that aren't good on her: sheath (straight tight skirts), more or less tailored. So she usually (reluctantly) gives them to me after she tries them on (I buy them from her, of course). Well, this day, she had one dress I absolutely loved— just perfect for business and fit just right. It was much too tight for her and the style was no good on her either. But she wouldn't part with it (it was $1.50; I even offered her $5.00). No soap. She said she would lose enough weight to wear it by fall—if she didn't, I could buy it from her then. Well, I've needled her ever since—each time she comes over I offer her fattening food. When we go out, I buy her Frostie cones, etc. She HAS gotten thinner, and I was getting worried (about "my" dress, not her).

Well, I met her back at her house for a quick lunch before Rummage Sale No. 2 (the Episcopal one at Holy Redeemer), and we looked over each other's loot. I kept the sexy blue lame hidden until the very last—she did not know I had seen the other two stop her (twice) from latching on to it. When I unfurled it from the bottom of the bag, her face was <u>very critical</u>: "Oh, no, Dottie. The color is all wrong for you. Makes you look so gray! (and old, she implied) and the low neckline is obscene— and really, it's not your type at all. I hope you didn't give more than a quarter for it—it's awful!"

"Well," I said, "I guess I got carried away—it is pretty bad on me. You try it on; let me see if it has possibilities. I could change it around. I like the material."

"No, Dottie. The stuff isn't worth it. If you changed the seams it would show, and the color really makes you look anemic!" (Me? Anemic?)

So, with trembling hands, she fitted her voluptuous curves into its contours; and IT FIT— EVERYWHERE! Shelly swished around and around while I sunk down in the couch muttering "Perfect, made for you. Wear it on New Year's Eve. I'll GIVE it to you—it's so much YOUR dress. It's yours."

Around and around she sashayed, so happy, looking like a Mae West-type mermaid with a split tail.

Then, at last when I was sure of success, I said, "Shelly, bring me that black dress I liked that you got last summer."

Over the summer I had even made sure she kept it aired it out and sprayed for moths; nagged her to do so. She said she forgot where she had put (hid) it, and that we'd better hurry. But I had an ace up my sleeve, a lovely suit (which had come in late, so she missed it), and I now used that card too. It was too short-waisted for me and too tight in the shoulders.

That did it. I now have my dress—I'm so-o-o tickled, and so is Shelly. She thinks she got the best of the deal, and so do I (I think I have). All business should end so happily!

I WAS SEVEN YEARS OLD when they married; and Linda; four years younger, somehow remembers some good times. Otto became the only father she ever knew. "Remember 'Pop' would make homemade doughnuts on Saturday mornings . . . and scrambled eggs with bologna?" Homemade doughnuts were a pretty big undertaking, and I also remember he loved and often made corn fritters. Mommy made apple fritters.

Maybe the strangest aspect of Otto was the seemingly complete metamorphosis he underwent after entering this marriage. I would

Otto, a war hero.

guess he took a big roll of the dice in taking on our motley group of wayward woman and wayward children. Maybe he never had a date or a girlfriend until he was introduced to Mommy. Maybe he was dazzled by her good looks and fun personality, from which he suffered a deficit.

But beyond all that speculation, we do have some evidence he was an outgoing well-liked fellow before we knew him. He had served honorably in the Army in the ski troops in Belgium and maybe Germany, receiving a Purple Heart and taking shrapnel in his head. (That slick spot on the back of his head and steel plate under the hair that covered most of the spot proved worrisome over time.) He was president of his class at Mastbaum High School in Philadelphia, which I believe was a school for gifted students. He was certainly gifted in math and music (and surely other things not revealed to me as a most unappreciative stepchild). He was an esteemed member of the Mastbaum Glee Club, singing in a quartet group as the bass or baritone. Music was one passion he shared with us, educating us in opera and classical music. We were often made to listen on Sunday afternoons after church to an opera or symphony. He would often sing along in a really great baritone. We didn't appreciate it, of course. It was difficult not to be able to play in the woods instead, but there was something pleasant about listening, because he was nicer. It was the soberest and best day of the week, a welcome respite. Blue laws kept the bars closed in that era. And he was a Mason! The highlight of the Christmas season was our family getting all dressed up in finery made by Grandmom, pretending we were a nice little family, and attending the Masons' Christmas party. Each of us received a ½-lb. box of hard candy that sparkled like ornaments on the tree. We each got our own box! Then there was his church affiliation as the choir director and organist in his Lutheran church. I never heard him play either the piano or organ, though he loved organ music passionately. But his roles in his church seemed to have just ended when he married.

"Remember when he presented me with that new TV when I was seven, still black and white, but *my* gift alone. I wasn't allowed to touch it, though . . . Remember him helping me with my math homework? . . . Remember he was happy when I started studying the Bible when we went to Faith Chapel?" Linda remembered it all.

Faith Chapel was a small independent church at the edge of The Woods. The young siblings, Danny and Nancy, attended with Linda. This worked out well for them, because they could walk to church on their own. Mommy started attending too, getting her first (but not last) dose of holy roller fundamentalism in a milder version. I don't remember people speaking in tongues, getting slain in the spirit, or prophesy (usually from Revelations and downright scary), but I do remember the altar call. Never done at our Lutheran church, it was a regular event at Faith Chapel, causing untold pressure on those who hadn't come forward, to answer "the call."

Contrasting the holy atmosphere of the little chapel, the shack of the Dugan boys was only 50 feet away on a hillside in The Woods. The three brothers were utterly frightening bruisers with wide noses broken more than once, deep-set porcine eyes, self-administered buzz haircuts, and necks as thick as the average waist. They lived in squalor in a structure on the side of a hill that would have been normal in the backwoods of West Virginia mountains but alien to our little suburb. Their single mother attended the Faith Chapel while they cooked up trouble. The brothers scared every kid in the vicinity with torturing and bullying as they roamed "their" woods. For sure, they'd be there waiting for their victims when church let out.

The pastor's name was Alvin Virgin, and the sign at the beginning of the little dirt driveway to the church shortened it to "A. Virgin." Later we always wondered if he was. He was a small man with a high voice, weak eyes and an ineffectual manner that failed to inspire me to spiritual heights. It was hard to imagine him being anything but a virgin, and it often got my mother snorting with laughter during the service, just over the way she pronounced with a long a, "A Virgin."

Otto didn't go to church that I could remember when he was in our household, which seems so strange in retrospect, considering his high level of church activity before marriage. My mother's devilishness must have driven his faith in the Almighty right out of him.

The good traits of our father and stepfather were easy to forget because his behaviors were so consistently awful to frightening. Linda felt a warmth for him that was unfathomable to me, but after she was married and had triplets, he was quite grandfatherly to her and the babies. At that time, he was retired and not in good health and living on his pension and social security; and when he needed care and feeding, we three sisters took care of him the best we could. Nancy and Danny, his "real" children, have described to me that they felt sorry for him. He was their father, and it is understandable.

I REMEMBER OTHER THINGS, NOT quite the pleasant memories Linda had.

We neighborhood kids were often embarked on a theatrical production, something that we put real effort into as a way to bring in money for the movies or a day at Chez Vous.

One day we were working on a "Tom Thumb wedding", starring three-year-old Nancy in one of Grandmom's fanciest creations with my crinoline under it for additional fluff, and appropriately, small Tommy Rheimer from up the street. The real Tom Thumb and his bride Lavinia were married in a lavish wedding put on by P. T. Barnum; and after that, Tom Thumb weddings were not unusual, often elaborately done by churches and organizations as fundraisers.

My favorite dress that zipped off for my jeans in a minute

Ours was to be a spring wedding, and our many cast members were in the basement working up the scenes. J. G., at age eleven or twelve, was watching our rehearsal, having just ironed his Boy Scout uniform and dressed and waiting for Mommy to arrive and take him to his Scout meeting. Uh-oh. She was late again, and Otto decided a punishment was required. He dismissed all the kids and had J.G., in his uniform, scrub the small area in the basement that was still dirt floor, on his hands and knees with a scrub brush and bucket. When she arrived, he was, of course, prohibited from going to the meeting. J. G.'S uniform was ruined, muddy and sopping wet. Otto stood there and supervised in his cruel way, blocking her from interceding.

That night of degradation may have been a turning point, as the hostility between stepfather and stepson grew deeper. J. G. was her first-born son and "protector" of Mommy. Otto's strategy of splitting us up didn't work. We stuck together, supporting her in her rebellion, and supporting each other to stand up to him in whatever ways we felt were "safe."

He would often choose the closed door of their bedroom for physical aggression. Never quite sure what his demands were, I would guess today it was for sex and her refusal of it.

"Ouch! Stop that! Get OFF me . . . leave me alone."

Sometimes she would scream or howl in anger and come running out of their bedroom, with him behind her, pushing and shoving her back in. It became a regular event. We children thought she was being beaten up from the sounds emitting from the closed door. "Leave her alone or we're coming in," we'd scream. In the upstairs hallway, we'd huddle and wait, with an armory of books, containers of water and assorted other stuff to drop on him if the tussle got taken out into their hallway directly below our armaments supply. It often did. He'd be pushing her back in with his barrel chest, saying, "Honest to God, Dottie—WORK with me, woman!" It was so creepy and terrifying.

In spite of his verbal and emotional cruelty, I was always surprised that "Pop" never hit us, which must have taken a great deal of discipline. He had many other ways of expressing his displeasure in each of us. He would call me a whore if I, when I became a teen, wore any make-up at all; he'd tell me my outfit was disgusting, and to "cover up!" The fashion of the day was already quite covered up, but he'd find something wrong.

Just once, he did hit me. I must have been about nine. Annie was having a bad day (probably waiting for Mommy to come home). I laughed at something silly; but in her bad mood, she thought I was making fun of her. Otto dragged me into Mommy's dining room-turned-office and whipped me with his belt until I lost control of my bladder. I can still remember it ruined my favorite dress now soaking wet with urine.

I had not committed the sin I was punished for. Humiliated, I went into the bathroom to take off my wet stinking clothes and rinse off in the tub. Covering up for the loss of his temper, he claimed I had made fun of Annie. We loved Annie so much—she was our savior in normalizing our lives. It broke my heart that she'd misunderstood my antics.

I BEGAN THE FIRST STAGE of my "exit strategy" without knowing it was such. Now that I was a Girl-Scout-certified babysitter at about age eleven or twelve, I began getting regular jobs through Mrs. Gorman's agency. I kept 50 cents an hour of the $3.50 she charged. Once at the home, I saw the parents out, assuring them all would be well, and I then had wonderful "regular" food to eat! I gorged on foods that rarely saw the light of day in our household: sliced roast beef, Jell-O puddings and whipped cream (my habit was to simply spray almost the entire can of Reddi-Whip into my mouth, a trick Janet and I had picked up outside the Acme Market from their cold box where early morning deliveries were left before the store opened). My employers also often stocked lunch meats, pastries, white bread—I'd even pour spoonfuls of white sugar on their buttered Wonder bread, a virtual unknown at home.

I worked hard at leaving an over-the-top impression by making the kitchen sparkling clean and the rest of the house tidied up (feeling all the while like an intruder and freeloader), which made me a very popular regular. After eating all the great food left for me and my charges and putting the children to sleep, I had the fun of looking through my employers' clothing drawers, medicine chests and closets to see how "regular" people lived. The searches revealed that most people had a whole bunch of stuff we didn't, and I marveled at the order most homes were kept in, the generous supplies of food, cleaning products, clothes, band-aids, bath soaps and shampoos, cosmetics, perfumes, and pretty things in these homes. Their rooms had "accessories." There was so little luxury in our household that seeing and examining these generous artifacts of life was a satisfying evening's work for me.

Not only did I feel like an intruder, I also was somewhat of a petty thief. I couldn't help myself. With unquenchable curiosity I would ransack their personal belongings; and on a regular basis I would carefully select and purloin a belt, a lipstick, a "preppie" piece of costume jewelry such as a circle pin, an alligator clamp sweater clip — usually something small I felt would enrich my life but not ruin theirs by much. At a younger age I found myself doing the same thing in Woolworths or Stitchberrys, our local five- and ten-cent store in the neighborhood. There I snitched silly little things that represented whimsy, something of which I seemed to be in very short supply in my daily life. I remember a yellow and red plastic bird, a cat's toy. I loved its brightness and silliness.

Somewhere during this time I arrived at adolescence; and as a fatherless child, I needed to find out whether I could be attractive to the male sex. Adolescent girls with fathers get to practice by flirting with them, but I and others in my boat have no frame of reference for acquiring female skills. I didn't count my late-arriving stepfather as my father, since he was so verbally abusive to me; and my mother was usually too preoccupied to educate her daughters on how to be a woman. This lack led to problems I experienced as a teenager.

Another part of female adolescence is experimenting with make-up. I was going way overboard on make-up about the time that Nutrilite was introducing a new line of skin care products and cosmetics called Edith Rehnborg Cosmetics, which were a huge bust. They were named after the wife of the genius who developed the Nutrilite supplements, Karl Rehnborg. The creams were heavy and greasy, and the cosmetics were dated before they were born. The lipsticks were drying and trended to dark reds and oranges, which worked well for Edith, with her fair coloring and dark black hair she wore in braids on top of her head. My mother's product loyalty was made clear: if I wanted to wear ANY make-up, there was only ONE brand I would be allowed to wear, and its initials were ER on every little sample tube of bright lipstick. The result was that I looked like a little harlot.

Later, the convenience of acquiring nice things I couldn't have gotten any other way expanded to my wardrobe. Up to this point, my clothes were selected by my mother at rummage sales, and she was quite often off the mark. My friend Janet became my partner in crime, and we often shoplifted the same clothing items so we could dress as twins at the dances where we were such hot stuff. White Stag was our favored brand, and I can see right now the navy striped jersey tank tops and the white pedal pushers we coordinated.

My mother would have been horrified to know this about me. Did I have guilt about it? Not then—I was simply filling a desperate need. But now that I don't need to resort to stealing to get nice things, yes. I believe this could be called situational ethics. I do buy most of my clothes now at Good Will Stores for $3.50 an item and find thrift shops where I just go wild and spend maybe $10 on a pair of fine Talbot's slacks. Maybe it's my way of doing penance. But more likely, I think I inherited the thrift gene.

I DON'T KNOW IF OUR stepfather's big excavation project in the basement was to impress our mother or to create for himself a getaway spot in a crowded household, since he built a long workbench like his cabinetmaker father had.

For Mommy it was too tempting: she had every available surface already covered with her "stuff," and she soon appropriated his space. She mapped it out: the workbench could function as the perfect spot for a big project that just sneaked up on us.

It began with her unusual journey to New York City. To leave Drexel Hill was to travel afar to Media, or 69th Street, or occasionally into Philadelphia. New York City was like the first Moon Shot in our estimation.

Shoes molded right on the foot.

She arrived back home several days later with what proved to be the proudest possessions of her life, her new bright red leather "Murray Space Shoes," hand-made and costing about a hundred dollars plus hotel and travel costs.

These had been built ON her feet and molded to each foot's exact shape— over several days! The bottoms were perfectly flat, but inside they had an arch that conformed to her own arch. Each one of her toes was clearly outlined in leather on the top side of the shoe. The overall effect was that of two large red clubs affixed to the ends of her slim calves. To us it was a signal that she had arrived at the very edge of the lunatic fringe, but by this time we were in the rhythm of the decline and had accepted it. We declared we could not be seen in public with her if she was going to insist on wearing them. She got that self-satisfied, devil-may-care look on her face and said, "These are the only shoes I'll need for the rest of my life."

It turned out to be true. They became a permanent part of her costume as a natural progression in the healthy way of life—she was rubbing corn oil into her skin, with apple cider vinegar rubs in between for vigor, swilling the vinegar, and adding the corn oil to our protein shakes (because after all, you can't even UTILIZE your vitamins A, E and D if you don't have oils in your diet).

Already preaching good health to everyone she met, she now opened her sales pitches with a subtle reference to their poor footwear choices: "Those godawful high heels are going to kill you!" she would say to perfect strangers. Or "Your lymph system can't possibly be functioning with your feet at that angle!" Maybe she got a "commish" on space shoe sales, but over time her customers and her troupe of Nutrilite salespeople began sporting them too.

The other radical change took place in her costume. As a 50s fashionista, Mommy had always worn (along with fashionable high-heeled shoes) dresses, skirts and suits, always very smartly tailored with interesting detail and then re-worked to be her original design—and all obtained at thrift shops and rummage sales once she became a single mother. Her legs showed well in her wardrobe choices. Women were still regularly sporting hats and gloves as part of their wardrobes, so pants were out of the question for your well-thought-of lady of the times.

With the Murray Space Shoes, the dress-up look was a little harder to carry off. Enter the skipper-blue jumpsuit, a one-piece snugly fitting zippered outfit with a self-belt. We were stunned. Pants on our mother? To us she looked like she was a new recruit for the Space Project—which hadn't even been conceived of yet till Sputnik got America's attention. All she needed was a helmet tucked under her arm. She was no longer a '50's woman.

"What do you think? Think it will hurt my sales?" She turned, throwing in a few of her now-famous bumps and grinds, hands on hips and jutting her chin out in a defiant way.

We were against it, having gotten used to her womanly clothing. But once she found it, she rarely shed that blue jumpsuit—maybe on Sundays when she dressed for church. The Murray Space Shoes and jumpsuit became permanent fixtures.

Pretty soon Mommy announced a grand plan to benefit both her family and the world. She would need to make another mysterious three-day trip to New York, she told us. I thought she was going back to have her shoes "adjusted." But no; she returned home having taken classes in how to MAKE Murray Space Shoes! Her new-found mission: to help people get comfortable, affordable footwear—because she would custom-mold them at a price way less than she had paid, yet giving her a nice profit. A pioneer Murray Space Shoe factory right there in Drexel Hill! Shoes for her children constituted Step One of her apprentice program. She'd develop her skill and use us as display pieces for her new enterprise. Once again, her guinea pigs, for an alarming turn of events.

As a true Lutheran, Mommy had never been a demonstrative parent, giving us a quick peck on the cheek at bedtime, sometimes a random hug. If any of us ever left on a trip of a week or more, we could get a kiss planted on a cheek and a quick embrace. With the hug or kiss came the disclaimer for it.

"Behave yourself," or "Be good," she'd admonish, as if her reason for pulling us in tight was to issue the command in a way that we would remember. It was like the spoonful of sugar with the medicine. But to me, the reminder was as sweet as the hug. It meant she noticed.

She had already waded into foot reflexology, making it a regular part of her Nutrilite sales repertoire. She would massage her customers' feet as she told the Nutrilite story, guaranteeing a rapt audience on which she now had not only an emotional hold, but also a physical hold.

This practice was also her way of being physical with her children without being overt about it. She could pour out her love to us while poking and pushing on various areas of the foot, identifying whether our ascending colons were blocked or our livers or spleens a bit sluggish. She'd poke until she found a tender spot.

"Owww!" we'd yelp, jumping out of her grasp.

"Aha!" she would say. "I'm stimulating your pancreas—hold still!" She could examine how well our intestines were working. If she found a tender spot, she would remind us to Fletcherize our food to get more saliva to help digestion. She could find blocked sinuses and ear problems while activating our pituitary glands. Mine worked fine; I was 5 feet ten inches in the fifth grade, towering above any boy in my class by about a foot and a half. And my feet were already size 9, which excluded me from the hopscotch games at recess because the blocks were too small for my feet.

Not given to long-range planning, it may not have occurred to Mommy that our feet were still growing and that this shoe project would have to be repeated on a regular basis once a year. But the shipment of supplies for building the home-grown Murray Space Shoes arrived; and she set up shop on that workbench. She had a kitchen chair perched up there on Otto's erstwhile workbench where the victim would sit for hours while she practiced. I, the first victim, would be overcome with the stench of "100 PERCENT PURE LIQUID LATEX," according to the stenciled words on the one-gallon shiny tin containers. Instead of working with leather to make the shoes, she had a bolt of terrycloth and extra-long scissors, various dyes, a punch to make the shoelace holes, and a colorful variety of shoelaces, to give each pair an individual look. "Oh, great…rubberized terrycloth," I thought. Exactly.

Since she was early in the learning curve, these sessions would truly last for hours while the latex set up and she practiced shaping the shoe on my foot. That gave me, the sacrificial lamb, plenty of time to lament the death of my carefree childhood.

I visualized the end of my status as a co-leader of all 30 or 40 neighborhood kids. I saw my future chances of a real social life and eventual marriage going away. My hope chest with the single item, the Rogers Bros. silver-plate, meant nothing now. All my aspirations, now being washed away by thin layers of latex draped and sculpted into the terrycloth while I kept my feet perfectly flat on the workbench for hours till my beige rubber clubs dried. Later, she explained, she would take the long scissors and cut around my ankles to give a nicely finished upper edge, and I alone could decide where I wanted the laces: down the side, or down the front.

I conjured that fleeting moment people talk about just before death where one's whole life passes before the mind's eye in a flash. But my images weren't fleeting.

Another image came to mind: my friend Janet's new black patent leather Mary Janes. "Why her? Why not me?" My eyes stung with the injustice of that annual shopping ritual. I wanted a pair just like them so badly I ached. It was almost Easter, and Janet always got new shoes, as well as a new outfit, gloves and straw hat for Easter Sunday.

I only got new shoes when holes appeared in the soles. To facilitate this happening, I had been riding on the back of Janet's bike and dragging the soles of my shoes to hasten the appearance of the holes. I had thought to time their appearance about a week before

Easter. That way it would make good sense for Mommy to go ahead and purchase my own black patents. But she had other plans. Shoes for five kids all at once got costly, and I believe that she had figured those lessons and supplies from New York had just eliminated her need for any future children's shoe purchases and would coincide with Easter.

My hopes for the black patents dimmed. When Mommy's mind was set, you didn't argue with her: She was a true Taurus the Bull. "Honey," they'll look fine when I'm finished — and they'll be the most comfortable shoes you've ever worn! You'll never even WANT to wear any other kind of shoes."

I don't remember any protest — maybe in the back of my mind I was finding my own method of her favorite ploy, passive resistance. But I sunk lower and lower as her victim. The acrid smell of the latex is in my mind today, as is the vision of my mother's deft sculptor's hands shaping the wet rubberized terry around each one of my toes so that they were perfectly outlined like an animal's paw. She tried to appease me in her no-nonsense way by allowing me to pick out a conservative color, suggesting, "How about black (like Janet's Mary Jane's) instead of red? Where would you like the lace holes to be? Why don't we go with red laces for a just a touch of color?" she asked excitedly. The laces she finally directed me to were black and red argyle plaid.

When the black dye was applied and laces installed, she had her first finished product. Every time I put them on, I stank of that awful rubber smell. I could not have been more out of step with my cohorts if I were a cavewoman suddenly appearing in their midst carrying a club and wearing animal skins. My mother's gay promise was that I would NEVER have corns or bunions, but what child even *thinks* about corns or bunions?

Janet and I often walked to school together when I wasn't late. Alas, I could not even bring myself to wear them the half-block distance to Janet's house. I hid the shoes in the thick yew bushes under the bay window and walked barefoot to Janet's house. She kept her castoff pair in her bushes for me. There I would scrunch my size nines into her size seven and a half beat-up old Mary Jane's and hobble thankfully to school with her.

After about two weeks of this surreptitious routine I had blisters on all my toes and both heels, and I could hardly walk in ANY shoe. Puzzled, Mommy began to think I was allergic to the latex; and I did not discourage her from this line of thinking. She proceeded on for a few more weeks working out her other children's "designs," but my blisters and hobbling shuffle did the trick. She gradually dissembled her grand plan to build Murray Space Shoes for us—and then the world.

Eventually, I did get my one pair of Mary Janes. And today, decades later, I always have at least one pair of black patent shoes in my closet—I continue to be attracted to them, as a symbol of victory and autonomy.

As it turned out, the Murrays really were the last pair of shoes she ever bought for herself. She wore them almost exclusively till the end of her life. I would give a lot to see her swishing around our living room, teaching us how to do a Cajun waltz or Zydeco jitterbug in those shoes and her blue jumpsuit.

WHILE THE NUTRILITE BUSINESS CONTINUED to be a sustaining part of her income, there was always that new enterprise grabbing our mother's immediate attention. Somewhere around this time she began selling the Niagara Cyclo-Massage products, which had two basic offerings: the "hand unit" and the flat heat/massage pad. There was even a line of luxury massage chairs.

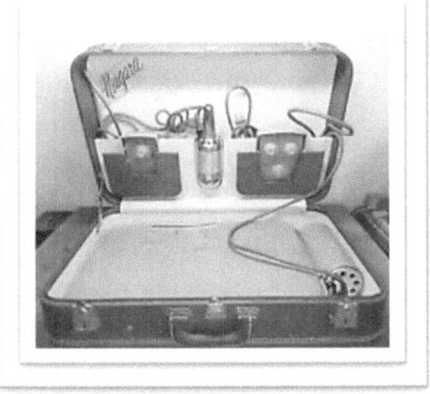

Mommy's demo case for the Niagara

This very cutting-edge invention required weekly sales meetings and serious training in door-to-door tactics, as well as skillful closing techniques to cinch the sale. She knew her closes: the trial close, the warm puppy close, the take-it-away close. Between the World Books, Famous Artists, and her short flings with Fuller Brush, Baby Butler, Pennyrich Undergarments, the Slim Gym and Kirby vacuum cleaners, she was a practiced professional when she concentrated on it.

To round out this latest endeavor of "the Niagara," she also offered a lower- priced product. She enthused all who came in her proximity about this simple and fun device called the Twister, a one-square-foot Masonite platform mounted on a solid rotating base like a lazy Susan arrangement. Mommy would sometimes bring it to the pool and casually set it out until someone asked, "What is a Twister?", as the name was emblazoned on the platform. She would have to demonstrate it, of course, and show how one could use this anywhere and anytime to whittle away their waistline. She could often make an appointment to further demonstrate the Niagara (for those who further wanted to melt away some pounds while they simply laid on it and enjoyed a massage). This was around the same time that Charles Atlas was no longer getting sand kicked in his face at the beach because he was now so muscled up from his workouts.

While shapely, her robust figure was not a solid testament to either product; but her enthusiasm and belief in the Niagara products has continued to live on in each of us. We still have the Niagara in our family today — it's one of the big items in our inheritance — and it gets passed around between family members according to need. "Do you need the Niagara?" means "how bad is it?"

Her scribbly copybooks were filled with sketchy methods for getting in the door: "ALWAYS open the storm door after ringing the bell or knocking: it indicates your intention to come in. When the lady of the house answers, begin wiping your feet on the doormat and put your head down while you pick up your demonstration case. This works well; they generally step aside so you can enter. If the storm door is missing or possibly locked, when she comes to the door, lean backwards expectantly to send a signal that she should open the door to you."

There were as many closing techniques as there were for getting in the door. The Choice Close: "Would you prefer your unit in beige leather, or the mint green?" The Warm Puppy Close: "Let me leave the hand unit with you so you can give your husband a massage when he comes home this evening."

I'm not sure how many housewives spent the afternoon experimenting with the hand unit for themselves, but the marketing brochure hinted at a few good ideas . . .

. . . just the right size . . . when you are trying to massage those hard to reach spots - behind your knees, around your elbows, or near your neck or face. It conforms to the shape of your body so it's easier than ever to comfortably massage areas that are hard to reach by yourself . . .

What I do know is this: Totally by accident, that fine piece of equipment delivered me my first explosive orgasm at age twelve. Just experimenting, I applied the hand unit to one of those hard-to-reach places, and thus began a deep friendship with the hand unit. It had a variable speed dial connected by a thick wire between the unit and the

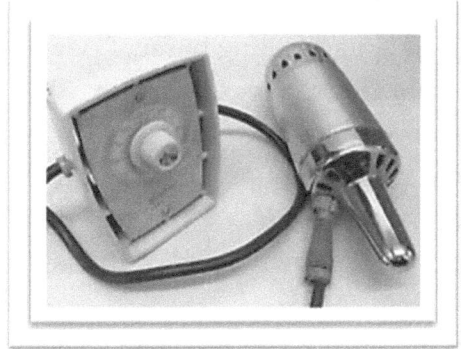

My new best friend

plug, offering a variety of experiences for those hard-to-reach spots. I hardly knew what sex was, but I knew how good that felt. I had a new best friend.

The Niagara products were a big income booster. The Twister, on the other hand, was an instant sale and easily demonstrated on the spot at the pool, a family party, or at the home of a loyal Nutrilite customer. She always kept a supply, like the Gold Bricks, for quick sales and cash for dinner that night.

J.G. WAS JUST REACHING THAT "magical" age of puberty when all hormonal hell breaks loose in the most placid of family situations, which was not what we had. My brother had become angrier and angrier as he suffered Otto's abuse and saw what he was doing to our mother. This testosterone anger usually reaches its peak in boys about age fifteen, but he didn't make it that far. One night, Otto was getting rough with Mommy; and J.G., in a seething burst of power, tried to push him down the basement stairs. It was time to pay our stepfather back for the time Otto pushed her down the stairs when she was pregnant. J. G. recently told me his memory of that night. "I wanted to kill him; it's what I planned to do." It was not clear who was going to kill whom, but it seemed that by the end of the night someone might be dead.

Mommy knew that this couldn't go on, and she made a very difficult decision: she arranged for J.G. to go to an *ORPHANAGE* called the Wallingford Home. We children were all devastated for him and thought it an unfair turn of events that J.G. would have to leave, rather than Otto. It would have solved a lot of problems if Otto had been the one sent away.

I remember visiting on one Sunday, after Mommy had made a real attempt to get Grant, our disappeared father, to start connecting with J.G. She had sent a letter to his brother, Art, whom she knew lived in our county, asking him to forward it to Grant, wherever he was.

Little did we know that he lived so comfortably and so close to that orphanage. Grant wrote J. G. one letter and sent him a football, to remind him of Grant's big claim to fame, the high school football team.

"Didja hear from Grant?" We jumped up and down, excited and hopeful, looking for that contact from what seemed like Outer Space.

"Yeah. He sent me this football and a note," J.G. said, with the longest face imaginable. That was it: duty discharged; request fulfilled. Our hearts broke again. It was such an important moment: a hope, a prayer, that maybe we three would get our real father back in our lives and everything would be good again. J.G.'s and our hopes were splintered.

We spent what seemed like every Sunday visiting J.G., and the pain at our separation from him seemed palpable. We would all come home in a deep funk, Mommy included.

The orphanage was run by the Presbyterians and was considered a good orphanage, as orphanages go. The kids were nice kids, well taken care of, and provided with a caring home. They were required to go to Sunday School and church at the Presbyterian Church in Wallingford and later in Media, PA, about a mile away. Each kid had his own space and also had a small work assignment like sweeping a hallway or waiting tables — much easier than our work details at home under Otto the Terrible. J.G. endured the separation, but I always thought he was miserable for this period, till maybe age sixteen. Recently I asked him to tell me how he felt about being thrust into an orphanage.

"It was great! I got three meals a day, had really dumb little chores to do, and I could sneak away on weekends and hitchhike to Jeff's house and go hunting and fishing and hang out with his family. They never noticed where I went. I just told them I was going home for the weekend."

"You mean there were weekends when you COULD have come home, and you didn't?" I was wounded to hear this recently. The sense of loss we each had felt for him over the years had left its mark. So much for our profound pity.

"Why would I want to do that"? Come home, he meant. That was his answer. I had never looked at that possibility. Home was where all the trouble was.

J.G AND I AND OUR other siblings each found our respective escapes from our difficult lives. Linda and I spent a lot of time at the Addisons' home and on vacation with them, and several times I got to be Uncle Dan's and Aunt Janette's mother's helper on their vacations. J.G. had his long stays with the Liptons before and after he was at the orphanage, where I believe he lived from age fourteen till he was sixteen. But we always had to return home to reality eventually — and the increasing ugliness gradually became a regular event.

It was also a regular event that Mommy would go into the dining room to her desk as soon as she could escape after dinner to make phone calls, setting up business appointments for the next day to sell whatever she was currently selling and to contact her distributors. We children cleaned up the dinner dishes while Pop sat there drinking beer, smoking cheap cigars, blowing smoke rings and preparing his nightly rant.

Unable to abide her absence, Otto would interrupt her phone calls loudly in his Master and Commander voice, "Dot-EEEE!" He'd repeat it, louder, then louder still. She was supposed to respond by ending her calls and going to him, bowing and scraping as she went, to stand before him as a servant and ask, "Yes, Master? You called?" She often parodied just those actions and words, to entertain her and us and ridicule his command. But as long as she could delay, she would completely ignore him, going about her business—which never sounded like business with all the laughing and storytelling.

Now drunk and in an ugly mood, Otto's anger level would rise like a creek in a raging storm. As he downed his beers, he'd stew over this woman who liked everybody better than him.

One night he got up from the breakfast room table, crashed through the French doors into the dining room-turned office, and simply ripped the phone right out of the wall while she was using it.

That night the temperature was close to 100 degrees. We knew he was always worse in the heat. He started pushing her around and screaming at her, getting more physically abusive quickly. He backed her into the china closet, knocking her against it and breaking some of her never-used porcelain gold-rimmed family china. He started with his favorite mantra through gritted teeth, his voice shaking with anger.

"Honest to God, Dottie, lighten up! WORK with me, woman!"

Pushing at her, shoving at her, he wanted compliance. He wasn't physically hitting her yet; he just kept pushing at her with his barrel chest until he had her in a corner, talking obscenities to her and exerting physical power.

Backed into this position with no escape route, she made a move. Catching him off-guard, she heaved herself past him, picked up one of our two antique cane-seat chairs and slammed it upside down over his head as hard as she could. His head parted the cane and punched a hole right through it. He stood there, stunned, with the parted seat framing his head like a clown with a ruff made out of wood and cane, totally stripped of dignity and power.

Then she made a tactical mistake. She knew he wasn't hurt by the parting cane seat; and she couldn't resist laughing at the comical sight. She may have felt she made her point that she would not give up her means of income and become his helpless victim. Shocked for a few seconds by her physical anger, her strength, and the blow itself, he exploded when she laughed. With the broken chair still hampering him, he grabbed her by the hair and started yanking her around like a puppy with a stuffed animal until she pulled away to escape the inevitable blow.

Surprise! As she struggled away, he found in his hand a huge hank of her hair, with scalp attached. We were all there, scared to get near him, shocked at what he grasped. We saw that shiny bald spot on the back of her head, about three inches around.

"Go next door and call the police," she shouted to whoever could hear her, "and quickly escape to a neighbor!"

We were a well-oiled machine. We each ran out any door we could reach, in fire-drill fashion, before he got there to body-block us from doing so.

When we banged on our neighbor Sissy's door that night, she answered quickly, ready to help. Sissy could both see and hear the catastrophes and knew the drill. There was no 911 then—just the slow process of rotary- dialing "O" for the operator, asking her to connect to the police, and hoping to catch the interest of someone at the station who'd heard from us all too often.

It's painful to remember the feelings we had waiting for the police to arrive, pacing on the sidewalk in front of Sissy's house, scared of what was occurring inside our home and hoping the crisis didn't deepen before they got there. Usually, when they did arrive, Otto, though still drunk, was usually sensible enough to appear docile and calmer, his head like the steam vent on Mommy's giant pressure cooker after the steam had released.

That steel plate in his head...did it cause these crazy tantrums? Or was it just my mother's obstinate defiance to what she viewed as unreasonable demands? That security her friends had convinced her she needed (and which perhaps she herself even hoped for) just didn't happen. We now had less security and more fear than we had before he showed up.

The nausea and fear I felt as I saw what he did to our beautiful mother was like that scene you see in movies where someone sees something horrible and then throws up. When you watch it in the movies, it never seems quite real. I know what it feels like in real life. Fear, uncertainty about whether the violence would keep increasing—none of us would ever be the same. That bald spot on our mother's head lasted for many months. The one on his head never went away, and we suspected it even more as bad wiring.

IT IS EVENTS LIKE THESE that steal a little child's life away. Without even knowing that it's happening, children like us lose our dreams, our sense of expectation. Hope for the future and belief in any good about to happen become dulled. Like little adults in a war zone, we develop a heightened sense of alertness and watchfulness. We learn to distrust those positive emotions a little child should have, becoming experts at acutely observing, scanning the horizon for the next impending event. Every encounter is guarded, like soldiers must do when entering an enemy zone. Those senses become so sharpened that we never let down our vigil—for to do so invites vulnerability. The happy feelings, the belief in the wonder of life, the sense of expectation that defines a childlike outlook, are not to be trusted.

As adults, we wounded children often become "control freaks," not knowing why—just knowing we want things to "go right." It may show up in the perfectly kept home; in the collections of an addicted collector, providing visual proof that order is restored; the need to be the unquestioned final decision maker in relationships; the too-strict parent who can't play with their children. We grow up needing that absolute control in all areas of life—that one thing we never had as children.

Our home was that place, and I became that person. Things were out of control most of the time. I became a child-adult, always trying to make things better, make the house nice, get events happening in an orderly way so it didn't all come undone. But nothing works for the wounded child — except fear and vigilance.

As a parent of a toddler, I remember identifying a palpable pain inside me to see our little boy playing and enjoying himself. I wanted him to be miserable, and I didn't know why. My anger was so real I was showing cruelty to him. I didn't realize I was experiencing flashbacks of a sad time in my life that my brain had graciously wiped out of my conscious memory. All I had left was the pain, now suddenly resurfaced.

Like many other damaged children, I had to find my way to a new place called happiness. I was lucky to find real answers in a book by John Bradshaw called *Homecoming.* His book gave me the keys to understanding why I continued to live in fear and pain when it was no longer appropriate. He helped me unravel that period when my biological father left for good. I cried with relief, fully able now to identify the pain I had covered up and put away; his writings also helped me understand it's OK to cry. The pain is real, and tears are healing. I didn't even know how to cry or feel pain. It was just a big blank that I had obliterated from my life. I know there are many adults who can identify this from their young lives.

I also give credit to another book called *Born to Win*, which enabled me to dare to revisit mentally that place of pain and heal from it. One of the exercises took me into my family's living room as early as I could remember and describe everything I could from that scene. I found I did not want to go there, because I was all alone, when my siblings had been sent away and my mother was in mourning.

The third book that helped heal my wounds taught me how to use neuro-linguistic programming to essentially reprogram my beliefs and thinking patterns into ones that served me more effectively. That book is *Awaken the Giant Within*, by Anthony Robbins. To even to be able to identify *un*-empowering beliefs, as the author calls them, is a rare opportunity most people never get. To learn the technique of installing empowering belief systems in place of the "bad programming" is, as they say, "priceless."

Children are born to be delighted with their world, and when it doesn't happen because of shattered plans, negativity, disappointments and constant living in fear, they find alternate paths to their lives.

I (and my siblings, I believe) were also victims of simply absorbing my mother's belief systems, of experiencing the empirical evidence of sheriff's sale signs nailed to the front door time and again, of seeing our entire side yard sold to a builder to erect twin homes there to keep her afloat, of never having enough money or food, of her oft-repeated reference to her "ship coming in," that proverbial ship, and to the poor choices she made with all her talent and personality. She was a child of the Great Depression and a father who was too controlling, which also left their marks. Parents instill their belief systems into their children in what they believe to be the best way to protect them from disappointments and bad decisions; but along with passing on their beliefs, they pass on their insecurities, their negativity, and their fears.

I didn't realize when I was small—nor did the professional world of psychologists— that such a thing as Attention Deficit Disorder existed. Kids with what today are called learning differences or neurodiversity used to be called "Dunce" and made to sit in a corner wearing a tall cap with that word lettered across the front! In the ideal world, our mother would have had a husband who enabled her to use her talents and support her in her flaws (as my husband does). She had a bad case of ADD—or a fabulous case of it, as revealed in her zany letters. Today, ADD is a diagnosis in the DIAGNOSTIC & STATISTICAL MANUAL OF MENTAL DISORDERS, a real thing. I think of her version as glorious and yet problem-causing:

- Failing to pay attention to details *(check)*
- Making careless mistakes *(check)*
- Having difficulty sustaining attention during presentations, lectures, lengthy reading tasks, etc. *(check—she usually did drawings instead of taking notes)*
- Failing to follow through on instructions or finish chores or workplace duties *(check)*
- Having difficulty organizing tasks and activities; e.g. messy or has poor time management *(check)*
- Seeming not to listen when spoken to directly *(check—unless she was in a sales situation, she was usually busy cooking up her next prank)*
- Avoiding tasks that require sustained mental effort *(check)*
- Frequently losing items like keys, wallets, and phones *(check—" has anyone seen my keys…glasses…checkbook?")*
- Being distracted by unrelated thoughts, activities or sounds *(check)*
- Forgetting daily responsibilities, such as paying bills, keeping appointments, preparing dinner *(check—she rarely committed to a certain time, and if she did was late)*

With her many flaws, I have always been grateful to my mother for her sardonic and novel sense of humor, right down to the last words she uttered. I've appreciated her ability to rise above her circumstances and find a joke, an adventure, a diversion — and often bring us along with her. She taught us to laugh in adversity. She taught us to explore the world when there was nothing of interest evident, and by example she showed us how to find it or make it up. She found wonder in the ordinary and got us excited about it.

If we were not along on one of her adventures off the main road to success, she'd regale us later with the stories. Today, as a close family of five siblings, we can get together and still laugh, reenact those crazy scenes and dance her Cajun dances.

A.D.D. NOTWITHSTANDING, MOMMY, IN her quest to maintain sanity and humor, was focused on a variety of ways to lighten the atmosphere in her dark world. Her humor could not be quelled, no matter how much Otto wanted that.

Otto ate the same lunch almost every day, that braunschweiger liverwurst on rye from Nessell Brothers deli around the corner, with onion and slabs of the "Jewish pickle." She filled the Stanley thermos that fit inside the lunchbox with coffee. This was a ritual lunch he rarely wanted varied, and it was maybe the one early morning task she performed with regularity. She let us in on the reason she got such joy from her task.

The last thing she did before she slapped the sandwich shut was this: she'd pull a nice long strand of hair out of her head and lay it across the sandwich. I can see her doing it now: if she had an audience of any of us, she pulled that hair out with great flair, and with a bump and grind thrown in and that devilish grin.

We would beg her to divorce him, but this seemed to be a conversation we weren't going to have, just as she never again spoke of our first father, Grant. With Otto, she did not share with us whether she loved him (one of her letters revealed her feelings). She just kind of endured him—along with our nagging. We wondered why, and I'm still not sure. Maybe she felt she had made a commitment in the eyes of God—though that commitment didn't last through the whole twelve years of marriage, I was to learn much later.

One night after coming in about midnight from a babysitting job, I was washing my face in the bathroom. I saw on the linoleum floor a rolled-up and rubber-banded wad of cash. It could only be Otto's wad, which he kept very secret, in his underpants, I would guess, from us and Mommy. Knowing he would have gone to bed drunk, I determined he must not have noticed he dropped it when he used the toilet. The next morning I showed it to Mommy, who quietly took it. "Shhh," she said, index finger to lips.

Otto came home that night in a high state of distress over his missing money roll. She was prepared. "Maybe it's not the smartest thing to keep money rolled up in your underpants. You probably flushed it down the toilet." He thought about it and quietly concluded to himself that might have happened. He was prepared to take the toilet apart in case it had gotten stuck. But the toilet was flushing just fine.

Here was where our mother shone. She began developing a convoluted and complex Great Scheme. In full thespian mode, she made a pretend call to the county sewage treatment plant.

"Hello, my name is Dorothy Fech, at 4030 Berry Avenue, and I'd like to ask your help. My husband has lost a large amount of cash . . . " With arched eyebrows looking over her glasses at my stepfather, she went on to explain in minute detail his sad story and ask if there was anything at all they could possibly do; her husband was frantic. She came back grinning, with that scornful look. "Well, you might be in luck. They gave me some detailed information. From our street corner the sewage takes five days to reach the treatment plant, and I got permission for you to get down there when the Berry Avenue poop starts shooting in — they estimate next Saturday morning around 9:30 a.m. They're going to allow you to come in early, around 8:30, and start watching the process. As it gets toward 9:00, they'll give you a strainer hootenany they keep there so you can be ready and start sifting through it. They say this kind of thing happens from time to time — wedding rings, lucky rabbits' feet, etc. — and if you can catch it at the right time, you'll probably find it." She delivered her lines with total straight-faced equanimity. Over the next five days, Otto apparently contemplated the sifting work and came to realize his wad was just plain gone. But it gave Mommy five days of pure satisfaction in the tennis match, and years of great storytelling.

WE LIVED ON A LARGE corner property that fronted two streets, with our house on Berry Avenue and our driveway around the corner on Drexel Avenue, which remained our driveway even after the new twin homes were built on our former yard. Next to our driveway was Danley's Auto Repair, there since the beginning of time. His shop began the commercial section of small businesses that went around the block onto Garrett Road, where a good part of the commerce of our lives was conducted. After Danley's was the Army-Navy Surplus Store, the Nessell Brothers Deli, and Doc Raymond's Pharmacy. After Doc's was the entrance to the alley behind the stores, then Pat's Hoagie Shop with pinball machines, O'Donnell's, the bar where Otto soused himself up after getting off the trolley two blocks away. On top of all the stores were apartments in which some of our friends lived, and the expansive roof of Danley's Garage, with two huge skylights that opened with long chains to let out the hot air in summer. We children regularly accessed this upper level of our world by climbing our giant maple tree, boosting one another up to the first branch on shoulders and backs and pulling the last one up from above. From the tree limbs we could step onto Danley's Garage's big roof and survey our empire. We could then continue to the apartments of our friends and come out their front entrances right in the middle of our shops.

Otto would stagger by these stores and Danley's every weekday evening as he headed home with his two quarts of Schmidt's. One night he arrived home highly agitated, beyond his usual level of frustration at my mother's behaviors.

The problem: somewhere he had lost his glasses — and he really could not see without them. We universally felt we were all better off with his vision fogged over, so there was no rallying cry to find them for him. For once, he was *our* victim.

Next morning after Otto had gone off to work blindly, Mr. Danley came knocking at our front door, whistling and twirling a pair of glasses in his hand. "Anybody we know possibly lose these, Dorothy?" he asked. Of course: they had to be Otto's. My mother's brain mechanism switched onto joke mode immediately; and she and Mr. Danley got busy cooking up a scheme. Danley was well aware of Otto's habits, since he passed his garage every night near closing time. One of us children was engaged to help carry out the prank, and we set the scene for that evening when Otto arrived home.

Not quite ready to spring the joke, Mommy's cruel streak may have shown a bit, as she let him suffer for several days with no glasses. At the appointed time several days later, after Otto groped his way home, Mr. Danley came knocking at the front door, an unusual occurrence. "Hey, Otto, can you come down to my shop? I need your help. There's something driving me a little crazy, and maybe you can help me out." Otto, puzzled and ego-stroked about how *he* could help out Mr. Danley, followed him out the back door this time and down the driveway, like a cat following tuna fish.

Danley brought him into the garage and asked him to look up. Otto was wearing his scratched-up Army-issue twenty-year-old sunglasses he had dug up, and he squinted up as Danley pointed to one of the big skylights. "Do you see what I see?" he asked. He stood there patiently, whistling again. Otto looked, shook his head as if to clear out the booze, and did see what Danley pointed to: the faint outline of a pair of glasses against the skylight. "Do you think what I think? Think they could be yours?" Danley asked matter-of-factly, fully in the spirit of the joke.

Otto couldn't quite answer, because as my mother had planned, he was busy trying to calculate just how drunk he must have been to do something he didn't know he could do: climb up that big silver maple and drop his glasses on Danley's roof. And how had he gotten down, if he was that drunk?

Danley just kind of shrugged and said, "If you think they might be yours, maybe you can get someone to climb up and get them for you. I just keep wondering how you got up there, pal."

Otto came home and never said a word to Mommy about where Danley found his glasses. We got the report from Mr. Danley. Otto must have gotten someone from the bar to get up there somehow and retrieve them, because several days later he was wearing them again. Mommy never said another word to him about it, nor did we.

Yes, Dorothy was the mistress of the joke. Our mother had always had these kinds of pranks going on, since childhood. Her brother Dan, sister Harriett and best friend Bernice have told us time and again about the same three or four classics she pulled on them. They have each told us the same few stories more than once, calling them "dirty tricks" and describing her as cruel and unfeeling.

From Aunt Harriett: Probably when they were teens, Mommy planted some cigarettes in Aunt Harriett's luggage, and their father found them. He was apparently quite a stern man whom Mommy described as punishing his children prophylactically by giving them a spanking before he left and whenever he returned home from one of his long exploration trips. I guess he dished one out to Aunt Harriet that day.

Mommy with "Hubbsy," the one that got away

I've heard described these same so-called dirty tricks and have thought they were great fun. I've pondered as an adult why these people who were so close to her felt wronged and why they couldn't enjoy the fun the way we have.

I now believe they'd been mad at her all her life because she apparently turned off some high-powered suitors with success, money and family connections who really fell in love with her and could have provided her a very nice comfortable life. "Hubbsey" was one of those high-falutin' guys she shocked with her angora sweater and the blonde "underarm hair poking out from the sleeves". She apparently hooted long and loud in uncontrollable laughter, embarrassing and making a fool of him. Those kinds of pranks didn't always go down well with the influential types, future power brokers, who were used to being taken seriously.

That "nice comfortable life" was the stated predominant goal of young women of her day — and she spurned it all because she couldn't resist that prank, practical joke, or "dirty trick". I think her friends and family stayed angry with her because she came up so short — two bad marriages and sometimes needing to be propped up financially and emotionally by them. However, I rarely every saw her "lose her cool." She was a stoic. If she drew some bad cards in the deck of life, she just bided her time and played the hand.

WE HAD A FULL SET, including serving pieces, of Melmac, the very latest in unbreakable dinnerware, first generation. Ours came from a thrift shop, which must have been donated because they were pink, and they stained terribly. Spaghetti stained the worst. They also retained grease even after scrubbing with dish soap. So J.G. and I, the official primary dishwashers most nights, would sneak out the shed door and eventually, one piece at a time, sail like Frisbees every one of those pink Melmac dishes over the top of our garage roof and into the back weedy area behind the stores.

Our next collection of table and serving ware was the spun aluminum stuff, with colored tumblers and a huge shallow bowl, which could be filled with enough spaghetti and sauce to feed all seven at the dinner table. This meal was one of our mother's premier offerings: it was plentiful, filling, and made something quite special out of a pound of ground chuck, sautéed onions, and a package of Spatini instant spaghetti sauce flavoring stirred into a large can of tomato sauce. Those little packages were the very beginning of the era of packaged seasonings, and they seemed like a magic act to us.

One evening Mommy brought the steaming platter of spaghetti to the table, but it was one of those nights that found Otto particularly peevish and more than a little drunk. He began the evening grace as usual, with one of us saying our meek "Come Lord Jesus be our guest, and to Thee this food be blessed." But then He took over for the real meat of the prayer period. His tirade of pleas to God to correct my mother's errant ways went on . . . and on . . . and on. It got nastier, with the usual foul language punctuating the prayer. There our hot dinner sat, cooling quickly — part of his master plan, to turn us against her.

We knew to keep our heads bowed while the rant went on, because if we caught the eyes of a fellow sufferer, we tended to lose control of the moment. It was a bad night for that to happen. One of us sneaked a peek and gave a small titter of derision. His response was usually to give a smack or flick his finger smartly on the face of the miscreant—I don't remember who it was because it happened so frequently and because of what happened next. Our mother usually handled the worst he could throw at her (or us), but the atmosphere was ugly and tense on both sides tonight. Mommy looked openly angry, quite different from her usual stoicism.

As he finally finished with his farcical " . . . in Jesus' name we pray," she stood up (as if to begin serving). She picked up the huge platter of spaghetti and balanced it in one hand, palming it to get control of its heft. She then heaved it like a shot-putter clear across the table and right at him. She sailed it like she had been training for the Olympics for months, in a beautiful arc that hit him smack in her target area, his face. If she had actually been performing in the Olympics, the crowd would have gone wild over the accuracy if not the distance. Not all of it landed on his face. His shirt and place setting in front of him were well covered; it also continued beyond him to hit the back wall of our beautiful ivy wallpaper. Plenty of it oozed down onto the marble-topped dresser, and the precious World Books on top of it. The platter bounced onto the faux brick linoleum floor, endlessly rimming like a basketball deciding whether to go in or out of the net. Our dog Socks (always under the table during supper for the parcels we shoved at him that we considered inedible) leaped into the feast on the floor as if he were a paramedic called to the emergency, all action, not a second wasted.

The only sounds to be heard were Socks' lapping noise and the electric whir of the gaudy brass clock that featured a little boy sitting on a bridge pulling up a fish, over and over.

Otto was speechless, sauce and spaghetti dripping from his face; and so were we. He was stunned; we were scared. No one breathed or spoke. None of us knew what Otto would do. We knew the violence was increasing in frequency and intensity, and that both combatants were becoming more intolerant of the other's behaviors. Mommy had almost never reacted to his behaviors with violence herself, except for the chair-over-the-head event.

Fearful as we were about what would happen next, her dramatic anger seemed to quell him. We children silently began cleaning the mess up, following up on Socks' work. It was such a mess we didn't know where to begin.

I don't remember what Otto did, nor do I remember what our mother did next. I do remember a huge lump of pain and fear in my throat as I did my part, tears streaming down my face. I have no memory of how old any of us were, as it's another experience my mind has gracefully dulled down to soften the edges.

We did not eat dinner that night, for obvious reasons. After silently performing the clean-up we sneaked away quietly to our bedrooms, just relieved he didn't become more violent.

CHAPTER 42 – THE BIRTH OF AMWAY®

THE SPAGHETTI STAINS ON THE wallpaper had marked another turning point, but what it was I didn't know. Our seemingly intolerable lives dragged on, settling down to a routine again.

The drama of the event seemed to help my mother focus more intently on her primary business and passion, selling Nutrilite. I believe now, as I piece together the flow of her undated letters that there may have been another cause of her high level of focus on making money: possibly the beginning of a grand love affair and a clear decision to end the marriage.

After adjusting to strictures of the FDA consent decree some years before, the Nutrilite marketing company of Mytinger and Casselberry had changed the deal to put the income more in their favor, paying less to their distributors – a shock to many who'd been making a good living. Mommy's Nutrilite business was still mostly what we lived on.[2]

In a dramatic move, two of Nutrilite's top leaders formed a distributor association called the American Way Association, which soon resulted in the formation of a new company with the shortened name of "Amway." The founders started with just one product to market: an all-purpose, coconut-oil-based cleaner called "Frisk." Mommy brought home a case of it and pronounced in her assertive way, "This is what we use for everything from now on: We're going to brush our teeth with it, wash the dog, do the laundry, the dishes, apply it to burns and wounds, wash the car, take baths with it, clean the floor, and we're going to find out what else it will clean. This is our job, and this is my new business."

We became the research arm of an evolving business. Mommy had already been through many "new businesses," so we didn't take her too seriously at first. While she certainly continued as a Nutrilite distributor, she and others had now started in this new direction, away from Nutrilite. The paper labels fell off the Frisk bottles, and it was inconsistent in viscosity from one bottle to the next, but it was an amazingly safe and versatile product.

The chemist who developed the product was apparently a heavy drinker (which explained the inconsistency of the batches), so before long the founders were able to buy the guy out and get the rights to manufacture. At some point, the product acquired the glamorous new name of L.O.C., or Liquid Organic Cleaner, and we did indeed use it for everything. I still do, every day.

The product line expanded by fits and starts, with many flops, all of which we lived through as part of their first research and development department. There was a battery additive that seemed to, upon replacing the battery acid, drain the car's battery and immediately end its useful life. Any number of "big ticket" items were tried out, all rather dismal failures: bomb shelters, an automobile generator, a water softener device of some kind, and more I've forgotten.

Then they got smarter and started developing products with repeat business. There was one product in which a great deal of hope was placed. It was at a time when we often had snow and icy conditions in our winters before global warming had even been thought about. This exciting product was called Liquid Tire Grip. It seemed like a natural for big repeat business, something no driver would want to be without. When the car was stuck on ice or snow, you simply would spray this red, white and blue can of gunk onto the back rear-wheel drive tires, spinning the wheels very slowly; and you could then drive right out of the slick spot.

To demonstrate it (all the stuff was sold by authentic and effective demonstrations) my mother and compatriots would look for victims stuck in the icy conditions of winter with a car they couldn't move. They lived for these opportunities! Every time our mother had her big chance, usually in a driving snowstorm, to demonstrate Tire Grip, she'd holler, "Hoop-La, I got one!" as she pulled over in back of the stuck car like a cop ready to give a speeding ticket. She kept a case in her car to be ready when opportunity struck. She'd give the driver the instructions on spinning the wheels, and there she'd be hunched over in the snowstorm, spraying first one tire, then struggling around to do the other wheel. Finally the wheels would grab, like a miracle! As they got traction, the grateful drivers would roll down the window and give a big wave, hollering out, "Thank you!" as they pulled away, grateful to be moving again, but without buying the now-used Tire Grip. Soon that product was discontinued.

Gradually a line of about seventeen products was rounded up, some excellent and some real dogs. They introduced fragrances in tacky plastic-netting-covered bottles, which smelled terrible and looked like colorful hand grenades. One was romantically called "Egyptique" and would not have sold to a gas station owner to deodorize the shoddy bathroom. The water softening compound and other powder products hardened into solid concrete-like blocks that we had to break up with ice picks and sharpening steels before they could be sold. We hated seeing those cases of products arrive, knowing we would be spending hours hacking each one in the case of twelve into a salable state.

The toilet bowl cleaner came in a turquoise plastic hourglass-shaped container, and its contents also solidified into one solid hourglass, which was not too easy to break up because it resulted in piercing the plastic bottle. Scented moth crystals, same-shaped bottle but purple also hardened beyond usability.

The Amway business began in 1959, about the same time I was sixteen. I was still the general housekeeper, taking care of the three younger ones now ten, six and five. At this point, I was dating, and I was sure looking for a way out.

I remember my guilt when she enrolled Danny and Nancy in The Red Feather Agency's Daycare Center, to where they were dispersed after school. I would guess that Nancy was in kindergarten and Danny in first grade, probably about 1957 or 1958. The center was just across the street from our Garrettford Elementary School where the three attended. The concept of daycare was virtually unheard of then. Usually kindergarten was the first "socialization" experience kids had. Good mothers and wives stayed home and took care of their children, and only desperate and poor people would cast off their children to such a place so they could work. We all felt the pain of "abandoning" them, but Annie was now long gone. She and husband Alfred had reached the point of no return with my mother's erratic ways, Otto's tyrannical behaviors and finally, our boarder Scrappy posing as my mother's "Japanese houseboy" and dismissing Annie. Scrappy had hoped that with Annie out of the way so he could have a permanent position and save himself from more jail time, which you may remember, didn't work.

If my mother was to go on without household help, she and I both needed some respite, and the daycare center was the solution. Since all three young ones were in elementary school, poor Linda got saddled with the daily heartbreak of delivering them to daycare from school. It was, of course, usually quite late when Mommy arrived. Ours would be the last ones to be picked up; and all staff would be waiting, pacing with crossed arms and anxious faces, looking out for her arrival so their day could end.

Nancy recently told me that on her first day there, she didn't like it and simply left and walked the three blocks to Annie's house, where she spent the day. Since we had no phone at the time, Annie couldn't call home to say she had Nancy safely with her. At day's end, I believe Alfred delivered her home after a frantic daycare staff and my mother tried to piece together how they had simply lost Nancy on her first day.

With Annie gone, we were back to our former routine, with Linda and me trying to dream up some meals from the odd assortment of ingredients, and little Nancy helping with her Betty Crocker cookbook for children. The cookbook didn't include recipes for chicken livers and oxtails.

---

[2] As my mother told it, two of the big achievers in Nutrilite, along with several others, began organizing what might be akin to a workers' union, calling it the "American Way Association," hoping to get some strength and voice to reverse the changes in the marketing plan. They formed a board of directors and began inviting other "Key Agents" to join forces, and the association grew. One of them was my mother's sponsor, a successful Wharton School MBA who, with his wife, had sold Nutrilite to put himself through Penn. Upon graduation he was reportedly making more money than any company was willing to pay him—so he never worked for anyone.

THE EMERGING AMWAY BUSINESS WAS often hilarious but filled with conflict as animosity grew between Nutriliters and Amway folks having a romance with this new business. In her usual pattern, Mommy wandered back and forth between both businesses. She also recruited a few stragglers into Amway and got "jazzed up" over the different kinds of products being regularly introduced.

ADD types are often attracted to the novel, the new. She rose to the occasion when a new product caught her attention—but there was one particular introduction that stood out like no other one had: "The Queen."

"The Queen." I still use it daily.

One of the wonderful but scary outcomes of a multi-level sales organization is that the head of the organization loses control over who populates his or her "group." What often results is one of history's greatest naturally occurring experiments in worldwide multi- culturalism. I speak personally from my mother's experience and later, my own.

Here's how it goes: Mary joins up, and she has a cousin in the Bronx whom everybody loves and who can round up the whole neighborhood to learn about how to make money part time selling Amway products.

"Hot damn!" my mother would say, looking at a way to double her meager group in one weekend. So the leader gets her leader (the Wharton School grad), and they drive up to the bowels of the Bronx. Some big tough-looking guy appears magically and volunteers to guard the very nice Lincoln Continental of the "upline." The meeting leaders find themselves hoofing it up eight dirty and pissy-smelling flights of stairs in a sorry-looking building with broken-out windows on almost every floor, carrying ten white alligator-pattern-embossed plastic suitcases containing the newly minted sales manual and seven tiny bottles and jars of demonstration products: a starter kit to future wealth and dreams for those who would.

The living room with only one bare light bulb in the corner would be filled with a hapless crowd of excited and curious people, chattering away in a different language (there would often be a translator standing next to the presenter, who would pause after each sentence for the translation, killing some of the fever of excitement and lengthening the presentation to double the normal hour or so). The people in the audience, who'd never had a real chance at free enterprise until this moment, would acquire that fever of excitement, despite the translation. In the other room would be all the tinfoil-covered dishes on the kitchen table, ready for the main event after the marketing plan presentation: the food!

Over time we found ourselves, as children in "the business," often in attendance at these more local events, meeting people from different cultures, with different colored skins, speech patterns, and eating habits than we had ever encountered. Though we were familiar with the entrails dishes, it was never a happy experience to encounter them on the menu. The tinfoil would come off, and surprise! There would be a casserole of chicken feet swimming in some delectable sauce, and pig's feet stewed up with rice and cabbage, arroz con pollo with *el pollo's* back, neck, feet (again, the feet) thrown in, along with that part where the tail feathers meet. The samosas and curry were most attractive to me.

From one of these events held in South Philly there emerged a distributor who became one of my mother's dearest friends, Miss Jean Washington. Miss Jean was Black and beautiful, and gracious as my mother was, but in her gentle southern-lady way. In coloring they were yin and yang. In manner, Jean was imperious and commanding and, as is often true in a matriarchal culture, not to be messed with. In contrast, Mommy was a real ham—a gracious one, though.

As Miss Jean got drafted into Dorothy's "downline," Amway had just introduced "The Queen." It was a most spectacular set of stainless-steel cookware. QUEEN COOKWARE® was nineteen pieces of 18/8 stainless interchangeable, stackable pieces that could be used to cook an entire meal on one burner, which in itself was spectacular. To demonstrate this set was to sell it, if the woman viewing this miracle could lay hold of some cash (there was financing available, but no credit cards were accepted). It was easy to get the crowd together, because the key part of the demonstration was the proof of the pudding—sharing in the miraculous meal. The impact smacked of the original loaves and fishes event if the salespersons were doing their jobs well. That job was to show the quality, thickness, versatility, the Bakelite handles, and lids that stored right inside the cookware as it hung up. Then the layering and stacking up the of foods and pans on just <u>one</u> burner.

My mother and Jean Washington developed a highly effective technique for their demonstrations. Most of the cookware "parties" were held in South Philly, where Jean lived. It was a mixed neighborhood, but the blocks were either Black or White, very carefully set within the larger community. The Whites were mostly Italian, and cooking was a big part of their lives. The parties were generated by door-to-door canvassing, with Mommy taking the White blocks (you could tell the White blocks, because the homes were unusually redone to the nines: aluminum or shiny stainless steel siding, large replacement bow windows, elaborate wrought iron railings, a fig tree in a tiny plot (wrapped in burlap in the winter), maybe artificial flowers in the display window, or an animated holiday display like Lit Brothers had going in their center-city showroom windows, except instead of Rudolph and Santa these were usually more about the Virgin Mary and Jesus in the manger.

Reason would indicate that the folks living in a row home that had been redone in embossed stainless- steel siding looking very much like a food truck would naturally embrace stainless steel and likely go nuts to learn about the Queen Cookware. This proved to be true. Salespeople know these things, and Mommy was a master at booking parties with these folks. Jean found different touch points, but she also was an achiever in finding the quality seekers in her ilk.

On the nights of the events, Jean and Mommy would inevitably arrive late due to my mother's consistent inability to show up anywhere on time, what with Otto sitting on the hood of the car, locking her out with her demonstration stuff in the house, and that broken mental clock of hers.

With the crowd getting a little anxious wondering where the presenters were, they'd arrive and lug all the food and cookware into the strange house, heading for the kitchen and seeking the most opportune location to create their instant show of meal preparation and serving the attendees small portions of the courses, all the while, selling-selling-selling. It all involved lots of quick decision making and improvisation, sometimes with little or no counter space, bad lighting, the crowd drinking wine for the last half hour, and usually a baby or two crying or stealing the show wobbling around to the guests.

Mommy immediately began charming the crowd and engaging them while Jean set up the demonstration. If it was a Black group, these roles were reversed: Mommy would set up while Jean worked the crowd. Jean would start imperiously calling out commands to Mommy:

"Dorothy! Get the food prepared and seasoned. Dorothy! Show them how the edge of each pan is rolled for easy cleaning. Bring me that pan, Dorothy." In a confidential aside: "We *never* use the word 'pots' because pots are what you *piss in*." Uproarious laughter as they bond with the first Black woman ever to boss a White lady around.

Several times during the presentation, Mommy would get down on her knees and look subserviently up to Jean, indicating a subtle emphasis on who was in charge.

With a White crowd, role reversal. My mother would order Jean about, as if she were the Black cook in Mommy's employ for several generations at least. In Mommy's hilarious retelling, both crowds loved it and never knew it was part of their act.

First, they would horrify the group with the rusty cast iron frying pan and the dented but good quality aluminum pot, both of which got scrubbed with an Amway product called a Scrub Bud, one continuous strand of coiled stainless steel (they always sold them with the cookware using this demonstration). Jean would have Mommy take the scrub bud and swirl it around the black frying pan, removing bits of the metal, rust, and the black "seasoning" and do the same with the aluminum pot, which produced a grey slurry. Then she'd pour both results into clear glasses and have them passed from person to person.

"Anyone care to have a drink of this? How about this one? You might as well have a drink, because if you cook in this stuff, you're already ingesting it—and it's what you're feeding your family!"

Then they would discuss the poisoning effects of ingesting aluminum and excess iron into the body, scaring the audience and setting them up for the fabulous Queen cookware.

The cooking of the meal was the highlight and most miraculous part, as drama built: it began with chicken cutlets or pork chops (cutlets for White folks, pork chops for Black) seasoned lightly with salt and pepper only, browning over medium heat—never high. The meat would stick to the pan, browning and creating a layer of flavor. Then the heat would be turned down, and the meat would "release" and start to make "gravy, a word the Italian women identified with. Then whoever had the lead role that night would talk about "shrinkage" and how meats roasted in ordinary cookware would have lost almost twenty-five percent of the original weight after cooking. Then they'd show how the cookware could be used to do a pot roast (retaining that twenty-five percent, because of the low heat). They'd arrange the pans demonstrating all the various configurations and uses, all the while moving the cooking along. Fresh raw vegetables would be added to the meat: cabbage, carrots, onions, and potatoes with skin on to preserve the minerals. The lid would be put on.

When the lid started to rattle from the steam being produced, the audience would be alerted. Something important was happening! More drama unveiled, they would show how the lid "rides on a seal" by spinning it gaily and explaining that that was why it's called "waterless cookware." No moisture was lost during cooking. In fact, they'd gush, only a teaspoon of water was needed.

This was the signal to turn the heat down to pinpoint, thus sealing in the flavor, juices and *nutrients* (and here, with this key word, was the set-up for Nutrilite food supplements pitch).

Now the dome cover would be put on the large sauté pan. The next part of the meal—which was usually peas or green beans with just that teaspoon of water—was started, cooking this pan of vegetables over a candle only (this wowed the crowd beyond belief:

the savings in energy!) and now with its lid also rattling happily. It would then be stacked on top of the first cooking vessel. The next part of the meal was usually raw apples and a bit of cinnamon, quartered and seeded, but with skin left on for the nutrients. The flavor of just apple, no sugar, was a miracle itself, which they owed to "the Queen." The crowning glory: the *CAKE*, poured in batter form and stacked on the *very top* in the utility pan, until completely and perfectly baked. Since the heat transferred right up the sides of the pans and the inverted pans also served as lids for the next layer, the entire meal could be cooked on one burner. No one would quite believe that this method could produce a complete meal on the one burner with a tiny flame, and the crowd waited in suspense for the results and the proof while my mother pitched Nutrilite. The distraction of waiting for their tastes caught the (Italian) women so off guard that they failed to notice there was no pasta or bread.

While the food was gently cooking away and smelling delicious, all the qualities of the cookware were discussed, accessory products shown, and more depth on Nutrilite supplements introduced. The vegetables were utterly flavorful without any more seasoning than salt and pepper, the meats delicious and tender, and the cake served with the apples cooked in their own juices ladled on top.

Penn and Teller, the magician team, could not have pulled it off any more dramatically. Loaves and fishes with just a slightly different menu. No discussion of pricing happened publicly until the food was served, and by then the attendees were mesmerized and converted into apostates. Over the meal, Jean and Mommy would go from person to person, closing the sale.

"I know you don't want to keep letting your old pots steal another 25 percent of your butcher bill anymore, do you? We have a beautiful six-piece knife set to offer as a thank you gift for purchasing tonight, Carmella." It was a rare night that cookware wasn't sold. I still have the gift knife set with the faux bone handles and use it regularly, and I still cook my meals on the same Queen cookware set that my mother wowed them with in South Philly.

The entire show was reenacted for us (minus food, just the raucous description) later when Mommy regaled us with mishaps, colorful descriptions of participants, and how each one was "closed." Every event led to her receiving a standing invitation to come back for an Italian dinner any time she was in "Philly."

CHAPTER 44 – MY FIRST DATE AND TROUBLE BEGINS

I HAD JUST TURNED FIFTEEN, and the highlight of my year was the purchase with my own funds of a brand-**new** bikini bathing suit in a stunning Hawaiian print, with drawstrings at the sides of bottom and top, allowing me to alter how much skin I wanted to show. The suit was real high fashion, and I felt beautiful in it. It was the first bikini worn at Aronimink Swim Club, so I dared not risk showing my belly button, too much thigh or décolletage. The currently favored two-piece suit had "boy legs" and a sexless top going straight across the chest that disguised any reference to breasts. Up till this time, most of my suits were my mother's hand-me-downs, with the ladylike crotch shield sagging across the pubic area, stretched-out elastic around my legs, and gaping sides where HER breasts that had nursed five babies had resided.

By age fifteen, though, I was approaching Lolita-voluptuous—which was what I had been working toward at full speed. Neither the daring bikini nor my improving looks were enough to gain me entry to the "in crowd" at Aronimink, because it was clear after many years of membership that we were poor, with only one parent in evidence, who rarely showed up for the swim meets. But the bikini made me vibrate with a newly heightened sense of my sexuality, and I was looking for ways to use it.

My first real date with Greg and my brother J.G. and date Sue

My sophomore year in the new senior high school was a disappointing year. In spite of my new looks and more interesting clothes I was purchasing or shoplifting, I could not snag the interest of any of the guys I fell for. Yes, I continued shoplifting occasionally with Janet. My mother would have been so ashamed of me to know that. My desperate need to move away from whatever my mother dragged home from the rummage sales and thrift shops fostered the continuation of this sad act. At least my little sisters had my fashionable hand-me-downs secured one way or another at a real store. They, too, would be disappointed in me to know this flaw in my character.

Besides having no boyfriend, the other circumstance that destroyed my sophomore year and beyond was even more sorrowful. It happened at a meeting at the end of ninth grade in junior high school. My mother, the guidance counselor and I were meeting to "decide my future."

"Anne, your grades are excellent, but after talking with your mother, we think it would be best for you to begin taking the secretarial courses in high school next year," the guidance counselor said. My mother was quiet.

"College would not be something your mom could help with very easily, and she and I think you would do very well learning to be a secretary. There are excellent business courses, such as Bookkeeping and Accounting, Shorthand, Typing; and of course, you'll have English classes and all the other studies such as Civics, Geography, and Social Studies. "

My mother continued her silence, apparently devoid of either resources or imagination. There was no discussion of grants, loans, or finding a miraculous way to get to college. My grades? I was an A student, dammit! I loved learning. I loved diagramming sentences and writing compositions. I loved history. I did not love algebra, but I never had a good teacher, either. Mr. Jochen was renowned for preferring to discuss cars he had owned over equations and the finer points of algebra.

Right at that moment I learned that going to college would not be an option for me. I would be a secretary. So there! My future had been decided — just like that. It was a terrible fate for me. I proved to be inept at my appointed field, and I wasted five years of my life finding out how badly suited I was. I can't say I *expected* to go to college, because I had become conditioned not to expect much of anything. I've often wondered how my mother felt when she was assigned to the dressmaking school instead of college herself.

Maybe I had vaguely hoped, but I had never been given any direction to plan for the future. What I had been conditioned for was to expect failure and disappointment. There was never a time when my mother sat me down and told me of her dreams for me. I guess she was too busy coping from day to day.

J.G. clearly was not going to college and had not shown any real interest in learning — though he was quite smart and read non-stop, as I did. Maybe he was possibly still licking his wounds from being shunted off to the Wallingford Home, I thought. When he escaped the home in his junior year and was plunked into Upper Darby High

School, he seemed withdrawn and disinterested in almost anything school related. I remember Mommy taking him to see a psychologist, with whom he refused to engage. He just sat there and grunted yes or no till he wore the guy down. J. G. was into guns, cars and trapping. He and one of his classmates, Bob Pounds, (my future husband) had talked of joining the Army when they graduated, to get their six months of Army reserve duty out of the way. At that time, the draft loomed over every young man's head, and it was better to attempt to chart one's course as best one could by signing up.

Bob had gotten kicked out of Friends Central School for stealing his neighbor's car — which he considered partly his, because they had built it together. He just used it for a few days and probably disappeared in the process, enjoying that car all for himself. So he, too, was now limping through his senior year at our public high school, shamed by having to leave the prestigious Quaker school, where his brother was a football star. The event seemed ordinary to me, because J. G. often stole my mother's car when she was asleep — her best one yet, a 1953 Oldsmobile we called The Grey Ghost — when she was asleep. I remember one early morning he came drifting into the parking spot in the front of our house, engine and headlights off, to find both my mother there and two policemen to arrest him for stealing her car. It seemed to get his attention. I'm doubtful he went to jail, but they helped to "put the fear of God in him," as my mother would say.

Both J.G. and Bob were noted in the yearbook as follows: "Team color: Purple. Class: General." No activities, clubs or achievements of any sort. They joined the Army Reserves the day after graduation.

There I was, suffering through that first bad sophomore year in senior high, sitting through General English classes filled with "General/Purple" types like my brother and Bob and knowing I was much smarter than where I had been stuck. I was studying shorthand, bookkeeping and typing, where I couldn't seem to get past ten net words per minute, even after summer school. How was I going to succeed at being a secretary?

Then something to lighten my life happened at the very end of that sophomore year, in June. Another friend of my brother needed a date to their senior prom, and J. G. suggested he ask me. Less than a week before the big event, Greg got up his nerve and asked!

There was an awful lot I had to put aside. He wasn't my type — didn't read or have good grammar. He was actually shorter than I. He had a dark front tooth. And he was a grease monkey — he thought, ate, slept and dreamed cars and engines. If he had been James Dean, I could have bought into it, but, alas, no.

Yet I found myself filled with excitement at what was to become my first date — to a senior prom! What was it that excited me? Maybe it was just that someone who was male and a bit older cared enough to ask me. When you are fifteen, a guy who is seventeen is an older man; so I was thrilled. I dreamed of a filmy silk organza prom dress and the grown- up feelings of being presented with my first corsage. I hoped for a wrist corsage.

Mommy began prowling the thrift shops, dragging me along and proclaiming the shops the perfect place to find a prom dress, because most were only worn once. I measured five feet, ten inches with broad shoulders and wide hips. It seems that most girls who have gone to proms are tiny elfin creatures, size five or so. Finding the perfect dress for me in a thrift shop was no easy feat.

What she finally settled on was a pale blue silk ballerina length gown that was endowed with ruffles from hem to breast. Believe me, that jaw was clenched, her eyes half-closed; with that look of determination that conveyed I had no say in this matter. Draped on my big frame, the dress resembled a mobile wedding cake in blue. My fifteen-year-old reasonably shapely figure was well hidden in those ruffles. I believe Mommy thought this was a good idea. There were so many ruffles I had to hold my arms out from my sides, since they added about three inches of girth all around. She found flat white ballerina slippers to accommodate Greg's and my height difference. These she dressed up with little blue silk roses. She was resolute and insistent. We had found the perfect "get-up."

"Judas Priest! You're a vision in blue!" She was a little over-enthusiastic to counterbalance my sense of loss over that filmy white silk organza dress I had envisioned. I had briefly thought about shoplifting one, but this was a habit I was trying to leave behind. Besides, it seemed too high profile an item, and how would I explain to her that I wasn't wearing her pick? I was sunk.

If not a wedding cake, I could have been a lampshade from a South Philadelphia row home (she had often described the lamps in these homes from the cookware period). I felt like a football player in drag as I rounded my shoulders and hung my head, hoping to sink into the floor.

On that glorious night, however, Greg inhaled with wonder when I made my entrance. He presented me with that lovely wrist corsage of blue carnations and white roses. Suddenly I was transformed, now a fairy princess in blue ruffles. He didn't see the flaws! Oh, how easily I could be swept off my feet. My need for approval must have been screaming at 1,000 decibels. "LOVE ME!"

So began a seven-year relationship where he became both sweetheart and father. He had many flaws, but so did I.

W HILE NOT A SCHOLAR, GREG was brilliant in that one key area, anything car related. He could tear apart and build any part of an auto—body work, engines, interior, or chrome work. He was also a patient and interested teacher. I learned about feeler gauges, timing lights, carburetors, head gaskets, valve taps, oil viscosity, nomenclature of tools.

We spent most of our time together at junk yards or in his driveway building, tuning, testing and experiencing the rewards of informal drag racing on West Chester Pike with other motor-heads on Friday nights. My mother was not excited that I had fallen for Greg and she became less so over time. When he entered my life, she lost her sitter, housekeeper and cook, as Greg would pick me up from school and deliver me back home late at night on most nights. She also felt we were not a good match at all. He was a wonderful and generous guy in so many ways, but all I saw was a mirror of my mother's bad marriages when I thought of a future with him—or anybody. I never expected that I would marry anyone to whom I would stay married. It just didn't seem to work out that way from all I observed.

Greg graduated from school, did his six months' stint in the Army Reserves and became a worker at the Boeing manufacturing plant. Concluding that he was not likely to elevate her daughter to a better life, Mommy wanted more for me (meaning, I guess, she wanted me to "marry up," which was how you got your life better in her thinking, perhaps). Maybe she felt guilt about not helping me attend college. I think she also worried about whether I would get "in trouble," since I had just turned sixteen and was growing up fast.

She needn't have worried. I was smart enough to know I didn't want those kinds of problems. Sex consisted of "everything but." It was the culture of the day to save yourself

But he was the father figure I desperately needed who loved and cared for me, so I couldn't quite let him go yet.

CHAPTER 46 – IMMACULATE CONCEPTION

GOOD INTENTIONS AND INSISTENT YOUNG men are not always a match made in heaven. While avoiding the taboo of real sex, intimacy was expanding and increasing. Like other young lovers seeking a chance to be alone, we had some secret spots where we could be alone. My sisters only told me recently that the usual spot wasn't a secret spot at all, and that my mother was stalking me, taking my siblings to check us out at Lovers' Lane in Broomall. We never noticed. She was worried and wanted the relationship to end. In any case, we were becoming more intimate in every way but the obvious.

In November of my senior year I had a panicky thought. Could it be that I may have experienced an immaculate conception? Could it also be that our "everything but" approach to sexual exploration might have failed me? I could hardly believe this, but I had missed my period by a week . . . then another week, and another. There were no pregnancy tests, but I felt different—and scared as can be. Greg became tender and hopeful. I became frozen with fear.

"I have a good job, and we could live with my father until we get some money saved up for an apartment," he enthused. Suffering with morning sickness already, both visions made me even more nauseous.

"I'm too young, I'm not ready; I haven't even graduated from high school yet. I can't have a baby," I wept. So we did everything we could, short of the coat hanger or back-street-abortion approach: Greg got me big quantities of quinine from work, a sure remedy to end an early pregnancy. I swallowed about thirty-five of them. I remember sitting in a movie theater waiting for whatever would happen to begin, with my ears ringing, a headache, double vision—but no miscarriage. I tried jumping from high places. Then I tried horseback riding at a gallop, something that had always been thrilling until this point. I began to think maybe I wasn't pregnant, but as time went on, my swelling stomach and breasts belied that hope.

I went to school every day and worked at the candy counter of Murphy's Five & Ten in Manoa after school. Here I was, making some real money and getting a regular paycheck, driving my own car (a hot rod Greg built for me), eking out my freedom at last. And the candy! For the first time in my life I had unlimited access to all the candy I could want, but I could hardly bear to look at it or even smell the chocolate. I was nauseous from the pregnancy and from contemplating my fate: married with a baby at age sixteen to a guy I thought would make for a failed marriage. I'd be unable to finish my education, embarrassed and absented as many a young girl was at that time. This marriage idea was something I hadn't been able to face in the best of circumstances.

Late in my fourth month, desperate, I realized I would have to tell my mother. I didn't want to hurt her or disappoint her, but I couldn't put it off any longer. The only private room in our house, the bathroom, was the setting for my awful revelation. It was the same room where I learned at age eleven-and-a-half while at overnight Girl Scout camp that it was normal to be bleeding from my lower parts— Mommy had forgotten to introduce the subject to me beforehand. I had thought I was dying.

So here we were again, in that little room where we shared used bath water, deep secrets and problems; and this time the problem was that I was *not* bleeding. I wanted her to hug me and tell me everything would be all right. That didn't happen. I hardly remember her saying anything at all, except, "Oh, Anne . . . ". She was on the toilet seat, and I was on the edge of the tub. She lowered her forehead into her cupped hand and sighed. I felt her despair. She didn't express anger or show great disappointment; it wasn't her style. Some time passed, and I remember hoping she was coming up with a solution—what, I didn't know. She sat on the toilet with that distant look and the set jaw that indicated she was mobilizing for something big. I didn't know what to think, because there was no obvious solution to me except the obvious one: become a very young bride and say goodbye to my future—which I hadn't even planned yet!

I HID BEHIND THE DOOR eavesdropping on my mother's phone conversation. "Is this the Florence Crittenton Home for Unwed Mothers?" She had been silent and in deep thought all week, as my hope and curiosity accelerated. I wanted magic and envisioned she would save me somehow, but I was scared out of my mind at the limited possibilities. The name I heard said it all. Whatever the plan, I could only think of my brother being sent away to a "home."

She filled me in when she hung up the receiver. I could go to the North Carolina home or to one in several other states (there were over 50 of these "shelters"). There I could have the baby while attending a school either within the home or nearby the home, where only young unmarried pregnant girls would attend. I could finish my high school education. It sounded only slightly more wonderful than a shotgun wedding.

In 1961, to be pregnant before marriage was a scandal that branded a girl forever as "trash, ruined, easy, a bad girl." Even if she married the father, it was the first thing whispered in confidence at parties as an important fact about this girl. The father was absolved of guilt, since boys will be boys; but the girl's sin neither forgiven nor forgotten in the women's world. Mommy had gone through her own scandal when she became a "divorced woman," with the ladies whispering to each other behind their hands when she entered a room. My mother was trying to save me from that, but all I could think about was my brother and his period of banishment. Now I was headed for my own personal Siberia.

Mommy wanted me to get her program underway before I really began showing. I would have to leave school over the Christmas holiday and not come back till I had delivered the baby.

Since I was at almost my fifth month, I needed to be examined by a doctor. For my pre-natal visit she made an appointment at Lankenau Hospital on the edge of Philadelphia, avoiding our community hospital where I was born so my pregnancy didn't get recorded locally. As I entered the lobby, I saw a large section off to the right with giant 3-D color reproductions of artists' renderings of the growth of a baby from conception to birth, showing each month's stage of development with a word description under each huge board. She made sure we spent time studying the dioramas. There were no ultrasound screenings then, so the display was revelatory to new parents, scientific wonder revealed. The boards showed a little creature who looked like a curled-up being from outer space. Up until then I had not thought of what was going on inside me as a person. Those images jolted me into reality.

The next jolt came in the Maternity Clinic, set within the hospital but quite different from the rest of the hospital setting, which seemed to be for the affluent people from the Main Line, mostly Jewish, well-groomed and well- heeled.

This clinic was for poor pregnant women. Most were single young girls like me, and I found myself gazing into my future as well as my past. My future: me, a young unwed mother, always poor and teaching my child how to get along poor. My past: Another Red Feather Agency! It seemed I couldn't get away from these awful clinics, where the treatment and interest level of the charity-giving doctors was sub-par and sometimes dished out disdainfully.

I believe now, these decades later, my mother was knowingly shocking me on the hardest kind of reality, as she prepared me to accept what she had mentally worked out, the Crittenton Home, where I could have the baby quietly and give it up for adoption.

That course was starting to look like a slightly better one than marrying Greg and keeping the baby, as I looked around at the group of young women in the waiting room. Some had one baby with them and another pregnancy in progress.

The doctor who examined me seemed comfortable letting me know that I was a second-class citizen in my single pregnancy and my inability to pay. The examination was an embarrassing nightmare, as he dug deep into places I didn't know a hand could reach, describing clinically what he was finding in language he and my mother of five seemed to understand without translation. I was still hoping he would say out loud and with finality:

"This young lady isn't pregnant. She just has a *fiferfloffel fersluganah* (or some wonderfully treatable condition) that can be cured easily with a *thigamajig* pill."

That didn't happen. The examination was followed by some hard questions about various means I might have taken to end the pregnancy. In the course of the revelations about my many attempts to abort, the doctor asked me a question: Had I ever had German measles or scarlet fever? There had been some question about the scarlet fever during first grade; but it remained unresolved. I had gotten healthy as the proverbial horse, thriving on Nutrilite.

Beyond that possibility, I did have German measles just the month before. I didn't remember many ill effects from it; a doctor said it was simply German Measles.

I was given a blood test to confirm the presence of the rubella virus antibodies: there they were, those life- changing antibodies.

Now the doctor informed me and my mother that this could be a serious turn of events, with a high likelihood of the child being born with birth defects.

I really don't remember exactly what happened after this. I may well not have been included in their discussion that decided the baby's and my fate. Over the next week my mother simply informed me that, because of the German measles, it would be impossible for me to deliver the baby. I would now have to undergo a "therapeutic abortion," done by C-section.

This was not offered as a choice. I was told the chances of the baby being born deformed were so high that it was too great a risk to take. I don't remember my feelings about this baby, myself, its or my future. It is a huge blank—maybe a blanket of pain I pulled over myself. I don't remember discussing this with Greg or my mother. It just was.

Mommy laid the plan for me to have an attack of appendicitis and to be rushed to the hospital, allowing even my own family, as well as my closest friends and teachers, to remain in the dark about the truth. No one must know. Even Otto, as far as I knew, was not informed of what was happening. To my knowledge, Greg and my mother were the only insiders.

The surgery happened. I woke up in pain, with a huge bandage across my lower abdomen. When I was released from the hospital seven days later, I was pale, weak, and depressed. I gradually returned to my schoolwork, my job at the candy counter, and my impending graduation. With my stomach cut about ten inches across my former pubic hairline with big ugly stitches zippered across me and my painful breasts leaking onto my blouse in Accounting class, I had sunk to a low point, awash in guilt.

Lost in the ugliness of this event, I remember almost nothing as I dragged through the usually exciting senior class events for the next several months. I was simply dead inside. At the senior prom I finally wore that brand-new white silk organza gown I had long craved (purchased with my own candy counter money). But it had lost its meaning. I remember only dragging myself through the long night, now a blank. Some years later Mommy magically converted the prom gown into my wedding dress, a much happier event for both her and me.

It was a heavy fog that hung over me as I sorted out my feelings about what had just happened: One, I had escaped several awful fates. I was no longer sentenced to a shotgun wedding and early marriage to a person with whom I knew I would not stay, even if I had walked down the aisle to him.

Two, I had tacitly participated in taking an almost life. This had barely registered at first because I had been busy trying to take its life from the moment I suspected pregnancy—I accustomed myself to blocking out any association with an actual life, a person.

Three, I had become a changed person, no longer quite a child. I had become one with Eve in the Garden after this time, that place from which one can never return. I was Someone Else now and I didn't know who.

But I began thinking I no longer needed Greg's underpinnings to make my way—because it hadn't done me much good after all. Time to grow up and face my future.

I HARDLY NOTICED WHAT MOMMY might have been suffering, she who took it upon herself to decide my future. Looking back, I realize I was overcome with my own pain and a need to distance myself from it, as well as from her. I had a lot of guilt about the pain I had caused her.

As I look through documents and letters I've uncovered, I can now place the event of my pregnancy as a point of departure from her real world. She must have needed to distract herself from the many burdens in her life, some of which went way beyond my own troubles.

This distractibility was something she had proven to be quite good at anyway. When I was seventeen and recovering that summer, her younger son Danny was eight—and he was struggling in school and most other areas of his young life. So much like Otto, he was already the child who was easy to leave behind. And so she did, in many ways. Danny was showing early signs of being troubled and adjusting poorly to the daycare routine. Nancy was bright and happy and comedic, seemingly better able to survive. It was a rare evening when they were picked up from the daycare center earlier than six p.m.

I see clearly now that my mother had a great need for freedom and fun. Life had gotten heavier in so many ways in her second marriage, and she was finding her escape. Unbeknownst to any of her children or her husband, she was cooking up that distracting and entertaining scheme that came to be called The Great Sadie Fletcher Caper.

In retrospect, her side trips off the Main Road of Life were what made her so enchanting — and so infuriating to those around her — that order-loving second husband and her needy children. We children had already made our adjustments and were running wild ourselves, but poor Otto kept holding out that harness and reins for her to accept.

Today these types of people can claim the moniker of ADD as described earlier from the Diagnostic and Statistical Manual of Mental Disorders. At the time there was no such identification, which was unfortunate for us sons and daughters of Dorothy. Four out of five of us kids had probably caught the "disease" ourselves, and we were struggling with no real guidance from her on how to get ourselves "in harness." I regularly struggle with focus and getting steady work accomplished. For me, as it was with her, daily life must be equally fun and balanced with the hard work and life's burdens. When poor Otto tried to create order and discipline, we resented it because he was so heavy-handed.

ADD types often find ways to medicate and get through their work or school day with gritted teeth and some "help." My help was diet pills of Dexedrine, perhaps the early form of Ritalin. Danny and J. G. would have gotten great help from some form of it. Instead Danny found alcohol and marijuana as a young teen — neither of which helped him in school. He has now been in recovery and a leader in the A.A. organization for over twenty years.

Some of these types of people go happily along creating whirlpools of disorder and havoc on a regular basis. She continued right into her second marriage those many-faceted hoaxes and jokes she contrived as a young woman to distract herself from life's routines.

I suspect that my pregnancy and abortion caused her great pain, though she truly never said any word to sling guilt in my path. I hardly observed that Madame Stiff Upper Lip was downcast. But then I got busy myself finding ways to get over this sad event. I was hell-bent on recovering from my agony through wild times carousing in bars, driving Greg's new Triumph 650 TT motorcycle and racing the Corvette with him on the street or the track. I wanted to put the horror behind me as far and as fast as I could.

I guess Mommy hoped my relationship would split up after the abortion and that I'd move away from marrying Greg and eventually "find myself." But I was only one of five! She had four other worries on her mind as well.

Each of her children of Difficult Marriage One or Two was struggling deeply with one thing or another, just as our mother was: failures in school, verbal abuse by Otto eiither to her or us, uncertain futures, relationships, jobs, and more. It's hard to have normalcy when alcoholism is destroying the family life. Events don't always go as planned.

Nancy related a story to me recently about her first experience at overnight camp when she was ten or eleven. She attended Camp Sandy Hill, a Christian camp on the Chesapeake Bay, for which Faith Chapel covered half of the cost. Nancy was bunking with her neighborhood friend, Sheri, whose family also attended Faith Chapel. Through the week, Nancy related, Sheri had become unbearably bossy and demanding, and Nancy was desperate for the week to end so she could get away from her. A common camp rule is that campers are not allowed to call their parents but may write and receive letters. On the final day of camp, Nancy packed up all her belongings and lugged them down to the end of the road to wait at the snack bar, so she could see Mommy coming down the road. She waited for hours, long after the snack bar had closed. Finally, she told me, a camp counselor came to get her, telling her that she would be staying another week but in a different cabin, with a different girl. Nancy said she was surprised beyond belief that this mysterious decision had somehow been made. Maybe she was hurt or upset, but she didn't mention she was. It's possible that we had no telephone at the time. She stayed the second week. And she added, "The whole time I was there, Mommy wrote me a letter every day, enclosing my favorite comic strip, Brenda Starr." Maybe that attention absolved Nancy's anger and disappointment, but in an average day our family life, disappointments were a dime a dozen.

I feel sure Dorothy loved us children deeply. Her usual state of distraction often left us unsure when we saw her showering her affection on strangers, though. We settled easily for the leftovers, which restored us for several reasons. We had become used to her lack of attention to the details of childrearing and housekeeping, both of which slipped further on the start of every new business venture. And her easy sense of humor could put a manic spin on what would have been tragedies in normal children's lives.

CHAPTER 49 – THE SADIE FLETCHER CAPER

MOMMY HAD BECOME KNOWN AMONG her friends throughout her young and adult life for carrying out pranks, some of which she regularly pulled on Otto to lighten her and our days. Another was a crazy scheme called "Lucky Luke, the Two-Headed Boy," which acquired a legend status in her circle. I wasn't there, but I understand that the plot involved Mommy pushing a baby carriage in the cover of night, the carriage holding two large grapefruits nestled under a baby blanket, meant to portray her unusual two-headed baby, and her pretend interviews to find a nurse who could care for her unusual charge. To say that such a prank would not be considered politically correct in today's times would be an understatement. It was a story that many of her cohorts laughed about for years, though.

The Sadie Fletcher Caper was a prank of a higher order, rising to the level of a grand hoax that lasted several years and reached into faraway places in the world, all pretend, of course. As the Caper grew like a sci-fi character with tentacles reaching in every direction, we heard bits of it here and there when she would share pieces of the scheme's latest hilarity, but the actual plot eluded us.

Many years later, long after my mother was gone, her friend Shelly, who had become her close friend and partner in this crime, shared Mommy's letters with me. Among them were the Sadie Fletcher letters. I kept the large tote bag full of scribbles in my office closet for years longer. One day I got curious about what might be found in the almost impossible-to-read onionskin, composition book and hotel notepaper pages, and I began deciphering them with a magnifying glass. Mommy seemed to have started with handwritten rough drafts and then typed the final copies on her beloved "Miss Underwood" portable typewriter, because her handwriting was so illegible. Those penciled drafts, all that I had, took years to work through. As I did it, a chapter of my mother's life that had been mostly secret to me, emerged.

Her Sadie Fletcher letters to her hoax victim Andy, an illiterate crooked car dealer who apparently swindled Shelly on a used car deal were among the collection of letters. I also found a single letter from the one great love in my mother's life, a man named Gilbert—with whom she accidentally fell in love during the Caper, more thoroughly than she had ever been or imagined she'd be in her life.

Doesn't she make a perfect "Sadie Fletcher"?

The scheme began when Shelly, who like my mother in her first marriage had never driven a car, decided she had reason to begin driving. She had started a new hobby of playing bridge through a Nutrilite customer and friend of my mother's, Mr. Richie Kane. Incidentally, Shelly and Richie became lovers. I can't tell more of this part of the story, because it all was revealed to me only through inference in the letters.

Mr. Kane was a handsome (married) man in his 60's, I would guess, with a distinguished mustache and a suave charm that his female bridge students loved. The sexual relationship between Shelly and him was perhaps a natural, surely her first outside of marriage — which had gradually taken a downhill slide, with her husband Max barely speaking to her in between their producing seven children. Today, Max would probably be identified as being "on the spectrum." Our families were friends, and one of her daughters and I were quite close. When Max stopped speaking to Shelly and began covering every pipe in the basement with aluminum foil, Shelly may have grown tired of the marriage that had begun when she became a sixteen-year-old bride in the Bronx and began producing babies. Maybe a new hobby like bridge could get her through the rest of the marriage. The car would have aided the project considerably.

As my friend's mother, she was in my life almost daily, and I never had a remote idea that she was anything except someone who loved to cook and care for her children.

At the same time, the doomed marriage between Dorothy and Otto continued to degrade. Yet, while juggling all the challenges of dealing with a curmudgeon husband and operating her businesses, the Queen of Distraction found yet another way to keep the fun in her life.

Charles Darwin would have understood: it was survival of the fittest; and she soared above as her marriage and spouse sank down. With twelve children and two difficult husbands between Mommy and Shelly, what started out as a silly form of distraction from their awful routines — the Sadie Fletcher Hoax — became an obsession that led each of the women into torrid love affairs.

I believe the year was 1961 or 1962, and Maria Beale Fletcher had just been chosen as the new Miss America. At that time, the Miss America contest was something all America hung onto, watching every event raptly. Using that national experience as a jumping off point Mommy adopted a faux persona, posing as Maria Fletcher's wealthy grandmother, a young merry widow, subtly sensual and sending signals that she was a "woman of interest," She named herself "Sadie Fletcher." The Sadie character in actuality never physically appeared "in the flesh" to the victim of her hoax, the used car dealer and gas station owner named Andy Iocono. This fact is important, as her letters have her slipping fluidly in and out of her several characters.

Allow me to introduce my mother to begin the story in her own words, in a letter she wrote:

> . . . **He owned and operated a Blue Sunoco gas station in Morton and was a crooked car dealer on the side. I got to know him when I sold him Nutrilite—at cost—and he said if I referred any car sales, he'd see that I got a good commission. I wasn't about to sell any crooked cars for him, but then he got in this neat Caddie. Knowing Shelly was looking for a car, I took her over to look at it. We didn't let Andy know that we were friends. I told him she was a cousin of one of my customers, was Jewish, and always paid cash and to give her a good deal, as her brother was a Philadelphia lawyer. He started at $475.00. She got it at $400.00. He cheated me—or us—out of the $100.00 commission (which Shelly and I were going to split). The reason we, or she, got it so cheap was there was a bullet hole in the windshield and bloodstains on the upholstery; also, the upsey-downsey windows didn't work. He later fixed those. Outside of these flaws, it was a real dreamboat. It did make us nervous to ride in it if the mind turned to thoughts of the Mafia.**

And that's how they schemed to get even with Andy. Both Shelly and Dorothy had been "had." I believe he later convinced Shelly that the Caddie had problems and to turn the car in for a lemon, a further trick, which incited their scheming further.

Mommy and Shelly began sending the "Sadie" letters to Andy, eventually enticing him into a series of never-completed romantic trysts with Sadie in Atlantic City and nearby. Her letters made him progressively eager to meet her, possibly bed her, and then when the moment was right, fleece her. This seemed to be his habit.

As the prank apparently deepened, I was busy trying to sort my own next steps in life, as her children each were. I was working my summer job at Murphy's and recovering from my interrupted pregnancy and escape from early marriage, but still seeing Greg. Linda, Danny and Nancy, now about thirteen, seven and eight, were mostly on their own with school and homework—except for projects like dioramas, when our mother got drawn in. As rich as our imaginations were between our No-TV era and our collections of fairy tales and World Books, none of us could have conjured her Sadie Fletcher character. Unaware of her "exterior" activities then, I think we all felt increasingly separated from her life, but I think I can say that as her children, our lives went on, and so did the rest of hers—her marriage, her businesses, her garden-variety side trips, She made it all mesh somehow.

As well as I thought I knew her sense of humor, there is no way I could have known the inner workings of her mind—or understood the depth of the relationship in which she became entangled. The letters revealed her as a woman of great warmth and passion, a writer of poetry, and a spinner of well-crafted and sometimes hilarious tales. They revealed frailties I never knew of, dreams I didn't know she dreamed, and hopes that had never seen the light of day until she found her love. As our mother, she was strong, tough and stoical about life's disappointments, always forging ahead with new energy.

When the Caper oozed into an affair, as far as I knew with the little knowledge I had, she was still a married woman who held fast to her marriage vows. In a vain attempt to provide some of the flavor of her tales, it is only fair that I provide some of Mommy's side of this story.

(NOTE: Her own colorful language best tells her hilarious and often poignant story. Here is an excerpt from one letter (twenty-eight typed pages) she wrote to a woman she never met, the sister of her lover, several weeks after he died an early and untimely death.)

. . . Our ROMANCE didn't develop from two people being thrown together and then sex rearing its ugly head – not a bit of it. Every one of our encounters were miracles of planning, intrigue and luck aided by interested friends and relatives.

Now then: this old guy, Dick *[Richie]* **Kane, who also was one of my Nutrilite customers and was also interested in this nutty correspondence I had going, allowed me to use "Custom Decorators, No. 7, N. Chester Ave., Pleasantville, N. J. as a mailing address. Dick owned a property that his friend Gilbert also used as a studio when he needed to meet with a decorating client. Richie allowed me to use his address as a mailing address for Andy to send return letters to. Andy found the phone number through the information operator and began calling Sadie there. When he couldn't reach her,** *[no answer ever]* **he sent special delivery letters.**

When Gilbert read both sides of this wild bunch of billets-doux *[I don't know how he got copies of the* *letters she sent to Andy]* **and wanted to hear the whole story from the beginning, so he kept after Richie to arrange a meeting with this Sadie Fletcher character. I considered this my chance to find out if this story was really funny for people who didn't know any of the real characters involved. And that's how I met Gil. We four, Shelly and Richie, and Mr. Gilbert Kline and myself met at Richie's house not far from me—so he drove up from Atlantic City for the occasion.**

Well, I did a reading of the letters from the very beginning; and Gil laughed so hard he was doubled over with the tears were rolling down his cheeks. Old Mr. Kane held his teeth in his hand *[from laughing so hard]* **after we got started. Trying to read my (Sadie's) handwriting—and Andy's handwriting wasn't easy, neither a prime example of good penmanship. I kept getting interrupted by Shelly and arguing with her about the sequence of events; and she kept telling parts ahead of time. Some of it I had dreamed up but hadn't gotten down in writing yet**

Anyway, Dick had told me a little bit about Gil, but of course he was completely different than I had expected. I'm sure no one ever met Gil for the first time without thinking this—a completely unique guy. Let me tell you how he looked to me that first time on March 25th.

We were introduced and shook hands. He was so very different; warm and so much nicer than Mr. Kane—whom I like very much; he's nice, but not very. Gil clearly was so intelligent, and he didn't

act like he expected me to really be Sadie Fletcher, in spite of his interest in the letters. I felt comfortable with him, and I liked him! I liked him immediately.

After changing from my Murray Space Shoes to heels, I sat across the room from him, and Dick gave each of us one of his cocktails that looked and tasted like the B-twelve tonic I used to buy for the children in a gallon jug. Very nice, actually . . .

. . . Getting back to the evening of the Sadie Fletcher readings:

At a certain point we left off the readings—our cheeks hurt so much from laughing we declared an intermission until after dinner. . . . We all drove in Gil's car to 'Walber's on the Delaware' so we could drive past Andy's Sunoco station. He wasn't there, of course, as he tended bar at night in order to learn the business, so he could buy a tavern when he got hold of some of Sadie's money.

At the table, we four got back into [my stories of] Sadie's life and times, and we were laughing so much again that the nice colored waiter remarked he'd never seen people enjoying themselves so much and we hadn't even had anything to drink.

Ol' Mr. Kane gave him (the waiter) such a glorious testimony for Nutrilite—which I had placed a portion of next to everyone's water glass—I could see this waiter was on the hook. At the right time I excused myself and found him in the lobby and spoke to him. He indeed was interested in obtaining some Nutrilite—he gave me a $20 bill, and I arranged to meet him at the Philadelphia airport the next day at 2:30 with the pills. I was only gone from the table for a few minutes—they all thought I'd gone to the 'Ladies,' but Gil saw me talking quite earnestly with the waiter; and he saw me put the $20 bill in my pocket. He thought I shouldn't meet him alone, but I told him he was a very nice fellow. His name is Benton Page; he has worked at Walber's for ten years and is married and has four kids; and he is interested in becoming a distributor! I'll meet him at the Atlantic gas station by the airport in broad daylight— perfectly safe!

. . . We both said we'd never had a better time in our whole lives. I almost always have a good time, and so does he—but that evening was a rare one.

When I was back in my car, he kissed me through the open window—like he would kiss you, his sister. I drove home and told my daughter Anne all about the fun we had as I washed my face. I certainly wouldn't have washed off that kiss if I had known it was the beginning of our love.

The first letter from Sadie to Andy, the used car crook, began like this:

Dear Mr. Iaconni,

I'm the elderly lady in the dark sedan that got a grease job and lubrication off you last Saturday. While you were doing your work, I took advantage of your nice Ladies' facilities and absent-minded-like must have driven off with the key. I am so sorry to do such a thoughtless thing—I think you and the road-wearied ladies have been

inconvenienced so long.

[She went on to discuss her foiled plans for getting the key back to him, having some extra keys made, getting the keys mixed up with other keys, and basically stringing him along and not getting that key back to him.]

I don't know how I can ever make it up to you—do you like pie or cake? I have an idea . . .

You are such a pleasant man—and your flowers in the front of the station are so pretty. The tomatoes and beans looked nice, too. Do you can?

That was a very satisfactory lube. Might have been one of the most successful of your career. I'll know in a week. If so, I shall certainly give you the business.

If I'm selected again to collect funds for the children's shelter, I think I'll call on you *[to donate]* **if I have the nerve—you seemed so pleasant.**

Mrs. Sadie Fletcher

Next, this. . .

Dear Mr. Iaconetti,

Well, I finally got hold of Johnny (grandson #1); and sure enough, he had the key to the Ladies. My, but he laughed at me, traipsing off with such an important item.

I baked a special surprise for you. I always put dimes in birthday cakes for my kiddies, so I baked your new Ladies keys in one of my Boston Shoo-Fly coin pies. I eat them all the time, and they keep

up one's strength. If you want the receipt, I'll oblige. It has lots of healthy stuff in it. Gaylord Hauser gave me the idea years ago. It's the yogurt in the crust and the blackstrap molasses that really makes it, I think. Don't worry about biting into the key, because I boiled it good—same as I used to with the dimes. She never baked him that cake, of course.

You are such a pleasant man. My cold is all done with and I am up and at 'em again. I'll soon be hitting the road. I visit around to the kids and spoil my grandkids, straighten out my sons- and daughters-in-law, cook up some of my specialties for them, and give a few lectures here and there. Ever since my man kicked the bucket, I've been having a real ball—no disrespect to James, he was a wonderful man. But now he's gone, and he wouldn't want me to sit around and mope—he never did.

Well, Mr. Iaconetti, I must get back to the bomb shelter plan we're going to have installed in the back yard. It'll be a doozy.

Yours truly,

Mrs. Sadie Fletcher

(Please keep in mind, Dear Reader, every bit of her descriptions about her life are completely made up! It never existed; she's never lived in Berks County – or been there, as far as I know – never had a Momma anyone like she describes, as her mother had died at age fifty. This is all her imagination to create a persona designed to lure in a randy man she considered a crook.)

Dorothy (Sadie) to Andy, August 1961

Dear Mr. Iancelli,

I wish I knew your first name—it is probably easier to spell than your last—which you could change for just ten bucks.

I'm visiting Momma for a few days—she had her 90th birthday yesterday; she always has open house and bakes for it during the whole month of August. I'll have to diet for two weeks to get back to my old sylph, (ha-ha, get it?). I'll bet over a hundred freeloaders were here yesterday eating up Momma's goodies. Well, that is what she loves: feeding kinfolk and friends. All Berks County knows about her cooking.

She wants to meet you. I'll drive her down when she's done canning tomatoes and peaches, which are at their peak now. I told her the funny way we met, by the way.

Jim has been dead for a year now, and Momma can't rest until I latch on to another good man. You sure didn't act like a married man—seemed kind of hungry-like. I'm looking for a robust man in good health who will last a while. It's too hard on a woman to love a man, learn his ways, get herself slimmed down, get so comfortable with him, then have him kick off. It doesn't make up for the heartbreak of it all.

I got this Ladies' Room key made at the hardware store. The man said it ought to fit—if not at first, just file it a little. *[Neither of the keys she apparently sent fit his "Ladies," by design and certainly to frustrate him.]*

Please take think of me as "Sade."

Mrs. Sadie Fletcher

And now the first letter from Andy Iacono, handprinted and dated Sept 20, 1961.

> **Dear Sadie, I am looking forward to the day to see you. I am glad you sent a return address. I try to call you yesterday and the operator try to get me your number but there wasn't any phone listed under your name. When will you be down this part of the world, would like to see you and hope it is soon. I hope I get my key back soon someone else walk off with the other key we had. I am not much for writing, do hope to hear from you soon.**
>
> **P.S. Sadie Here is my phone number if you want call me. Person to person I love to talk to you. KI 3-9649 Andy**

And so began the Sadie Fletcher Caper. My best guess is that it began in about 1961, and I imagine the prank was well under way when Gil was introduced to her for the "reading," since there were only one or two times she ever seemed to date her scribbled drafts.

I GRADUATED IN THE TOP tenth of the 1961 class of four hundred having completed the business courses through twelfth grade. That was the easy part. The hard part lay ahead, that of finding a job I knew I would hate, doing tasks I was not suited for. As with each of us, we were on our own when it came to charting the next leg of our journey in life. I remember slogging out on interviews dressed in a suit and heels on the hot summer days and failing to attract anyone's interest in me — including my own!

After struggling all summer to find that secretarial job, I finally found a man with a heart, a gentle Jewish man named Moishe Hurwitz who was the comptroller for the Penn Meter Company, perhaps the most colorless place of business in the City of Brotherly Love. It was humiliating to conjure a career here, but I had consistently proved unable to pass the simplest of typing tests. He hired me! I was given an electric typewriter, my key to survival as I climbed from ten to eighty words per minute.

Over the next several years I discovered that I hated the office environment and the work, and the dreary lunchroom scene with obligatory card game and gossip with other goal-free people. I had no goals myself but sensed these people weren't going places either. I don't think I'd ever heard my mother utter the word "goal," so I and my siblings didn't really know what a goal was or how to create one.

At home, the negative environment continued, but I avoided home as much as I could now that I had a job, money, and a car. Otto was still part of our scene. Both J. G. and Greg were usually ready to attack Otto physically at the slightest provocation.

If I was home, Greg was often there with me. One evening Otto started getting physically aggressive with Mommy, chest-pushing her out of the kitchen after dinner. Greg, sensing trouble, charged into the kitchen ready to unleash his hair-trigger temper. He grabbed the cast-iron frying pan, grease flying everywhere, raising it over his head. Otto backed up and grabbed the butcher knife behind him on the counter. The rest of the family, still at the dinner table, froze, now fearful of entering the fray for fear of losing our own lives.

In seconds as Greg began lowering the frying pan toward Otto's head, Mommy jumped between them and screamed "STOP," shoving Greg back with all her strength, the frying pan clattering to the floor. Otto, somewhat drunk, took a useless swipe with the knife. All three froze, shocked at the intensity. Silent, the combatants reassessed; the moment passed. Mommy shoved Greg out of the kitchen, and Otto's steam valve had been released. Everyone was scared, including Otto.

The day-to-day downward slide, punctuated by that bald patch on her head, the spaghetti heave, and now the almost-murder, was wearing my mother down.

(Here are a few more revelatory excerpts of that long letter. They describe events we never knew of at all, and also tells why we only found one letter from Gilber):

. . . Eleanor—now comes the bad part.

Two-and-a-half years ago when I was getting the divorce, Otto got into the trunk of my car with a screwdriver and got all my precious letters from Gil. They were wrapped in foil and hidden in my sales kit. I guess I had driven to the office with

someone that day because I was probably training them. He went to Orlowsky, his lawyer; who called Elaine *[Gil's wife]*. Then Elaine, Otto and Orlowsky had a real witch's convention. Now: during that past year Gil had serious back trouble, and I had a slight stroke. If it wasn't for Gil, I would certainly not have recovered like I did; but he kept me fighting and urged me not to have any dye tests or spinal taps. All the doctors were so strong for this, and of course, Otto. He would have been happy to have me become an invalid.

So at this maladjusted meeting, Otto wanted to sue Gilbert for stealing my love and causing me to have a stroke--which is ridiculous. I had consulted a marriage counselor when I was pregnant for Danny in the third year of our marriage, 1952. I earned $6,000 that year I had my fourth child *[apparently a good sum then]*. Otto drinks and is a miserable neurotic. Well, I'll spare you the whole story.

I had seen a lawyer before Gil and I had met but stopped the divorce procedure after meeting him because I was kind of afraid to be free. But when Otto confronted me, I told him in front of my children that I loved someone and wanted Otto to leave. There had been no love to 'steal' for many years.

During this period of turmoil, she was strangely driving The Sadie Fletcher Caper at high speeds in full throttle, still leading him on into thinking he was going to "score" with Sadie eventually.

(Dear Reader, please remember my mother, as far as I knew, had no knowledge of life in Berks County where she claims as Sadie's home, had never been to the Hershey's factory, had never gleaned leftover broken chocolate, and surely had never made ninety chocolate pandowdies! This was a dish we had never tasted in our home kitchen!)

Dear "Andy,"

Hasn't this heat been awfull Hershey's had more chocolate waste than we expected. The machine went haywire and broke up the bars wrong for 2 hours—ruined near 80-some pounds, We get all the broken bars, so we left with the 80 lbs; and it all melted together on the trip back home! Well, I'll tell you: if Momma's kitchen wasn't air-conditioned, I think we would have given up. We made over 90 chocolate pandowdies and froze them and chopped them up with a hammer. They are in the freezer now, except for the dozen or so the boys ate up.

It's a relief to know the Ladies isn't locked as I feared. Better put up a neat sign that the door doesn't lock, so they aren't caught with their— well, you know what I mean.

You were very pleasant and seemed to have the right vibrations—and that's so important.

What is your birthday? I'm Taurus. Sincerely,

(Sade) Sadie Fletcher

I FIRMLY EMBRACED ROCK AND roll, but Eloise was nuts for jazz — and the epicenter of jazz was New York City. I and my two friends Eloise and Carol made the decision to have a big-girl experience in the big city.

Eloise convinced Carol and me into a whole weekend in New York. She just had to get to this jazz club called Birdland. The club was near Broadway, which would be dazzling to us Drexel Hill types. It cost money to get into the club, but all three of us were prepared to spend some new working girl wealth to hear someone famous like Charlie Parker. Eloise had many favorites, so anyone would thrill her. Dizzy Gillespie, Thelonious Monk, Miles Davis, John Coltrane, Stan Getz — they all performed there. At eighteen, we could order drinks right at the bar, and we could dance till five a.m. A real jazz club in New York City!

We took the train and arrived in the thrilling buzz of New York City. We found our tiny room in our hotel and got busy applying extra make-up and perfume and dressing in the most sophisticated outfits we owned. Poured into an emerald green sleeveless satin sheath dress with a matching green satin purse and 4-inch black patent heels, I expected to turn heads of even the most jaded New York jazz fan.

"I'll have an Old Granddad and Seven," I told the bartender after we paid and entered. Dizzy with excitement, we had crossed the line, no longer children, but sophisticated young women. I felt ready for what the evening would bring. Much of my life had been a death of hope and dreams, but here I would begin to experience Life at its apex.

Carol and Eloise were dressed for the city also, but Eloise was the bulky type with a face that looked old when she was born. No matter how interesting the clothes were, her appearance was not. She usually danced with a cigarette hanging out of her mouth, and her heavily made-up eyes were like a giraffe's in mascara. Carol was cute and perky but always had a look on her face as if she had just been hit with a blackjack from behind.

Eloise was always tough and sarcastic around guys, but Carol was a perfect counterpoint, full of fun and innocent cuteness. They each were engaged in animated conversation with several guys, Emily talking out of the side of her mouth and Carol giggling away. On my own, I was casting out bait, seeing who would nibble, downing my grown-up drinks as I took it all in.

Soon I was approached by a good-looking guy who exuded sex. Flattered and slightly intimidated, I was thrilled to be the one who got the cool guy paying attention to me. I set the hook. We danced once or twice, and it was clear we clicked. He invited me to a party on the other side of town in a hotel with drinks, music, food, and

Birdland in New York City

lots of interesting people. Yes, there would be a good jazz band. It was tempting and now I was getting into the jazz. But there I was at *Birdland*, settling into a New York state of mind, enjoying Stan Getz's mellow sound.

Why leave? What if the music wasn't as good as this was? But the food sounded enticing and maybe the people would be too.

"We can grab a cab," he said, "and be there in ten minutes," he crooned in my ear while he pulled me to him on the dance floor. I had never been in a cab.

Always drawn to an adventure, I told Emily and Carol I was on my way to a big party. They were jealous, but the invitation had been extended only to me. We agreed to meet back in the hotel room later, and I left with my cool guy.

"Is this where the party is?" I said, as the cabbie dumped us in front of a shabby hotel. I wasn't sure what New York standards were—I only had our own small shopworn room at our hotel to compare it to. This was maybe a peg down. We walked in and the guy held his hand out to keep me back, saying, "Hold on." He said something privately and quickly to the night clerk and slipped him a bill. He turned to me.

"The party is on the 7th floor—let's go have some fun,"

And up we went in the creaky and dirty elevator. He seemed somewhat drunk, and now I noticed I was too. My grown-up bourbon drinks had dulled the details that I should have been alert to. We were in the room with the door closed and locked before I realized that the "party" was just him and me. He turned ugly quickly, commanding me to get my clothes off. I hesitated; he grabbed me and tried ripping my dress off, but he couldn't get the fabric to give enough. He threw me down face forward on the bed and ripped the zipper down the back.

"Get the dress off! Get your clothes off."

I remember feeling sick that I had given off such a sexual aura and that I had been so excited to be attracting the leering eyes of strangers in a strange city. I had felt such a sense of power scarcely an hour ago. And now I was helpless because my ego had misled me. He opened a dresser drawer and pulled out a black revolver, gesturing with it to continue stripping. "C'mon, lemme see what you got," he hollered.

My brother had a .22 for shooting squirrels, and I had shot a shotgun once with my cousins, but this was the first revolver I had ever seen in my life, except in the movies.

He opened the chamber to make sure I knew it was loaded. Under its threat I stripped off my stockings and slip while he watched. He was drinking from a bottle wrapped in a paper bag and waving the gun at me to move faster.

I wondered if he would kill me after he finished with me. Would I die on the night I had thought my life had finally begun? My mind and heart were racing. I hesitated for a second, hoping to come up with an idea to save myself. What would my mother do here? She would do something ridiculously funny and catch him off guard or get him laughing. Mommy at her best, poking fun and getting right out there on the edge of danger, seeing how far she could take it. But I was not my mother.

"Please don't do this to me." My face contorted into a tearful mask of pain. No other words came to me. He grabbed me and held the gun at my neck, throwing me down on the bed and stripping off his own clothes. By this time, he had consumed the contents of the bottle and flung it across the room. He set the revolver aside and fumbled at his clothing, planning to rape me.

I saw that the whiskey had ruined the sexual prowess he had planned. The next ten minutes were a frustrated attempt to get his limp member operating correctly. It sickened me more to watch him prepare himself to violate me. He got angrier and began pushing my legs apart with his knee, no longer seeming to care whether he could penetrate me. Thrusting wildly at my pubic area until he finally managed to weakly spurt some semen on me, he soon changed his mood, becoming disinterested. He drifted off and seemed to lose interest in me.

Had he passed out? I lay there quietly, calculating my options. Testing, I moved away an inch, causing the gun to fall onto the carpet. He jolted alert for a second from the noise. I froze, holding my breath. If there was one thing in which I was experienced from life with my stepfather, it was quiet observation and calculating that exact point of no return when a drunk stops being dangerous. I inched away and lay quietly, watching.

I waited for the snore to begin and the mouth to fall open, trying to control my shaking. His breathing became more regular. I took a chance and rolled onto the floor carefully. Still quiet.

Nudging the gun slowly under the bed with my foot, I low crawled to my dress. I stopped. Still passed out. I threw my ripped dress halfway on, leaving my underwear and stockings behind. My purse was under him. I couldn't risk it. I wanted my life more than I wanted that purse or to be fully dressed. I ran down the dirty stairs, afraid of yet another predator on the elevator. I felt as dirty as the stairs were. There was no one at the desk. Feeling grateful, I broke out of my prison.

Regretting my four-inch heels, I began walking. Never before having flagged a cab down, with no money anyway, I limped across the mostly deserted city. I cringed at every passing car, sure that each one held another man who could victimize me again. Surely, I looked like a prostitute who had tangled with a nasty john. Me in my emerald green satin dress.

I had no idea where I was or how to find my hotel. I had been so dazzled by the city when we arrived off the train, Eloise had taken charge of getting us to the hotel. I only knew the hotel name. I found a woman to ask for directions—she may have indeed been a prostitute. She didn't know the hotel. I wandered for a few hours looking for anything I could identify in this strange city, tears running down my face and staining my now-torn dress—that dress in which I had placed such confidence. My ticket to a good time in the Big Apple, I thought ruefully. I passed telephone booths, longing to call my mother and cry to her, but I had no money. I thought of the times she had already bailed me out: my five-month pregnancy surprise, my arrest in Somers Point for underage entrance to Tony Mart's with my crudely falsified license, when she had had to drive down with all the cash she could muster to get me out of that ugly little jail. I couldn't disappoint her yet another time. There was to be no comfort for my most foolhardy act yet. She was not the comforting type anyway. She was the steel-jawed pragmatic type. And I didn't want her to know the shame I felt.

I kept asking people for the location of my hotel and made my way back, exhausted and drained When I dragged myself to the front desk, I asked the night clerk for an extra key, saying that I had had my purse stolen. With my tear-stained face and my torn dress, he saw I was distressed and scared; he discreetly gave me a key.

Five a.m. The sky just beginning to lighten. I let myself quietly into the room to find Eloise and Carol sleeping like innocent children, New York makeup still on. Stained and dirtied in contrast, I crept into the bathroom, stripped my dress off and put it in a laundry bag. I sneaked it out to the hallway, covering it with trash. I couldn't cover my shame, but I didn't want to explain my stupidity to my friends. I just wanted to cleanse myself of him, horrified at the thought of being pregnant, fumbled as it was. I stood under the steamy water, hoping it could wash away my perpetrator and absolve me of my yokel ignorance.

Within minutes of the shower, I found I had just begun my period. A bit of unadulterated luck. I embraced those cramps that usually stole a day of my life each month and made my decision: I would tell no one. I was used to pain and horror and violence — but this time I had brought it upon myself. I crawled into bed and silently cried myself to a troubled sleep, stunned at my naivete — and my luck. I cried for my mother, but I cried alone. This pain she

would not have to bear. What a long way I had come from Birdland.
I died a little that night.

Later that morning Emily and Carol prattled about their thrills
and adventures — what guys they had talked with, who asked them to
dance, who bought them a drink. Innocent girl talk. I had to make an
excuse about losing my money, my wallet and my purse, saying I had
drunkenly left it at the party and didn't know where the hotel was.

"So how was the party, anyway? What was it like?" Jealous, they
were.

"It was a blast," I said. "A cool bunch of people, great music, and
everybody was dancing. I danced till I thought I'd fall down." I told
them when the party was over the guy had hailed a cab and paid the
driver to take me back to the hotel, like a real New York gentleman.

CHAPTER 52 – WILD TIMES

THAT FIRST DAY ON MY new job at Penn Meter Company was a company shutdown, and only my forbearing boss and one other "skeleton crew" person besides me remained. She became my good friend with the first two questions she asked me over our greasy spoon lunch: "Do you have a boyfriend? *[Yes.]* Are you sleeping with him?"

I laughed at her extreme directness. My own sisters wouldn't ask me that question. I didn't answer at first, then I poured out my story to her, telling her everything. We became close friends as I was invited into her home and family life, learning about how city Jews lived. Gilda made it her personal mission to thoroughly school me in Jewishness. I was invited to every seder, bar mitzvah and family event.

While I was learning about Jewish culture, Mommy was embarked on a similar quest, first with *her* Jewish friend Shelly; and then with that wonderful Jewish man she accidentally fell in love with.

Meanwhile, I realized I couldn't fill my workdays with flow-meter-related work, so I moved on to several more jobs. Most didn't last long. I left one job after realizing that all five men in the small manufacturers' representative office failed to notice that I was now running the office, taking and giving quotes by fax or teletype (for steel tubing, no more exciting a product line than flow meters), enabling them to be out on the road. I hated being alone for eight hours a day.

One day after my boss was particularly rude and cruel toward me, I took my two- foot-high pile of unfiled filing (my personal ADD nemesis) and slotted it randomly into various file drawers, handily dispersing in about five minutes two tedious weeks of work. I then rolled a piece of paper into my typewriter, switched the ribbon to the red half, and wrote, "3-6-9, I resign." I was my mother's daughter, to be sure. I skipped down the stone steps three at a time, filled with joy at my decision. Soon I had a better job.

I spent much of my free time in and out of jobs with my decade-older friend. Gilda. She was a living, breathing sex object who could not resist the game of attraction. She would be teasing under the table the foot of the president of the latest company she worked for and rolling in the hay with him that night. She was attracted to everything male, and the opposite was also true. She walked with an amazing way of swinging her "tuchus" while she held her left hand out as if to keep it from swinging out of control—somewhat similar to the outrigger on the port side of a Polynesian rowing canoe. Her hand was a kind of balancing mechanism—which also functioned as an overt beckoning mechanism.

Unfortunately, Gilda seemed to get pregnant by sexual osmosis—that mysterious "something in the air," like a contagious virus. Over three years, she got pregnant three times with her married executive lover.

In the 60s, abortion was illegal; but Harry made it easy. "This should cover it," he would smile, handing her a fat envelope of cash. "The address is right on the bottom corner, and your appointment is 8 tonight."

In each case, I was the driver to the back-alley abortionist in the sleazy part of town. I can still see the doctor, the waiting room, the ugliness of it all. It was a dangerous thing for a doctor to do, and dangerous for the woman having it: dirty conditions, sloppy methods and all of it illegal. Gilda handled these events as if getting a cavity filled. I think now that I handled the driving task with such aplomb because I had been toughened up by the ugliness of my mother's second marriage. After a while, not much bothers you.

Along the way, after work, I began taking literature courses at St. Joseph's University. The courses opened up a new world to me, and I loved what I was learning. Still no specific goal to get a degree, but I kept taking courses.

My ability to settle into my workday kept starting later over time, as I daily rediscovered how much I hated the work. No matter what time I managed to show up, I didn't kick into gear until about eleven a.m. — with the good help of the diet pills I was now taking daily. I could not have been a secretary without those wonderful pills steadily supplied to me by Gilda's doctor.

Getting my first prescription was an unforgettable experience. The good doctor who dispensed the large supply of pills insisted I needed a physical before he could "prescribe" them. I had to this point had very few encounters at the doctor's office: Mommy wasn't the type to take us for physical exams. We got by with Mercurochrome, honey and Band-aids in emergencies, and what is now called Alternative Medicine. Every answer was found in PREVENTION MAGAZINe or Adele Davis' books. The only physical I remembered had been that recent one where the doctor reached inside me to determine I was pregnant.

So when Doc Laboff had me take my clothes off and lie on the examination table and cover my naked body with a sheet, I complied, thinking it was necessary and that perhaps all doctor visits began this way. He seemed like a kindly man of about 60. How naive I was.

Nervous as could be, I lay there with face turned away waiting for it to be over. He would take various parts of the sheet off to examine me. He examined me pretty thoroughly as I wondered what he was looking for that might disqualify me from getting the pills. Gilda had said it would be easy.

Then the exam slipped into an attempted massage of my nether regions. At this point I started to catch on, just at the time I noticed he had his privates exposed, revealing possibly the most gigantic fully erect member on Planet Earth — I truly didn't know they could get that big. I bolted from the table, sheet wrapped around me and ran out into the empty waiting room, scared. My night of terror in New York City came rushing into my head. Venturing back into the examination room, I found my clothes and threw them on while he casually got his parts back under control and sheathed. He said not a word.

He gave me quite a large supply of the pills. He continued to supply me thereafter. I was so innocent that I never realized (till now) I could have blackmailed him for all the pills I wanted and started a business selling them. Those were the times then. I never told Gilda, and I never told anyone.

Those pills kept me skinny and kept me working, albeit in spurts. Without my pill, my day consisted of doing almost nothing except whiling away the hours as best I could. I had also discovered that pills came in handy on those wild nights of dancing and drinking till two a.m. The pill habit led to a great need for another one the next morning, of course. They were an important part of my life during those years to aid me in regularity and consistency of the hated work, as well energy for the life in the fast track. My sister Nancy reminded me recently that I had her and Linda taking them when it was time to clean the house.

Since Mommy didn't know about or have access to these pills (so I thought at the time but was to learn differently later), distraction was her medication, and it always had been. And she took regular doses of that.

Continuing with her "Sadie Fletcher" letters, as she expands her totally fictional role:

September 1961

Mr. Andrew Iacannoi *[she purposefully spells his name differently each time]*, Kedron Ave. Sunoco Station, Near track, Morton, PA

Dear Andrew,

I see I didn't have your name right after all. I'll think of you as "Andy," like the sign says. I'll bet you didn't get any of my letters because I spelled your name wrong.

Momma and I stopped on our way down to Ocean City *[where Sadie supposedly owned multiple rental and investment properties]* last Thursday night. I came off the turnpike at Valley Forge and got lost for a while, not being too familiar with the back roads around there. Everything was closed— except your Ladies, so glad it was unlocked, as we freshened up a bit.

[She goes on to explain that her grandson Johnny mistakenly took the key and is now traveling the country with the key on his key ring.]

For Momma's birthday I gave her a case of Christian Brothers brandy (her doctor advised one shot before bed from now on). She never drank before—wore the white ribbon of the W.C.T.U. At 32 snorts to a bottle, the case will last about a year with 19 extra shots to nip on when it's real cold.

We forgot to take her bottle along to the shore, so every night I had to take her over to Somers Point for her snort. (She just loved all the nice boys there.) I must say, she made quite a hit. Funny, she told the bartender what an ugly baby Maria was. Of course, everyone all around the shore is so proud of Maria being Miss America.

We had gone down to close up the Ocean City apartments, and I was reminded of when Maria was in that Atlantic City [*Miss America*] contest. I thought her act with the tap dancing and singing together was a little too much, but she won anyway. She is my oldest son Beale's oldest daughter. Beale has operated a dance studio back in Asheville, and he taught Maria how to tap those toes. This is the first time any Fletcher woman has ever entered anything other than a pie-eating or bake-off contest. Momma wasn't too happy about it but wasn't at all surprised when she won. She knew she would, but she still doesn't like the vulgar publicity—imagine!

Maria got a lot of loot besides the scholarships. Well, Momma gave Maria her good pearl lavaliere, and I gave her my phi beta kappa key (my first husband's). Maria bawled her eyes out—she knows they came from the heart.

We are going over to the Hershey factory next week to pick up 50 pounds of chocolate bars(they save the broken ones that fall on the floor for Momma). She'll make her chocolate pandowdy in the fall, a whole freezer full.

We are going to stop at Theodore C. Auman, Inc. funeral home in Reading. Momma wants to view "Stone Willie," the mummy. He was about her age or a little older. He would be even better preserved than she is! She believes she might have known him. While we are there, she intends to get measured up and make her own arrangements— she's afraid we might go overboard because she is the great-grandmother of Miss America.

Well, "Andy," I expect that key will be back east about the 20th of the month.

Sincerely,

"Sade" Sadie Fletcher

Mrs. Sadie Fletcher "Eagles Nest"

R. D. #4 Hershey, PA

CHAPTER 53 – "THE INSTITUTE"

I MOVED ON TO MY fourth job, all with the title of "private secretary." This time it was in the negative atmosphere of a prestigious WASP Philadelphia law firm with about fifty lawyers scrapping for business. I was going up a ladder of success I had zero interest in climbing. (My days consisted of racing to beat my boss to the office so I could bring him coffee as he arrived from the Paoli Local train); I would often still be at my desk past two in the morning to prepare briefs for William R. Hancock III while he looked over my shoulder and clapped his hands loudly every time I typed a mistake on the quadruplicate copies, fuming while I erased four tissue copies. When we passed in the hall, he would turn away from me to avoid eye contact.

I wrapped up this segment of my career shortly after I passed him and a colleague at a full gallop one morning so I could beat him to the office to prepare his coffee.

"Well, well, well . . . look at the gazelle leaping across the savannah," he smirked to his companion. "Must be a lion chasing her."

I was humiliated that he ridiculed me while I was hurrying to perform my menial duties as his faithful servant. I suddenly realized I didn't want to be his faithful servant. My mother hadn't raised me with an attitude of servility. I gave notice that day and left on the day

President Kennedy was shot—the only good thing I remembered about that bad day we can't forget.

At the time I never really blamed my mother for hanging me out to dry on the education issue, but in retrospect, I believe she should have tried harder, found some resources, or at least directed me to find some. I obediently accepted the sentence pronounced on me by her, through that so-called guidance counselor.

Next I became secretary to the technical director of a prestigious non-profit research institute whose mission was to elevate the discipline of marketing to a science. It was located near the University of Pennsylvania's Wharton School. The environment was intellectually stimulating and served as the beginning of my own intellectual awakening.

Still going to night school writing classes, I didn't see getting out of my "secketary" rut any other way. I found I loved writing, but Momma hadn't taught her children about having a vision—I had no plan for where my courses might lead me. I had already put on the mantle of hopelessness, hunkered down into Life's rut: oozing toward inevitability, my other secret life and classes were mostly to distract me.

At my job, I was surrounded by the great thinkers of the world talking about data sets, survey bias, probability theory—-such lofty ideas, and I felt myself shrinking by comparison. I didn't see where I could fit in or how I could make the leap—didn't even know what the leap might be. These bright people dazzled me into emotional paralysis. I felt like such a loser in those surroundings.

Mommy had given me excellent coping skills in the worst of situations, but a vision was apparently something she lacked for herself. Unknowingly, she had passed on the belief that what looks good at the moment will surely turn to shit at some point. She was the proverbial Sisyphus pushing that boulder up the hill, knowing it would come rolling back down yet again. In spite of all her talk about that ship coming in, I believe her interior language was so sadly self-canceling—at least until she fell in love deeply.

When my boss wasn't holding court doing complex mathematical calculations with friends on the blackboard or telling his latest jokes, he was massaging my neck while massaging his turgid penis against my back and asking if I could stay late. I was revolted, but since he had a mistress and possessive wife, I was able to shrug him off. In the "Me Too" world today, this is a high form of sexual harassment, but then it was an unspoken right, which men in positions of power assumed and enjoyed.—Just like the doctor who supplied me with diet pills.

As the pressure to give in to the insistence from my boss got worse—which of course it did—my vision for a new career loomed once again. I began to think I had to get out in spite of how stimulating the intellectual environment was. Now I began thinking another secretarial job would be a continued march toward a kind of doom. "There must be something I could be good at," I moaned to myself, but I didn't know what.

During this period I was very detached from my family life anyway, staying at Greg's, Gilda's and only occasionally at home. I continued to get no career guidance from Mommy. She was involved in Nutrilite and now Amway, and surely a few other enterprises thrown in.

In 1964 I was in a terrible car accident in South Carolina with Greg on our way to visit my aunt and uncle in Florida. The car had flipped five times down an embankment and landed upside down. Greg freed me by using that burst of adrenalin they talk about in such times with a broken neck, which put him in traction with a weight screwed into his head for six weeks. I broke my back and suffered other injuries, and when I was able to limp home, I drove our Corvette with no top, no headlights, and one arm. Once I was home, my brother urged me to recover by going to a picnic with friends on the Brandywine. Fun has always been our antidote for tragedy in my family, so it seemed like a good idea. I needed a ride and called his friend Bob Pounds, saying I would bring the food, and he could drive. We danced to the Beatles, paddled the Brandywine, and laughed till five a.m. In a word,

Our happy wedding

we fell in love that night and made a plan to get married soon, telling my mother when she came out to Bob's car to tell us to shush because we were waking the neighbors with our laughter. It was instant, and my mother was as happy as I was, with her fondness for Bob. We married in August of 1966, and my mother made me the most beautiful wedding dress.

I didn't know at the time of my wedding what terrible pain she was in, with her lover close to death and separated from her completely as he was dying. She never saw him before his death, and while she was busy making my dress and helping me prepare for our wonderful wedding, here is what she wrote in one of her last letters to Gil:

> **. . . During June and July I was terribly depressed—especially in July. My daughter's wedding was set for August 13, 1966, to a boy I love as my own son. He has been a favorite of mine since he and J. G. were little kids. We had a lovely wedding. I designed and made her gown, but in July I was so down I couldn't sell. I felt like the world was coming to an end . . .**

To think that she never shared her pain with me, not wanting to ruin my happiness!

About a year later, when I was a lost soul in my career path, my mother stopped by at midnight and opened the door to our little apartment and slid in the Amway Career Manual, with three words: "Here. Read it!" I did, and then I read it again. I found the possibility of a business in those pages, and I gave it to Bob to read. Overnight, we launched an Amway business, which we successfully built and ran over 30 years. In our first year we outgrew our apartment—that had now become our warehouse—and just at that time accepted a temporary home at my mother's invitation to move in and keep an eye on Danny and Nancy. She rescued us, and we attempted to rescue her from dereliction of duty. We stayed about a year before we found a home to rent. She did give me career guidance, after all, saving me from another secretarial job.

And what else was Mommy up to during this period? With her victim Andy now firmly hooked on her line, she continued chumming his waters as if he were a prize gamefish, keeping the bait fresh, tantalizing him and being a perfect imitation of a juicy morsel: a wealthy, high-class lady of a certain age, sexually interested and looking for a place to invest some serious money. Andy was following the bait. "Sadie Fletcher" was working at (a) getting him to buy Nutrilite through Sadie's high endorsement of the product and "that nice lady" Sadie named "Pocohantas" who sold the product [*her real self, actually*]; (b) tantalizing him into believing he could seduce Sadie and get a bonanza of her money to buy his dream nightclub-bar; and (c) setting him up to believe she, as the Sadie character, was absolutely wealthy and bored. In the letter below she pretends to be on an expensive cruise out of New York after an indulgent spending spree in New York City. Though she meets an attractive man who wants a shipboard romance, Sadie can only "pine" for Andy:

Dear Andy, It's been such a long time since I've written or talked to you—I feel out of touch, and so much has happened. Did Momma ever get over to meet you? I forgot to ask her.

Thank you so much for getting in touch with your friend Mrs. Fish [purposeful misspelling of Mommy's last name Fech]. She brought the pills down to the Rittenhouse *[Sadie's "city penthouse"]*—and we liked her so much, we had her come along to the ship for the bon voyage party! Ask her about the fun we had. You can tell her I just LOVE the Nutrilites—those pills sure put a "capital L" in Living.

She joined us for cocktails, etc., and we decided to call her Lady Pocahontas—do her kids wear those crazy shoes *[Murray Space Shoes]*, too?

I had a little chance to speak with Mrs. F. about you in the cab on the way to the pier and about my interest in you. Supposing that she knows you well, I asked her if you are honest (this is quite important in my book). She said, "No man—or woman— is completely honest; it is a matter of degree." But I still insisted on a direct answer.

"Andy is an honest liar," she said. I wanted so much to explore this further, but we arrived at the pier then, and there was no other chance to pump her any more about you.

The ship was full of beauty-parlor-special types showing off their finery to one another; a few real people as well. One of them was a man I met at the Captain's reception, who was somehow attracted to me, and I to him. His name is Charles Hubbs, a manufacturer's rep for Barr's products, from Harrisburg. His wife recently died, and his doctor ordered the cruise to lower his blood pressure. I gave him some of my Nutrilites and wrote to Mrs. Fish to mail some to him. He is a fine man, but his vibrations are rather low for me.

("Hubbsy" was a real person from her youth, the rich one who got away after she pulled blonde "underarm hair" on the double date — the blue-angora-sweater incident, remember?)

YOUR vibrations hit me just right, by the way. If only I could really get to know you. Are you still "no strings," or have you got something going? "Hubbsy" has been really rushing me. I've given up traveling with Maria and her Miss America party for a month or so, to spend more time with Hubbsy. Plus, I was fed up with all the hoopla and commercial b.s. connected with those appearances. My lands! If Jesus Christ and the Mother Mary came down from Heaven, people wouldn't make this big a fuss!

I spent a lot of time on the ship, sunrise to sunset, hanging over the rail, not seasick, but sea struck. A real soul stirrer, the sea is. There you are, skimming along between the immensity of the sky and the sea—the blood of the earth, so full of life. I get sad, sexy, even drunk looking at the sea. So much beauty, mystery, cruelty. I can see why people take up skin diving—what a kick that must be. I'm going to see about it, too and maybe try it out.

I hung over that rail until I felt all the radioactive

mental dandruff of the past years being blown out of my brain. Inner dandruff is the hardest to get rid of. I even wrote to you on the ship, but when I read it over, I tore it up and threw the pieces to the fish. How can I have such a passionate longing for some man I know so little about? One chance meeting—certainly no impression either of us was aware of . . . I wrote only because of losing the stupid key, but then I felt compelled to *[continue to]* write for some reason. Every time I hoped to satisfy my curiosity about you, we couldn't get together. Your note was enthusiastic, but no news. I hope you enjoy my letters. I love writing to you; but it beats the hell out of me why I do. When I've talked on the phone to you those few times the same vitality that attracted me at first is still there.

Did you save my letters, or read them once and crumple them up? I wonder...

Did you get that tavern you told me about on the phone? If so, you must be a very busy young man. It must be an interesting business. I don't know myself just what I am going to settle down to, but I'm sort of fed up with hopping around from place to place. At least I'm not stewing over where to put the bomb shelter—Momma bought one and has a contractor who's building her a blast-proof bomb shelter. She is also having him build a blast-proof outhouse—imagine! Well, it will be convenient; the old gals at her picnics and outdoor shindigs won't have so far to go now .

Sadie Fletcher

P.S. Please write. Don't try to compose or "snow" me. Just flow some of your thoughts to me—I'd love it.

S.F.

OK, I confess: I did write you a "hot" letter on the boat—it was a doozie. I couldn't bear to destroy it but yet didn't have the nerve to send it to you, so I put it in a bottle, corked it and tossed it out over the coast of Florida. There is, of course, only a remote possibility you'll ever receive it. But if you ever do, it might someday shake up your third marriage. The Nutrilite, the sea air and the sexy moment all affected me.

A favor? Could you please have "Pocahontas" send 3 boxes of Nutrilites to this address below? Thank you so much, Andy. I'd write myself, but the sea air is exhausting.

Mrs. Sadie Fletcher

C/o Custom Decorators

Chester Avenue Pleasantville, N.J.

A T AGE NINETEEN I HAD become the total party girl and into my fun job at the institute, now surrounded by interesting MBA students with whom I'd go out drinking and dancing most nights of the week—whenever I could break away from Greg. I was not-so-subtly telling him I needed some breathing room. Sometimes I would hit the bars in Powelton Village to shoot pool with my guy co-workers and the grad students. It was a seamy side of town, which at that time meant it was multi-racial. On other non-stop nights, my best friend Janet and I would drive our beautiful Corvettes (mine jointly owned with Greg) to the T-Bar, where the owner Tony would stand at the door, eyes taking us in as he ran his tongue across his top teeth suggestively and hugging us up in our hotter-than-hot outfits. There was very little time for sleep and so much (under-age drinking and) partying to do!

Janet and my other party friends shared my endless supply of diet pills, which were a great help to sopping up every morsel of insane fun we could stuff in. I was liberated from my home life and getting some distance from Greg, catching up as fast as I could to even up the score in my life.

On one of those days when I was recovering from one of those nights, feeling much older than my nineteen or so years, I was draped over my desk pretending to work while I waited for the Dexedrine to kick in. I got a call from my little sister Linda.

"Mommy had a stroke, and the ambulance just took her to the hospital. She wasn't awake when I found her on the floor, but after they gave her some oxygen she came to a little bit, and they put her on a stretcher."

A stroke? Our mother was only forty-seven years old! She was made of cast iron — I never saw her rattled or nervous or anxious in a way that made me worry for her health. She was the picture of health, for God's sake! And my little sister Linda: she had so much more presence of mind to handle this crisis than I. I panicked and was overwhelmed with guilt at my inadequacy. I, her right-hand person, had become so unavailable as Mommy dealt with more and more ugliness in the marriage. I realized I had contributed so much to her building stress. My pregnancy, my wild partying, the unendingness of Greg — and now this devastating situation for her and us! And her two boys were busy getting into their own trouble, with encounters with the police and overnight stints in jail. How would our mother be able to work again? How would we continue on, even keep our house, if she couldn't work? Her businesses were a fact of life that we took for granted, believing she loved what she did. We were all sick at heart, because we had known aspects of her life were intolerable, and yet we all had lived with Otto for so many years, and it didn't seem like it would end. She had a way of making life tolerable and even fun, but she acted as a shock absorber — with this as a result.

I drove right to the hospital and found a woman who looked vaguely like our mother, but old, twisted and greyish white. She couldn't talk well — words came out slurred and halting. We stood around the bed, tears rolling down our faces. It seemed like it could be the end of life for her and us.

It wasn't. The quick administration of oxygen had spared her from more lasting effects of paralysis. One side of her face was a bit different from the other, there was a slight slur in her speech; but she was still beautiful, and she bounced back with her usual equanimity to rise above it and get back to zaniness and hard work again. I don't remember knowing at the time what else had helped her to bounce back, and it wasn't really until I started reading her scratched-out letters that I really understood what else was going on in her life. She was continuing with her Sadie prank, but had also now fallen deeply into the love relationship outside of her marriage with Gilbert Klein, the Jewish interior decorator from Atlantic City, that began when he requested a reading of the Sadie Fletcher letters after hearing about the hoax from his friend Mr. Wane several times. He said, "I MUST hear this woman read these crazy letters!"

As part of that long letter to Gil's sister written after his death, she describes here her hospital stay when she had the stroke:

> . . . **Gil got into the hospital to see me, right under Otto's nose. He came with my brother Dan and his wife Janette and waited on the floor below. My brother raised his right eyebrow half an inch to signal the mission was accomplished; and Janette rolled her eyes and kissed me on both cheeks, whispering, 'You are as bad as Elizabut Taylor!' Anne helped me walk to the ladies' room (supposedly). I sent her to pretend to get some tissues from the nurses' station and scan to see if we could make a beeline; and with her help we ran to the elevator and went down one floor, leaving Otto with Dan and Janette. And the joy to see Gil and be with him briefly was better than any medicine in the whole world. I think it would have meant a great deal to Gil if I had only listened to my impulses and could have done the same for him** *[when he was sick and dying in a hospital]*.

The slight physical disability from her stroke was a daily reminder of the futility of her marriage. Shortly after she recovered, in 1963, about twelve years and two children into this second marriage, she announced to us, "I'm filing for a divorce from Otto, and he's going to have to get out."

Not one of us seemed sorry—just relieved. I think we all hoped for a chance at a life of normalcy now. We really didn't know what "normal" was. We were so worried she'd have another stroke.

She got a restraining order put on Otto and told him he would have to move out. She certainly had enough history of the police being called and hauling him to jail under a restraining order. (It turned out there was much more to this story than we knew then with the dirt he had on her, too. And it seems he used it. We had no idea she had a trunkful of letters from Gil. Much of the time I barely knew about him at all—except perhaps as one of her friends.)

Otto began to realize there was no way this could get better for him either. This failure must have been a bitter pill for him to swallow. I don't remember wondering how he felt, but I do now. I think Otto really loved our mother. Perhaps he wished he was more capable of change—I know he certainly wished she was. I don't know if his two biological children Danny and Nancy felt his loss when he left. I felt relief.

He moved out with her help into a tiny apartment on the bad side of Upper Darby. It was conveniently situated over a bar and across from bus lines to his job and back to his home church a few towns away.

Otto continued drinking for a while, but eventually stopped and tried to clean up the relationship, which was beyond repair. We daughters would visit him and bring him food (and a toothbrush, something he had not possessed heretofore), and we would talk to him about quitting drinking. He started back attending church. Sometimes he would take the trolley to our church in his brown double-breasted pinstriped suit and spectator shoes, trying to win Mommy back and find the life he had dreamed of.

Around 1972, a letter I wrote to Mommy does indicate he did start attending AA meetings. In any case, he stopped drinking, like it had never been an issue. He instead drank a lot of coffee and ate sweets, as many recovering alcoholics do. He got nicer. He got back to working on a long-term project that had been set aside along with the rest of his life's activities when he married. He had hand-carved a scale model of the Cathedral of Notre-Dame de Paris, flying buttresses included. He'd been a hope-filled bachelor, a war hero, an accomplished musician, and a high-ranking Mason. He was a man who took a chance on marrying a pretty woman with three small children. The Schmidt's beer and rye whiskey had loaded the dice from the very beginning. He hadn't quite bargained for the likes of Dorothy Elizabeth.

OUR MOTHER'S WANDERING PERIOD BEGAN subtly at first. One of her wealthy Main Line Nutrilite customers, Ginger Bascomb, and Ginger's paramour Gar fell in love with our mother's charms. They had a great time together. Ginger had a beautiful big mansion of a place with a lot of bedrooms decorated to the teeth, family antiques gracing the interior, surrounded by dreamy gardens tended to by both Ginger and her gardener. Gar mixed up martinis for his ladies every afternoon at five, and either Ginger or the cook prepared a dazzling dinner with great wines. The first night cocktail hour happened, Ginger suggested why didn't Dorothy just spend the night and go home in the morning, instead of driving all the way back from Wynnewood—just pick out a bedroom she liked. That must have seemed like a good idea. Mommy, whose imbibing heretofore was limited to a small glass of sherry and a reserve bottle of Lydia T. Pinkham's for fainting spells, never drank at home The cocktail hour was an unusual event for her. Ginger got her smoking the occasional Salem too.

Mommy had glowingly told me the story of her new friends. Ginger was was not married and pursuing a very complicated divorce with the usual Main Line Philadelphia 400 theme: wealthy father sets up daughter and young husband, including big property and money for hubby to finish law school and set up his own practice. Over time, father dies, leaving vast estate, daughter's marriage degrades, and now husband claims half of everything. Fighting the claim in court was Ginger's only job.

The marriage had produced two lovely daughters in their late teens, who, when not attending private school, were off playing tennis at the cricket club. The fun people, the setting and luxury of it all proved a siren call to our mother. She had had been presented with a steady diet of hard times since Grant left in 1947. She herself was the gracious and glamorous person who seemed able to fit right in with the landed gentry set. And perhaps it felt good and right to her.

Dear Gingy and Gar,

One of the nicest things that's happened to me in my prime of life is being friends with you guys. Wasn't that badminton fun? And that Cubby is really good at it! I think I'll join [the Merion Cricket Club] **if nobody blackballs me. I must admit, I'm a bit lame today—my right knee feels older than the rest of me! . . .**

At home, Linda had moved out of our family home to live with her good friend's family and avoid the daunting challenge of trying to prohibit her unruly younger siblings, now in junior high school, from conducting illegal activities. Danny at age fourteen had begun holding "parties" in the basement for which he charged an admission fee to fund his beer purchases. His enterprise was already proving to be the most interesting and successful part of his life thus far. School was a spiral of failure for him, as he had been somewhat ignored by our mother.

Unfortunately for him, his Otto-like personality may have proved to be a point of critical mass for her. She loved him, of course; he was her son. But he was difficult with personality too similar to Otto's.

Nancy was sometimes drawn in by the free-for-all environment, though she was working harder in school and hoping to attend college to study fashion design.

I, too, had abandoned my position of being caregiver and now prison warden of all three of the younger ones. I tried anointing Linda as the new Person in Charge, which was hardly fair, since she had been one of "the kids" till then. Suddenly she was asked to take a leadership role over unruly Danny and Nancy. It was an unfortunate moment for Mommy to grow tired of Motherhood, but that's what happened. She had none of those worries at Ginger's; it was all fun. I don't think any of us realized she was now conducting a full-blown affair. We just were wondering what had happened to her.

My three younger siblings: Linda, Nancy, ad Dany as teens

Ginger had a long-standing hobby of decoupage, producing picnic-basket-type ladies' purses personally decoupaged and signed by her. These items sold for a lot of money to the country club set, and I still have the personalized one she made for our mother. Mommy, being so artsy herself, joined right in. For a while, all we heard about was Ginger and her decoupage.

Nancy remembers pining for just one chance to meet Ginger and her daughters so that she could assess her competition and understand why those other daughters were more interesting to Mommy than her own were. She remembers feeling lonely and hurt.

"Remember redecorating Mommy's bedroom after Pop moved out? Remember how pretty we made it? We painted it and put up that Mod flowery wallpaper? And we found second-hand furniture pieces and antiqued them? And the decoupage on the furniture? I thought sure that would get her back."

We painted all the furniture pieces an off-white shade and decoupaged the hell out of them to lure her back to her home. Nancy still has that furniture in her bedroom today.

Ginger's decoupaged custom purse and the decoupaged furniture we hoped would lure Mommy back home

But it didn't work. The roving theme that her life had taken took a more distant turn yet. She made a big decision to actually go to work in her first real job in her life, with a company called Windsor Publications. She was hired to sell the local Chamber of Commerce on having her company produce an attractive book filled with scenes and statistics to attract new people to the area. The books were moneymakers for the chambers, because they would be filled with members' advertising, which Mommy sold. She also got involved in the layout, since placement of the ads was a key to closing the sale. It turned out she was good at doing the photos, laying out the book, selling the ads—all of it. She began carrying a camera. It may have been the first time she had found a way to turn her creative tendencies into real money. It also was the first time in her sales career that she had behind her a company who sent her on jobs, with an actual boss who liked her work, and with accountability to both.

At first it was Cherry Hill and nearby towns across the river from Philadelphia, then a few smaller New Jersey seashore towns like Pleasantville. These towns suddenly wanted to look bigger and better, with gambling coming to Atlantic City. In between her chamber sales and unknown to us, she was more heavily involved in the Sadie Fletcher Caper. The traveling facilitated the great love affair with Gil the interior decorator.

I BELIEVE MR. KANE KEPT a small apartment in Pleasantville, New Jersey to entertain ladies outside of his marriage. Shelly was at least one of the ladies, after starting as his bridge student. He and Gil had a relationship, either a friendship or maybe just business. Apparently, this small apartment said, "Custom Decorator;" in front, to where Mommy told Andy to send his letters, so she could purportedly have a place to receive his mail when she was looking after all her *[non-existent, fake]* Atlantic City properties. Maybe Gil decorated the den of iniquity and bartered for its use as a studio space for his design clients. A later letter I found, which is too long to be included, reveals that indeed he and my mother probably did redecorate the "love nest," but I am not totally sure of the nest's location. The crazy letter describes that Mr. Kane allowed Gil and Mommy to use it for a tryst, which ended up in some wild lovemaking in the bathtub, overflowing it onto the landlord's dining room table below during their dinner hour. . .which resulted in Gil and now-assistant designer Dorothy getting a big decorating job to do all his apartments over with a discounted refinishing price for the dining room table thrown in. But I can only guess her crazy letter to Mr. Kane was pure spoof.

Shelly, meanwhile, had graduated smoothly from being the former real housewife of Drexel Hill to now driving a car and regularly traveling to Atlantic City. Her husband Max, who never drove a car in his life, was apparently safely at home keeping an eye on their brood. Shelly was busily shaping a new life for herself with her bridge-playing partner in love, Mr. Kane.

The saga of the missing ladies' room key continues.

Part of a letter from Sadie to Andy:

> . . . I promise you the "Ladies" keys this week! Please keep any mail for me at your office.
>
> Momma and the girls thought you sounded "cute" from my description, and just my type. I was certainly glad to hear you say you have no wife and no strings at all—I'm in the same boat. I don't think I'll marry again—too confining. I love my freedom—it's exciting. I would like to have you for a friend. And since I talked on the phone to you, I am sure you do have the right vibrations, which is important to me. Please tell me your date of birth (the hour, too, if you know it). Gert Kenkel is an expert on astrology, and she keeps asking me if I found out about "Andy" yet.
>
> I'll call you again—the best time for me to call is at night, but you have always left your gas station by then.
>
> Would you be interested in a little money-making scheme? I have a good idea for you—no cash, no investment required. *[Set the hook!]*
>
> Please write to me again, Andy.
>
> Sincerely,
>
> Sadie Fletcher

Design work for Gil, a well-connected Atlantic City decorator, was getting plentiful. Her letters indicate that our mother began helping him by setting appointments to sell draperies and luxurious furniture and doing customer relations—an addition easy to accomplish when she was in the home selling one of her other lines and looking around. As a seasoned salesperson in the most challenging of any number of product lines, she must have found this work of selling Gilbert S. Kline, the decorator, a piece of cake.

More from her letter to Gil's sister to describe the very beginning of their love affair:

> . . . **Shelly stopped over** [*the day after the Sadie Fletcher letters reading*]—**it seemed Mr. Kline, the decorator from Atlantic City, wanted me to work with him when he got the deal with Penn Towers, still only a hole in the ground at that time. She thought I could probably make more money than with my pills. And also, she added—knowing I wouldn't ever give up Nutrilite—I could surely sell Nutrilite to some of the high-class people I would meet. They had given Gil my address, and he was surprised I had no phone—Otto had torn it out of the wall three times recently; and as long as he was in the house, I couldn't use it anyhow. So until I could get him out, I had given up on having a phone. I had seen a lawyer but was a long way from having the money for the divorce. The main thing Shelly wanted to get across was this: Dick was very fond of Gil, and Shelly and I have been friends forever. It would be fun having more group activities like last night, she cajoled. Sure, we had fun, I said, but I only came to read the Sadie letters—I scolded Shelly, saying "I don't**

want to become a cheating wife; I have five kids
to worry about." She scoffed, "Don't worry, it's
just for fun—Gil he said he never had so much fun
in all his life . . .

In about 1961 the groundwork was being laid for gambling in
Atlantic City, and people in the know were making their moves.
Resorts International purchased what had started out as a wooden
three-story boarding house, then became the largest military hospital
during World War II, and went on to become the venerated Chalfonte-
Haddon Hall. Resorts had a plan to open its first casino there. Then
Resorts bought 55,000 acres of land right on the boardwalk. Everybody
in the inner circles knew gambling would happen; and the town was
on a binge to dress up fancy.

Mommy at this point was often using Main Line friend Ginger's
home as a base for her many "irons in the fire," so to speak. She would
come back home maybe once a week with some groceries and to check
in. She would tell us all her stories of whom she met, how she closed
a big deal with Windsor, Gil's decorating business, or Famous Artists,
and bits and pieces of the latest events with Sadie Fletcher—which
were a little hard to follow.

Gradually we were introduced to just the very edges of her
relationship with Gil and what a wonderful man he was. Since at
beginning of her of revelation, she was still married; so we were a bit
upset to think of our mother in a friendship with a man outside of
marriage. She avoided at first saying she was in love, but her
enthusiasm was too big not to share. Over time she carefully revealed
the depth of this relationship. She was crazily in love with the interior
decorator from Atlantic City, also married in an equally unhappy
situation.

She withheld most details of the affair once she sensed our
discomfort. Her children, with the exception of J. G., were all pretty
involved with church, and it was "a sin in the eyes of God." She simply

withdrew more, to pursue what had become desperately important to her: the one chance she had ever known at happiness in a relationship. I imagine it was also the first time she had a clear goal and direction.

It was only through those penciled draft letters that I finally learned how deep and complex this period was. She was busy leading another whole life apart from her family, both as Sadie Fletcher and as a woman in love. Nancy remembers Mommy telling her once in the car as they pulled up to a stop sign that "Gil would lean over and kiss her every time they came to a stop sign." Nancy, upset, was struck wordless with shock. Our mother was a straight shooter. She had taught us not to lie or cheat and to do the right thing. She was a married woman, strait-laced at that! How could this seem so right to her? Otto was Nancy's father, and her heart ached for him in a new way, no matter how difficult a man he was. Danny may still feel some resentment over this, never really discussed.

The Windsor Publications gig was too lucrative for her to quit—even as she apparently added selling the Famous Artists Course and interior design for Gil. She was probably trying to find the money for a divorce, but it was not discussed with me. She had never before made such good money as she was with Windsor, because she had never had the discipline of someone else telling her what her next job would be. Till then she could wander off her track at whim—in fact, it sometimes seemed she was hardly ever ON track! Yet she had built a business (many, in fact) that sustained us, out of nothing but the drive to take care of her family and herself.

Her letter to Eleanor about how the relationship began continues:

> . . . **So then I got a telegram from Gil (since we had no phone in the house) asking me to please call him collect on Thursday at 4:15 and saying I was harder to get in touch with than the Prince of Wales. I had never gotten a telegram before! Well, I did call, and he said he was so delighted with my thank-you**

note, his very own original Sadie Fletcher letter. Gil said he was coming to Philly on a buying trip the next day; and he wanted to take me to dinner ALONE to discuss some business important to both of us. How were all the children, etc.? I was to meet him at Dick's [Richie Kane's] at 6 p.m. Friday. So I did. This time I wore one of Anne's knitted dresses and high heels. I had my hair a bit fluffed up, and earrings and white gloves on. I really wanted him to see I could be a lady quite capable of meeting the kind of clientele he could expect at Penn Towers. I was convincing (for years I had been selling to Main Line snobs, and they're just people, too).

Of course, I wanted to convince him to begin taking Nutrilite, but I decided I would simply give it to him.

Also, if he gave me a choice, I would request going to the Springfield Inn. It's close by, so Gil wouldn't have to drive any extra distance. Driving A.C. to Drexel Hill and back is enough for one day; and I knew the food was good there. I had eaten it many times at my customer Betty's home when I delivered her Nutrilite. She's a waitress there and brings their choicest food home every night. Since Betty had moved to a new house and hadn't yet sold her former home for seven months now, she had stopped taking Nutrilite, being strapped. I figured if I showed up at the restaurant, I might get her back as a customer; and besides, she would probably need new drapes for her house. So maybe I could impress Mr. Kline by getting him a little business . . .

Windsor assigned her to the Chambersburg, PA, book; then Harrisburg after that. We made field trips to visit her (and so did Gil, we later discovered). We had fine times and we, her untraveled children, got to see these pieces of the world through her eyes. She knew all the beautiful places and interesting attractions, since it was how she sold the ad space in the book. There was always a lake somewhere, where we went swimming in warm weather visits, the most memorable being in Lowell, Massachusetts, where she got us all to go "buck bathing" (one of her favorite pursuits) in full daylight across the large lake, suits in hand, put the bathing suits on and buy ice cream, then swim naked back across the lake.

IN A CONTINUATION OF THAT twenty-eight-page typed letter to Gil's sister Eleanor, she describes the intensity of their "first date" she didn't know was going to be a date, but a business meeting:

> . . . I had just finished delivering some Nutrilite that day and was headed home. I saw his car ahead of me when I approached home.

(So she completely skipped going home at all, following him like a dog to a bone, apparently.)

> I told him I'd follow him in his car. He said he had an important call to make, so we would go to Richie's house to call (since I had no working phone at home). I said (faking him out) that I also had an important call to make. He held my elbow as we went up the steps to Mr. Kane's house, and he was all shaky. Well, this old smoothie had a KEY to the house on his key ring! He let us in and went right for a bottle of Seagram's Seven—to make us a drink. No one else was in the home. It was clear he and Ol' Richie had this all set up. I had brought my briefcase in, as I decided to pitch the Nutrilite as soon as possible. He asked what I had in my briefcase. I said about $40 worth of

Nutrilite and the day's receipts of $80; and since I couldn't lock my car, I brought it in. It's the gospel truth.

He had taken charge to such an extent that I just couldn't pitch Nutrilite. He had bought me a pack of Salem's—that's what I smoke, no more than three packs a year.

([My mother did not smoke, but in those times smoking a cigarette still conveyed an air of sophistication, which apparently the high heels and white gloves did too.)

He lit one for me and gave it to me along with a drink. He made his phone call, a mixture of hearty small talk and some big talk about an enormous amount of money. Holy cow! Here I was smoking Salem's and drinking booze with a smart Jew from A. C. in this den of iniquity. I was getting a little shaken up myself—I noticed my hand was shaking.

Then I made my call to Mr. Wilson while Gil squinted at me.

So next Gil said he'd like me to name the place we'd have dinner, as he was sure I had a place in mind; but I decided to show him the map I kept in my briefcase. Opening my briefcase would give me an opportunity to get out some Nutrilite and open my sales pitch before pulling out the map. He didn't bite. I handed the box of Double X to him, pretending to search for the map; and he put it on the table without ever looking at it—not a nibble. I felt like such an amateur! He turned his full attention to the map. Together we plotted our trip on the map. We were two blocks from Baltimore Pike, and Springfield is two-and-a-half miles south. As if neither of us knew damned well where Springfield is, I thought.

Gil sniffed and said he liked my perfume. 'Shalimar,' I said, 'the last of the big bottle my mother left when she died . . . *[the bottle approximately seventeen years old then!]* . . . Several years later he gave me a bottle for Valentine's Day.

Then we decided we were starving, so we set out on our journey. After he made sure my car windows were closed, we got in Gil's car. I sat near him but not touching. I could see that his arm was shaking again. I wondered what was the matter—he looked so strong and well. I had to keep looking at him because he was way more beautiful than Abraham Lincoln. We smiled at each other, and I moved close to him without realizing what I was doing. He took my hand and said 'This is so nice. I'm so lucky you could see me on such short notice.'

'Oh, dear God!' I thought; 'He's so very nice.'

'Let's have a cigarette," I said, 'I'll light them." Two cigarettes so far—and I didn't even smoke! That's why young people start to smoke, I realized. Not that they like it at first, but they don't know how to handle this MAN-WOMAN stuff; and they're scared. We had more conversation, which I don't remember, because we were both so shook up. I had gotten the cigarettes mixed up, and he got my Salem while I got his lousy Winston.

We arrived at the Springfield Inn parking lot. He stopped the motor and looked around. 'Beautiful! You know just what kind of place I like.' Then he just beamed at me, and I was afraid he was going to kiss me. But he ducked his head and said, 'Come on, Mrs. Fech, you must be starved.' As we walked to the door, I had a plan to go right into the main dining room, sweep the scene with an eagle eye to locate the waitress upon whom I had designs, and then settle at her table. But as we entered the door Ol' Smoothie lightly put his hand on the small of my back and glided me into the dimly lit bar and sat us at one of those cozy tables where if you weren't lovers, you'd be miserable. He was terribly pleased with the situation and pretended it was all my choice. I was a little bit miserable, and it got worse after a while.

It turned out that Dolores, not Betty, was our waitress. I didn't recognize her, nor did she recognize me. I had seen her only one time before, at Betty's. They had both had their hair up in pin curls and rollers and scarves, and we were eating some leftover goodies from the Springfield Inn's previous day's menu.

For the first time in my life, when it came to ordering the food and drink, I heard myself saying, 'Mr. Kline, you order for me—I'm sure I'll like whatever you like.' Ye Gods, I was doing exactly what he wanted me to do, I thought. He is the only man I've ever known who could actually manage me.

The old-fashioned drinks arrived, and I began to relax and get used to him. He was telling the story of his career in the furniture business since the age of six.

The food arrived. He told me about his Cherry Hill deal and his plans for Penn Towers, and that he wanted me to work with him.

Meanwhile, back in the kitchen, Dolores told Betty there was a couple sitting at a table in the bar who had those expensive alfalfa pills Betty used to take sitting next to their water glasses. (I always get out my Nutrilite and place it in a pretty little dish.) Waitresses are nosy, so Betty came out to see for herself. She walked over to our table, spied the Nutrilite, then recognized me. 'Oh, it's Dottie, the pill lady,' she exclaims. Don't you remember Dottie, Dolores? She used to bring me the pills".

She went over to the bar for an order and told the bartender about my fabulous pills and hair. Some cozy place it turned out not to be! Except for Gil being there, I would have cleaned up on Nutrilite sales, but I was playing for higher stakes.

Gilbert didn't pay much attention to this series of continuous interruptions, but he said quietly and earnestly, 'You know I love you.'

I was shocked and disappointed that he would say this just to 'pave the way.' I said, also very quietly, 'I like you very much, Gilbert S. Kline. You are most likable, but I like hundreds of people. If I ever love you, I'll tell you, and it will really MEAN something.

Either you don't know what you are talking about—or it's worked very well for you before. Please don't say a thing like that until you know what you are talking about.'

'I know what I'm talking about. I've loved before. I'm 42 years old, and I loved a Sylvia and I've loved a girl named Barbara.' He went right on eating and talking. I was really miserable now; couldn't even swallow.

He said, 'Come on, eat, Mrs. Fech. You said you were starved. And anyway, I think you're beautiful.'

I'm a pretty good salesperson—but Gil was a real master that night. He went on to win me the same way he would 'win' a customer. I was just getting used to him again when he said,

'And I can tell that you love me. You're all shook up because of the change it will make in your life. But I'm going to make you very happy.'

He did not say he loved me again, but over the Drambuie's he said that his timing in these things was perfect. When we were back in the car, we didn't kiss. We both wanted to, I am sure, but we each felt we had gone far enough. Gil wanted to go somewhere and dance. I said no to that. I didn't know where we could go, and we would have to consume more drinks if we did. He talked me into going back to Richie and Anne's place, to which I agreed but made it clear I was not going to 'come across.' As we went up the steps to the front door, he told me we were becoming sweethearts and that he wanted to kiss and hold me in his arms, but the rest would come in due time—when we both knew we were ready. That's the way it was, Eleanor.

The next day I called him from the A & P booth at noon, as he had asked me to.

(Every time she needed to make a phone call of any kind, she had to drive to the A & P supermarket phone booth about a mile away.)

He wanted me to come to A. C. for an evening at the 500 Club—he had tickets. Of course, I couldn't. It was my turn to drive the kids to Youth for Christ. He was terribly disappointed, but he said that that was more important. I wrote him a poem on a piece of brown paper A & P bag. I called him 'Sam,' because 'Dear Gil' sounded like the old soap opera 'Helen Trent." I signed it Elizabeth, which is my middle name—I thought he might want to know that.

Continuing the Eleanor letter:

. . . And he had this thing about haircuts—every time we were together and still inquiring politely about our respective families' health, etc., he would either say 'did you notice I got my hair cut?' It was a big deal to show how important the occasion was to him. Well, I never knew a man so interested in hair styles before. He kept making tactful remarks about hair styles; how nice the waitress's hair looked (blonde in a French twist), etc. Ever since the Toni Home Permanent catastrophe . . .

(She left it on too long and turned her entire head of hair to mush.)

. . . I had gotten into the habit of cutting my own hair with the nail scissors to shape it; I got into messing with it as it grew in. Many times some of my high-class Nutrilite customers would say, 'Dottie, who cuts your hair? I love it; it always looks so smart—kind of French.' I think they were expecting me to say, 'Victor of Lord & Taylor.' So I enjoyed being artistic on my own head.

One time I showed up in a beautiful brown wig I happened to be selling at the time

(A new line Amway started carrying, and she of course had a wig in every shade.)

The style was very bouffant—I looked like a huge middle-aged Barbie Doll.

Gilbert looked as if he was going to throw up, so I took it off. I had a nylon stocking on my head— that really shook him up until I got down to my own hair and unpinned and combed out to the full two inches. Well, his final goal was reached when he made an appointment for me at a high-class hairdresser in Avalon and delivered me there personally. Naturally, he sold the guy some drapes and tables—we never went anywhere, anytime, not connected with his business (and sometimes I sneaked some in too). You had to really love that guy to put up with him.

The hairdresser combed through my short hair with a flick of the comb, snipped exactly two times—and he stood back and admired it and asked who had cut it. 'She did,' said Gilbert, like I was four years old. 'Beautiful!' said the hairdresser. Gil tried to give the guy a $5.00 tip. I gasped, 'He didn't even get $5.00 worth of hair out of it!' But Gil said, 'It looks better.' He was a great believer in THE EXPERT. The guy wouldn't take the tip—too much for the two snips. When we got to the car, we were both hysterical.

After that I never cut my hair again. Once, after it had grown, I even went to a hairdresser (which I never did normally) and got one of those glamorous hairdos that take two cans of hairspray. Gil really flipped—he loved it. After two days I washed it out—couldn't stand it. Now my hair is halfway down my back and I wear it "up. It's OK, but it was for him. So now all I've got is all this hair—and no Gilbert.

"I do not really know what Gil was for other people, but for me he was the square root of happiness. He was so wise and strong and foolish and tender, and so completely whole-hearted in everything he did.

I've been married twice, and of course, I've been kissed before, but since that time I could never remember anyone else kissing me. I would not trade the time we had together for anything on earth. Our hours probably do not add up to more than three or four weeks, but we shared more genuine happiness than many people have in a whole lifetime. Since we met, I was his dearest love, and he was the nicest thing that ever happened to me in all my life.

(So there we have it, my mother, completely smitten by this man.)

The lovers seemed to have written to each other almost daily and apparently met about once a week both to work together on Gil's decorating business and finding some passionate moments together. I have wondered how she got any work done at all. We never had the chance to read more than his one letter, but I've deciphered most of hers.

[no date, to Gil]

My darling:

. . . Since you have reached the point of saturation on my letters of love and nonsense, I shall write my next one to your wife—I sometimes feel quite close to her.

You can start breathing again—I won't send it to her, but to you. Then you can burn it, give it to her, or you can save it for a dull spot in your domestic life. If your curiosity gets the better of you (it will) and you read it, you will realize that it is a clever device to satisfy my addictions (of writing love letters to you).

(11:50 p.m.) We had an evening out tonight—we got all dressed up (somberly, of course) and went to a viewing: the father- in-law of the man Otto rides to work with (he died).

Last spring, I had an appointment one morning at ten a.m. to sell the father-in- law of this man a Niagara and Nutrilite.

(She goes on to say that her love affair kept her from keeping her appointment with the man.)

So I was in no shape emotionally to concentrate on saving this man's toes (diabetes—three weeks later, he lost several). Well, I never did get to him. Now he is dead at 70; and his wife will get the insurance money. . .

. . .so she might as well redecorate. This is horrible that I'd think of this—see what you have done? In luring me into your business, you have practically ruined the most passionately dedicated pill peddler in the east. This love business is certainly peculiar. I should really love R. T. Wilson!

Well, it's you I love; but it makes me sad to go to these funerals of people I haven't even tried to help. The only solution is to convert you *[to Nutrilite]* — I miss you. I just miss you. Dottie"

(She had apparently ridden the bus home from Atlantic City the day before, and I can only guess Otto thought she was at the shore on business.)

Sunday, after Church

Dear Gil:

Some nice lady saw me kiss you good bye, and I sat next to her on the bus. She indicated she would like me to sit with her, with me by the window in order to protect her neck "from the air-conditioning." We had some very lively conversation, I'll tell you. She remarked on our fond farewell and loves "true romance;" so I told her a very nice one, leaving out the details. She never married until she was 45—had a marvelous man, now dead.

So the two sisters and "Momma" (86 years old) live

together near Schibe Park. She sneaks off to Atlantic City for a change, now and then. All is routine and order in her life—so different from mine! So I told her the story of "Candide," Voltaire's philosophical novel. The characters live their lives through wars, earthquakes, the most impossible of hells; and all end up quite battered—but alive and united at last in a comfortable cottage, each doing their part for the welfare of all. But, in his heart, each longs for the excitement of the "good old days," although they keep thanking God (aloud) that " . . . all is for the best in this best of all possible worlds."

The lady kept saying, "I could never stand it!"

"Meaning the wild stream of life?" I asked. "It's much better than the dullness of secure, comfortable routine."

"When you're older, you will love it," she said.

Some bus ride—then she saw Ott and Danny meet me at the end—wonder what she thought.

I enjoyed being with you, so, so much. The idea of living near the sea is like a flower bulb in the cellar of my sub-conscious—taking hold and sprouting! Hoop La!

I love you, XXXXO Dottie"

ALL THE WHILE, MOMMY WAS tantalizing Andy Iacono (or Ianelli or Ionello, not sure) at an ever-increasing pace. Taking on her Sadie Fletcher persona, she pretended she occasionally worked in "client relations" for a funeral home, while "Momma" and her girls were also employed in the industry, making false teeth for the corpses who had neglected their teeth during life (who knew?) As Sadie wrote to Andy, "the girls" used the teeth money they made to play the horses and increase their wealth, which went to a charity they supported.

Below is a letter in which she had begun setting up Andy for their first "tryst," only subtly hinted at. The letter reveals how wildly her imagination was in play, as she pretends to attend a mortician's convention. I'm not sure if morticians even have conventions, a bizarre event to imagine, but she sure imagined it all:

Andy-Boy,

Well, here I am at the airport (N.Y.). I'm supposed to meet some big shot morticians and fly down to Washington with one of them, Mr. McCarey, in his private Cessna. It's a small plane, and I expect it will quite cold up there. I'm bundled up in my full-length mink.

(She never had any fur remotely resembling a mink. The closest we came to fine furs was in the famous cedar trunk, where some animal fur resided with fierce animal head that clipped to its tail. It might have been a fox in attack mode. We often employed him/her/it for Halloween. PETA people would be horrified to know what lurks in the closets and trunks of people from another age.)

We'll be attending a morticians' convention in Miami. We will spend a few days in Washington, D.C. first. It was so good to hear your voice, and so nice of you to ask about Momma . . .

. . . Tell Pocahontas *[Mommy of the Murray Space Shoes]* **I'll let her know when to send the Nutrilites as soon as I know where I'll be. Isn't she a fine woman? I hope I get to see more of her! She said some funny things about you—"don't ever give Andy any $100 bills; you only get 50s back." Not sure what she meant . . .**

(Neither am I, but I am pretty sure Andy knew the subtle reference was to how he cheated that "fine woman," as Mommy describes herself)]

Could you meet me after I return, on Sunday afternoon between 1 and 1:30 at the second-floor mezzanine at the Ritz-Carlton Hotel at Iowa Avenue and Boardwalk *[in Atlantic City]***? I thought it would be better than my hotel, which is small; and people are nosy. Then we can go to my friend's apartment—if you are not too timid. I'm really looking forward to our meeting.**

I will try to call you when I get back. Well, here come the morticians. I guess our work will really be piled up when we get back.

(Oh, how she loved the devilish pun and double entendres.)

God bless you, Andy. Sadie

Nothing about this trip really happened in my remembrance of her activities — this would have been a landmark event for my mother to fly in a private plane and a great story to retell to her children if it had happened. She made up one fantasy event after another to keep Andy guessing and lure him in even further, always off on a pretend lark involving spending "her money" freely.

She related below the safe landing in Washington D.C. after the hair-raising ride in the Cessna. Of course, she wrote on Willard Hotel Stationery and claimed she was staying at the top hotel in the city — only the best for Sadie!

Late Saturday Night,

The Willard, Washington, D. C.

Andy-boy:

The trip down here was a perfect nightmare. Mrs. McCarey didn't come! I think she chickened out; and the others flew T.W.A. I had the "honor" of being personally flown here by McCarey himself. He let me have the controls for about 20 minutes! But then he took over. He was one of the Flying Tigers under [*Major General Claire Lee*] **Chennault, and he made that old crate roll, loop-de-loop and do figure-eights. He had no mercy. I got air-sick and vomited all over my mink coat and orchid— clam chowder, too. I would rather fly solo with 2 rolls of scotch tape and about seventy-eight surplus pigeons. I'll never fly with that bird again!**

I suppose you've heard the news: right after most of the big-shot morticians left N.Y. for the convention,

the damned hearse drivers in New York and Pennsylvania went out on strike—most of these people I'm stuck with for the next few days are rather stuffy at their best, but this strike has made the lot of them more gloomy than usual . . .

In case you wonder what I have to do with these vultures, I am *not* a mortician. I am doing some extremely interesting research for Dr. Rhyne, of Duke University, concerning E.S.P.; and what I *seem* to be doing is acting as a hostess or arranger for families where there is no one else to fill the gap. Many things of an E.S.P. nature occur just before or after death; and that is my research project.

This aspect of dying is really fascinating, but the undertaking business as a whole horrifies me. If you have not made your final arrangements, you really should do it now. You not only save a good deal of money to settle it in advance, you also get by with simple dignity. You'd be amazed at the rugged, outdoorsy-type men I've seen laid out in a fashion that would horrify themselves but delight a prissy pansy: nails polished, hair marcelled, and the casket all shirred in white satin looking like a fancy candy box. Nauseating!

Example: Willy Koons, from some hick town in N. Y. state, [was a mortician who was preparing the body of] a shoemaker whose wife died ten years ago and who had made his arrangements with Willy beforehand. He wanted a plain oak casket, no frills, lined with his own tapestries he had brought from the Old Country (his own father had made them). His faithful dog Sam was put to sleep and was thoroughly embalmed, same as the man, and placed in his final sleep right at his master's feet. To me that was beautiful— but most of these 'morts' thought it highly irregular. Of course, it could be carried too far . . . an old maid with seven or eight cats would be a mess . . . or a large dog, or even a horse. But a small dog or cat I think is fine. And it isn't necessary to call in a funeral taxidermist; the pet can be properly embalmed right there for less than $50.00.

(She's swimming in the deep end of the pool now, imagination doing triple flips off the diving board.)

Whew! Excuse my going on about all this gruesome stuff—have to get it out of my system so I can sleep tonight.

Guess what we did this evening? A gang of us went out to the club to twist. I got along fine—Chubby Checker aside, I've been doing it for years and didn't know it! I have a little piece of equipment called "The Twister" that I use to keep trim, so I was ready when Chubby showed up. Momma uses it too, and she's a natural at it.

On account of my connection with the 'morts,' Momma's hobby is now paying off: She has Gert Kunkle, Mary Kauffman, and Pearl all working a couple of afternoons a week on teeth, getting "cosmetizing dental repair" work for most of the funeral homes in her area. Lots of corpses have a tooth or two missing, especially old people who have maybe had a fall and didn't get around to having a plate repaired. Momma is happy as a clam; the girls are making more money than they did with the quilts and pies, and half goes to the children's shelter. The other half they plan to play on the horses at the track in the Spring (only to get more money for the shelter).

I called and arranged to stay with my friend in Miami . . . If you call, do it person-to-person, as I wouldn't want you to call for nothing—better to write to me there. I'll be there from Wednesday to Saturday a.m., when I will return to Atlantic City.

(. . . to meet Andy for their first encounter – this letter she did mail, and it was received by Andy; he responds in the letter beginning "Sadie My Girl.")

In the following, she has arrived in Miami and writes a short continuation of the same letter from her new location, from where she actually had the letters mailed, creating a "paper trail" to fool him into thinking she was in Miami but hadn't had a chance to mail the letters she's written yet. She delayed having them sent, as she wanted to make sure the letters arrived after her requested assignation at the Ritz-Carlton. (She was not really in Miami at all—she actually had involved my aunt who *did* live in Miami by sending her the packet of letters and asking her to mail the letter from her Miami address so they would arrive too late, after Andy had shown up for the hoped-for romantic tryst.)

Andy-boy:

Didn't get to mail this yet; arrived here in Miami Tuesday in time for lunch. It is so nice and warm, 85 degrees and beautiful. I may stay longer than

I planned—it all depends on what I hear from you. I've had a gallon of fresh-squeezed orange juice already!

I came from D. C. on a BIG airplane—no more flying saucers for me!

(Up till this point in her life, she had never flown in any plane, ever.)

. . . Please, if it's not too much trouble, tell Pocahontas to send special delivery 3 (three) boxes of Nutrilites, one of them for McCarey. How many years have you been eating this stuff?

(She was telegraphing quite a word salad of mixed messages there. She is always "pushing pills" to keep Andy using Nutrilite and exhibiting her grandiosity toward others by ordering boxes and boxes of it for those nice people she meets.)

Wait until I tell you <u>why</u> the morts are meeting here: it is positively revolting, not because of the climate, hotels, or the usual reasons most conventions are held here, but because of the Cubans! Isn't that awful? Those poor people are arriving here in droves *[from Cuba]*; and most of them are destitute and have nothing, of course. Some of them die, and usually no one can afford to bury them, and no one claims the body. So the morts get them for a song! That way they have lots of material to try experiments and new processes on. Isn't that sad?

I truly hope you are the gentleman I believe you to be. The note I wrote you at the airport (arranging our meeting at my friends' apartment) may have sounded fresh, but my friend [who owns the apartment] is in Europe; and she keeps a maid and cook there, so a few friends will probably stop by. As I told you, I am interested in you, mentally, physically, spiritually, financially. As for sex . . . we'll see . . . I expect you to be very upright in your behavior, as I am a lady.

Good night, and may the Lord be with you, Andy.

Sincerely,

Sadie

(She continues on with another amendment to the never-mailed letter that is simply to later establish her paper trail to throw him off.)

Well, friend Andy, I have to go pretend to admire the work the vultures have been doing—I really can't do much contact work here myself, as most of these people don't speak English; and the morts are not really interested in people, and so they don't retain any stories I could follow up (for my research). Oh, well, it is still lovely being here, with waving palm trees and balmy breezes.

I'm going snorkeling this afternoon.
Looking forward to seeing you, Sincerely,
Sadie Fletcher
P. S. Please write your life and times, O.K.? S.F.

Monday, February 19, 1962 - Andy's verbatim response to Sadie, sent to the only address he has at Custom Decorators

Sadie My Girl,

Sure was nice to hear from you and I don't blame you for being afraid about the plane ride, wish I could of been with you on the plane holding your hand so you wouldn't be afraid. I would hold you

**in my arms so you wouldn't be afraid if you let me
hold you in my arms or are you bashful? I'll be in
Atlantic City if I am sure you are going to be there.
I'll call the Ritz Carlton and have you page before
I come I love to see you.**

Continuing, Andy goes on to explain his side of the story of why
there was any question about why the "pill-pusher" might have
questioned his honesty (the "pill-pusher" was, of course, actually my
mother and someone whom he DID really see pretty regularly as she
kept the multiple identities going and was working on keeping him
buying Nutrilite). I have left intact the lack of punctuation:

**This pill pusher is out of her mind about $100.00
and you only get $50.00 back. The story is and
I'll tell you the artist** *[Shelly, who really was an
artist and was painting murals for the Atlantic City
restaurants dressing up for the coming casinos]* **she
is so full of you know what, well the artist has a
wealthy aunt, and her aunt had sent her a
$15,000 check and she went to the bank and
cash it and put the money in a shoe box and she
brought the shoebox with the $15,000 in it and
she was going to let me have it** *[the fictional
$15,000]* **to open up a night club she knew I was
try to buy one and I was going to try and borrow
the money so she happen to be in the station and
over heard a conversation and went to her aunt
and her aunt let her have the money. So that night
[when]I was going to meet you** *[Sadie]* **and instead
you meet the artist she had the money with her.
She was mad because I wasn't over to the station
when she had the money with her, she the artist**

was getting afraid to take the money home so she went over to the pill peddler's house and she asked her to put the box *[of cash]* in her freezer with the $15,000 in it because she didn't want her *[Shelly's]* old man to find it. Well the pill peddler foul up. She was afraid her *[the pill peddler's]* old man would *[also]* find it and he is nutty as a fruit cake you know what I mean I hope. Well, anyway, the pill pusher put some of her old jewelry *[on top of the non-existent fifteen G's in cash]* in the box and took it to the artist home, and the artist thought her old man was in bed, he wasn't, he was down the cellar *[possibly covering the pipes with aluminum foil]* and then when artist went down to hide the box in the cellar she went down the cellar only to find her old man down there and he grabbed the box from her and it slip out of his hand and the jewelry and the fifteen g's fell to the floor. He kept the money because he hates the artist aunt. So the pill pusher raise so much hell about her jewelry gone the aunt's husband sent her $100.00 and a note. So one day she *[my mother, the pill-peddler]* come over to the station and the artist was there at the station getting some work done on her car and the pill peddler come in and said look what your husband sent me *[the check for $100 and the note]* and she said to the artist I can't accept all this money for the jewelry, because it wasn't worth that much. So the artist took the hundred dollars and she gave me fifty dollar of it on a bill she owed. She gave it to me to pay her bill. So the pill peddler set there for a while and she said Why did Shelly give you that money? I wouldn't tell her and that is why she said that to you.

(I don't pretend to understand his explanation, but I know part of the hoax was to keep this man thoroughly confused while pulling him in further in the hope of fleecing Sadie out of some money to buy his bar.)

I hope you don't think I am crazy because I am not. After reading about the artist and the pill peddler you will think I'm as nutty as they are and I am not nutty.

Well, I do hope to see you this weekend so long for now and may God bless you. I tell you more when I see you.

Andy

(No wonder my mother couldn't resist keeping this crazy prank going. It was the most fun she'd had in years!)

Andy-boy,

Just got my mail—stacks of it—read yours first. Oh, what a delectable, adorable thought, safe in your arms while flying thru space! You really are romantic, but I'm so glad. Of course I'm not bashful!

The rest of your letter about the shoebox full of money was most confusing—I know the artist was mad about you—remember I thought she was your wife? Andy, for her to be anxious to hand over all that money for you to achieve your dream, surely shows great trust and respect for your ability to invest with integrity . . . and I'll bet, love for you.

Did Pocahontas (I assume that is to whom you refer as the "Pill Peddler) . . . know what the artist intended to do with the money? I can't believe she (Pocahontas) would do anything to hurt you—she speaks so well of you. *[Now my devilish mother is lauding her own character here.]* I find her to be a very honest and sincere person. I like her so very much— you must remember the things she told me about you on the day I left for Bermuda. We were drinking cocktails—she is not used to them and hadn't eaten; also, I pumped her for information about you. Also, I know she is your good friend—she has made some suggestions to me concerning you that show this. I'm so sorry about her husband. Is he really mentally ill? Is that what you meant? My lands, she really has her problems. I'm glad I have been able to throw business her way—you should, too—and it *[Nutrilite]* has benefitted me. If you're not eating Nutrilite, you simply must! I feel marvelous; and my friends in Miami just raved about how much younger I'm looking . . . one always loves to hear that.

Andy, you didn't explain about her antique jewelry. *[The box of jewelry was actually rummage-sale costume jewelry.]* I'll bet it is quite valuable. Was she contributing that, too? How awful for the three of you to have such a loss!

Does the artist's husband drink? What on earth did he do with the haul? The aunt should get a detective. Do you have anything in writing with the artist? I hope so. *[More confusion thrown in, just for fun.]*

Well, we certainly will have a lot to talk about tomorrow when we meet. I can't wait to hear the rest of that wild tale. Two heads are better than one—maybe we can figure out an angle. This afternoon I'm going to do something reckless, something I've never done before: I'm going to a beauty parlor, Elizabeth Arden yet, for a "Miracle Afternoon at the Red Door." I hope they accept me—I'm all raw material! I'm afraid you are younger than I think you are. You know, I'm a bit past 50, but I feel 20.

You didn't mention receiving my long letter from **Florida.** *[She gives a phony reason for delaying having it mailed from Florida, which she never intended to have occur till after she stood him up at the Ritz.]* I'm not sure I mailed you the letter, in all the excitement.

God bless, see you tomorrow, Andy   Sadie

(Oops . . . Andy showed up at the appointed hour at the Atlantic City Ritz-Carlton, but Sadie was nowhere to be found . . .).

Feb. 20, 1962, Morton PA

Sadie,

What happen to you on Sunday. You said you would be in the lobby of the Ritz Carlton and baby I was there like I told you I would be. I waited until 3:00 for you and no Sadie. I was coming down last night so I called you at the Ritz Hotel room 742 and they told me there wasn't a room there at the Ritz, of 742. Did you forget the date you made or did you over-sleep and I had you page

at the Ritz Hotel. I arrived at 2:10 p.m. Maybe we can get together this weekend if so call me. Maybe you can come to Phila. this time. Well I do hope I hear from you and let me know what happen. Our phone conversation I told you I would be there and you said you would be there. What Hotel are you staying?

So long for now. Oh, by the way maybe you had another date and forgot all about me is that what happen? So long for now and may God Bless you.

Andy

PS I didn't see any one with an orchid or red dress and mink coat. Where were you.

This letter, from Sadie to Andy, is a cat-and-mouse pretension that she was there in the lobby, apparently in the mink coat and red dress with an orchid pinned on her so he could identify her, having just returned from the morticians' convention in Miami; but she'd had to leave after getting an emergency phone call while supposedly at the Ritz, about Momma taking ill. She made a handwritten note on scraps of Philadelphia Sheraton Hotel notepaper, to make it appear she was rushed. The scribbled note was ostensibly "left with Eddie the bellhop" — who was made to look like he apparently didn't do his job of finding Andy in the lobby and getting the note in Andy's hands.

Now the hoax takes a new turn, as Sadie claims Momma has taken quite ill in Hershey, which is why she wasn't able to stay long enough to meet him at the Ritz. Her next few letters place her back in Hershey worried about whether Momma will live after her "spell."

Dear Andy,

If only you will come early! I have just had terrible news: it's Momma. They have been trying to reach me. I left Miami earlier than my family knew in order to meet you. I got a telegram to come to Momma's immediately. The line at home was busy, so I called Dr. Klump *["Momma's doctor"]*. He doesn't know what is wrong with her. Momma had a spell Saturday and she is sinking fast. Andy, my mother has NEVER been sick. Oh, if only she pulls through—she wants to live to 100, and she loves life so. I told Dr. Klump I couldn't leave *[Atlantic City]* before this evening, but he said, "Sadie, leave now."

It's become urgent—I'll fly, I guess. Oh, if only you get here before I must leave. All the way from Miami I could feel your vibrations.

I guess Pocahontas didn't get my note on time— at least the Nutrilite didn't get to me in Miami. If only I could have reached your office before you had left! I am crying. I feel so anxious about Momma and so disappointed not to have the lovely time I planned with you—broiled lobster, etc., and our own chocolate pandowdy for dessert.

I was so ready to meet you! I had a memorable afternoon at Elizabeth Arden's yesterday . . . Andy, I didn't know myself! Until I got the sad news of Momma I felt like *[it was preparation for]* the senior prom, when *[the masseuses?]* with the phony French accents got there— scrubbing, steaming, rubbing, electrifying me; and at one point I had warm wax all over me up to my chin (I think that is to make you feel you're getting your money's worth). You know why they call it "Ze Miracle?" Anytime a lady my age looks this good, she's usually laid out. I'm very much alive, all dolled up for you; and now you aren't going to make it.

I didn't tell Zoe and Arch *[her make-believe friends with the Ritz suite, where the planned assignation was to take place, who are supposedly away in Europe]* about our planned date. Archie is always trying to tell me what to do—and he would have too much to say about meeting you. He thinks that every man who is at all attentive to me has his mind on money—he forgets what makes life really worthwhile.

I'll give this to Eddie, the bellhop, to mail for me.

Sunday, Feb. 11, 1962, Andy to Sadie:

SPECIAL DELIVERY TO SADIE FLETCHER C/O CUSTOM DECORATORS

Dear Sadie, I receive your two letters and was so glad to hear from you. When I receive your first letter and saw the address that you were in Pleasantville I call information for the phone of Custom Decorator. The operator said there was no phone listed for Custom Decorators, that is why I sent you the telegram hoping you would call me on the phone. Maybe we can get together this weekend. Call me if you get a chance or send me your phone number and I call you. How is

E. ANNE POUNDS

everything with you fine I hope. We sure have had some time trying to get together. I am sorry we didn't get to see each other when you came to the station and saw the artist there you should of come in. *[Andy had set Shelly up with a little 'art studio' in the back of the station and was charging her rent, I believe.]* I would like to know what the pill peddler told you, she called last week and asked if I had your address because she said she had receive a check from you and didn't know, where to send the pills to. I gave her the address and she wanted to know what you *[Sadie]* were doing down the shore. I told her I didn't think it was any of her business. Hope we can get together this weekend like I said before so let me know what your plans are for this weekend. *[He can smell that money now and feel it in the palm of his itchy hand.]* Hope to hear from you. So long for now and may God bless you and do hope to hear from you.

Your friend, Andy

March 10, 1962, SADIE TO ANDY, Sadie's Explanation of Why Momma Took Sick:

Andy-boy,

Our last conversation was unsatisfactory—I couldn't feel your vibrations at all. I hope you are not finished with me because I failed you last Sunday. I was completely exhausted all last week. Momma bounced like a yo-yo between life and death. The strain of the anxiety and lack of sleep had me down. Usually your voice thrills me—but it all seemed different.

Momma finally seemed much stronger, and for the first time in nearly a week I was so relieved I slept more than one hour, really until 3 p.m. I called Atlantic City and found I had to go back down to deal with property issues, so I stopped on my way at the Howard Johnson's on the turnpike to call your *[gas station]* office about quarter to five, to be sure you had been able to get Dorothy to talk to Dr. Klump *[about Nutrilite for Momma]*. You weren't there, and then your phone was busy.

Sometimes I get the feeling we never are going to get together—perhaps it is not part of God's plan. I'm still stuck here in A.C.—I expected to go back to Hershey Tuesday a.m., but for the storm. *[This reference is to the "March 6, 1962 Ash Wednesday four-day Nor'easter that hit the southern Jersey shore and eastern PA hard.]* It has been a real doozie. New moon, high tides and two storms coming together, and we ended up with a nor'easter producing thirty-five-foot waves. Atlantic City looks destroyed, and the diving horse's tower is destroyed. My properties and my car are a mess; the garage was flooded.

(Let us remember that my mother, in her Sadie persona, had no properties, no flooded garage, no friends with apartments in Atlantic City, and no sick Momma. It was all in her wild imagination.)

Andy: I would never forget our "appointment." After all, I came all the way back from Florida just to see you. I feel so awful, knowing you would be hurt. I delayed at the Ritz as much as I could, expecting you to show. I was so worried about Momma.

I'm sorry I was wrong about Zoe and Archie's suite number at the Ritz—I don't know how I got that number. The bellboy (I gave him a good tip too) didn't give you my note, I'll bet. Each time I've written you a letter lately all hell seems to break loose.

I talked to Dr. Klump early this a.m.; he has been wonderful. If Momma had been Elizabeth Taylor instead of just a sweet old lady, he could not have worked harder or longer. People are certainly wonderful—and Andy, your help in getting hold of Dorothy for us I deeply appreciate. Dorothy even drove up to Hershey again on Monday —I didn't see her, of course, since I was down in A.C.; but Dr. Klump, when I phoned him Monday night, told me Dorothy not only got everything going okay with Momma's nutrition by pulverizing some Nutrilites (she still is fed through a tube), but she stayed several hours with Momma. She gave her some sort of treatment with that *[Niagara Cyclo-Massage]* machine she sells and had Momma walking a little.

I would like to give Dorothy a nice gift to show how much we appreciate her kindness. Do you think she would be insulted if I gave her money, a nice sum—she couldn't refuse that? Please let me know what you feel is best, Andy.

(This casual mention of what could be thousands must have unnerved Andy; he wanted that money for himself so badly)

Dr. Klump has finally figured out what nearly killed Momma: that bomb shelter! As you know, she got that shelter dug in the back yard; and ever since Christmas she has been furnishing it and stocking it. Well, it was as complete as possible, and I think she just couldn't stand it just sitting out there empty, going to waste. So she decided to stay underground for a whole week to test it out. She persuaded Gert Kenkel to stay with her. Gert was mad at Fred anyway—he's drinking again. Anyway, Gert made several trips out of the shelter to pick up and deliver their teeth work for the undertakers. On the sixth day, Saturday, February 14, Gert went out to deliver a repaired bridge; and when she returned, she couldn't get the hatch open, even with Momma flinging herself at it from below and Gert hollering encouragement; and "Beware" barking like crazy. (Momma used to have a German Shepherd watchdog and had "Beware the Dog" signs at all the gates. When King died, Momma got this toy poodle; and she named her Beware, so the signs would still be relevant and honest.)

Well, Gert had to get Lem Gussert to break a hole in the damned lid with a sledgehammer. My God, Andy, they were almost too late! Momma was flat on the floor and blue looking, and Lem and Gert thought her dead. But Momma had made all the girls study the first-aid book when she got the shelter installed, and so Gert tried mouth-to-mouth breathing. (The ironic thing for Gert was to discover Momma had broken off two teeth on her uppers exactly like the one they had fixed the night before for a corpse at the Theo. C. Auman, Inc. parlor) Well, Momma started struggling for breath and Lem poured down her throat the last of the Christian Brothers, giving some to Momma and some to himself. Gert got a firehouse ambulance and Dr. Klump met them at the hospital—he thought she had had a stroke. But her blood pressure was not high. She was in shock, and her heart seemed good. Later he realized she couldn't talk because her vocal cords were injured. She had nearly choked to death, but it was no stroke at all!

She had set up tea and cake on the table, and she had even cut the cake, a special birthday cake she had taken out of the freezer for their underground tryout. Whatever stuck in her throat between Gert and Lem and the Christian Brothers moved a little farther down her trachea—not her lungs, thank goodness, but into her stomach. A few days later it got stuck where the stomach empties into the duodenum. X-rays showed some object the size of a coin, only irregularly shaped (but not so large as a teaspoon). We thought it might have been a small salt spoon she uses for sugar, but we found that in the shelter. *[Hmmm. Could it have been a still-missing Ladies' key? Let's say yes.]* Well, that is what Dr. Klump meant by U.F.O: to fliers this means unidentified flying objects, but medically it means unidentified FOREIGN object.

It will be awhile before she is allowed to talk, so her throat can heal; and Dr. Klump will keep her in hospital until the U.F.O. mystery is cleared up and he is sure she is OK.

When I got to see her late Sunday she almost died again. She was not fully conscious and (remember, I was all prettied up planning to meet you, even had false eyelashes on) she thought I had died too and that we were both in heaven (we believe that in the next life, all grown-ups will of be the age Jesus was when he arose.) Of course, it wasn't until the next day we could get her to understand that I was still here on earth with her.

Last Wednesday a specialist from the Chevalier Jackson Clinic came up to use a bronchoscope on her, but after studying Momma and the X-rays he decided to take a chance on nature handling the U.F.O. itself. We just have to watch and wait. I was so glad Momma didn't have to go through that bronchoscope!

We believe Nutrilites and protein powder really gave her the stamina to survive these things—Dr. Klump was so pleased about her this morning when I called. He liked our friend "Pocahontas" and remarked about her crazy shoes. Seems he is having a pair made for himself; and the fact that she has worn then for years really impressed him. I wouldn't be caught dead in them myself! Do you wear them? I hope not.

I just love to write to you; hope you don't mind, Andy. I feel you are a real friend. This horrible storm has made a lot of misery—such a mess—of course we couldn't have any funerals down there unless we wanted to bury them at sea! We could have actually done that right out the front door when the water was up, waves rolling right into the hotels! For now, this gal might just as well relax . . . when Nature's in her rampage it is no time to fret. I'll bet my *[non-existent A.C.]* properties have had a lot of damage. So I'll take it easy today, and tomorrow I will go back to see what must be done there.

Wish you were here now. I'm not making any more plans to see you until we both feel that it is the right time. Maybe I've been foolish to think so much of you. If you don't answer, I'll know you are no longer interested. After all, you're an attractive man and probably have had lots of girlfriends, and I know you lead a busy and interesting life. I don't want to write and call you if you would rather I didn't.

So long for now, Andy-boy. May God bless you and be with you always.

Your friend, Sadie

P. S. Here's Momma's name and address if you want to send her a card.

The letter above illustrates the lengths to which she would go to keep spinning Andy in circles. I believe it was for her sheer entertainment to insinuate that what caused Momma's near death was that she accidentally swallowed the key she had baked into a special cake she'd made for Andy, which happened when she had a mouthful of cake and had to hurl herself against the bomb shelter hatch to try to break herself out. (Remember the overarching theme of the hoax is the missing lady's key.)

In this letter, Sadie leads Andy on even further by describing another one of her supposedly profitable enterprises. She's back to using the setting of the Theodore C. Auman Funeral Home, and her crazy mind is at work again as she describes a garment she invented for female corpses so they look elegant in the casket. Her description of the garments, the setting in which she checks out the latest shipment of her designs she's just received, and what happens next is something I could never describe, so I must leave most of the letter intact. I cannot imagine why she seems to have this fascination with funerals, death and funeral parlors, but they all provide plenty of grist for her mill.

Dear Andy-Boy:

Hope you didn't give up on me—ever since the Great Storm my life has been moving so fast, I've just had to hurry to catch up with myself. Momma has recovered, and I brought her to New York for a few days to shop, etc. She and Gert Kenkel are taking a cruise. It'll do her good—hope she doesn't get into as much trouble on the ship as she did in the bomb shelter. She's taking Beware on the cruise, too; got her a complete outfit at that swanky N. Y. Poodle Shoppe. I'll bet she spent more on that silly dog than she did on my layette!

Since I didn't hear a word from you after we missed each other at the Ritz Carlton, I figured you might have gotten hitched, or at least found yourself a lady friend—so you might forget about your Sadie Girl. The Pill Peddler, as you call her, told me you were not married, and also that you had asked about me . . .

Well, anyway . . . Momma and I both want you to

come to her 91st birthday party (God willing). I'll let you know the time and place later, but it's the first week in September, probably.

Do you remember how I got stuck working with the undertakers after the Great Storm? Well, Ted *[owner of the funeral home]* and I worked shoulder to shoulder, and I came to admire him very much; he has a wonderful wit. And fine vibrations. The first feelings I was aware of were rather strong—and crude, frankly—but underneath, his vibrations were most subtle, like the fur of a northern animal: Pfffffttl I first became attracted to him when he made a speech at the morticians' convention in Miami. He spoke out against the *[funeral directors']* Green Stamps Incentive. In Greenville, North Carolina, it started when one mortician named Dave openly advertised that he'd accept 6,500 Green Stamps for a basic service. And then another establishment advertised 6,000 Green Stamps. And then a third establishment got in on it. You can understand how it got out of hand—like a gas war—hurts business; but in this business it is vulgar, to say the least. Imagine a widow having to consider the value of her Green Stamps at a time like that!

Well, getting back to Ted: we got to respecting each other, then admiration set in; and all of a sudden, sex reared its ugly head. And I thought it was love. Guess I might have married him and been stuck in the funeral business forever—except he was just a little too forward.

Well, to go back a little: as you know, I've been trying to project a little charm and glamour into the gloom this business has to contend with. One of my enterprises I call "Going Away Gowns, Inc." At first, I called it "Sadie Fletcher Shrouds;" but it is silly to include my name, as this sort of thing never will build up trade—you just take them (the corpses) as they come—or go, that is.

I'm proud of this line of gowns. They are sort of a cross between a negligee and the type of dress ladies wear to lawn parties. They should not look out of place in Heaven, but yet they definitely say, "This lady was a lively one on earth!" (When a lady takes this last trip, she's not only crossing to the other world, but also attending a bon voyage party—her funeral.) For these creations I use only very lovely and, of course, expensive fabrics; and, unlike negligees, they tie in the back. There really isn't a back to the garment, as the back doesn't show in the casket, so is unnecessary. And that is what makes my line unique and competitive! Less fabric, but of the best quality.

One morning a couple of weeks ago, this is what happened: We were getting the main parlor set up for a viewing, for a stout lady who was a very big deal in the Eastern Star. We were arranging the floral pieces, fixing the lighting, selecting the music, etc. The dressmaker delivered one of my new designs, a gorgeous pale blue chiffon with ecru lace. Ted asked me to model it for him. "Not yet," I said, kissing him on the nose. "Life is too interesting to get wrapped in a shroud yet."

Ted had some telephoning to do and stepped into his office. I took off my clothes and put on the blue chiffon and laid myself out in the casket (silver, extra wide, with ivory satin lining). Maybe it isn't a funny feeling lying in a casket all by yourself . . . I was there a few minutes, just relaxing and listening to the music—think it was Moonlight Sonata. There was a huge star of pink and white carnations at the head of the casket . . . the fragrance was absolutely intoxicating, and I felt kind of floaty and spiritual. Ted came in, and he was stunned seeing me like that. He stood by the casket just looking at me. Finally, he said to himself, "The neck is a bit too low," (I was still playing dead, so to speak) and he moved to pull the bodice up a little.

"Jesus!", I heard him say. At first, I thought he was moved to prayer, but he kicked off his slippers (he wears bedroom slippers if no funerals are happening—his feet bother him) and jumped in beside—or partly on top of—me. He kissed me roughly! I finally got free to get a gulp of air. However, before he could take out after me again, Mr. Petersen and Harold (head embalmer) came in. The usually suave and dignified Theodore, who could have nonchalantly said he had slipped while fixing the flowers or some such thing, instead sat there *[in the casket with Sadie, apparently]*, red-faced and all mussed up, and howled, "It was that Sadie! She 'got after me!'"

I'm so glad I found him out in time—I'm certainly against being married to a worm like that!

Well, we couldn't work shoulder to shoulder after that—all he had on his mind was the flash he had of the back of my crotch that the shroud didn't cover. So I've left! And good riddance.

I've been thinking about you, Andy. Do you still have the station? Did you get a nightclub business, or what are you doing?

Well, so long for now, and may God bless you. Sadie

P. S. I'll call you. Please write to me; I love hearing from you.

S.F.

THE SITUATION IN MOMMY'S HOME was degrading. For reasons we hadn't quite figured out, she seemed to view her children as former roommates, forgetting the needs of her two youngest, who were really struggling in school and getting wilder. Nancy remembers getting letters from Mommy with checks for $35 included. "Here's some money for groceries." The A & P was more than a mile away! Nancy was barely a teenager! It was hard to fathom how she could have abandoned Nancy and Danny, but we didn't know about her love affair and what it meant to her till later. Linda, who had moved in with a friend and her family, would come home frequently; and she and Nancy would sometimes go to the nearby butcher shop and buy steaks with the checks.

J.G. and I were also gone from our family home. Bob and I, newlyweds, were living in our first apartment. Bob was finishing his college degree at night school and working the day shift at the Inquirer magazine as a copy-checker, but I was a bit lost, having left my job at Penn for a failed opportunity in real estate. We had begun learning how to build an Amway business, but mostly I spent my days hiding under the covers, hoping the whole thing would go away. Not exactly cut from the same cloth as my mother apparently, I was scared to sell and afraid to talk to strangers. Bob was much better and full of enthusiasm. He kept selling cases of products at his new job, junior editor on a trade magazine. Four months in, he came home to announce that he, too, had quit his job.

In a short period of time with some frantically hard work we had a good start on growing a healthy business. We quickly outgrew our little apartment, with products piled everywhere and a veritable warehouse instead of a home. And then our landlord kicked us out due to all the business activity.

It was just about that time, when events converged. My mother, knowing her two teens needed supervision, once again sensed opportunity and asked Bob and me to move back into our family home to keep an eye on them. Timing was convenient; being offered a new place to live just when we needed it. That newly decorated bedroom we had made to lure Mommy back home became ours. It took the pressure off her and us, in different ways.

Our mother had other pressures, still unknown to her family, to handle. After she apparently had just spent an overnight with Gil in NYC, after much consternation about whether to go, she seems open to a plan I think he has proposed to be together, probably not in marriage at this point, but to work together in his decorating business for a start, possibly have her move down to the shore area, and to eventually divorce their spouses and marry later — my guess, since it's only hinted at in this letter. She has already started doing some client work for him. At first she writes a letter in which she seems to be forcing the issue for Gil to make a decision to leave his wife so they are both not continuing in an extra-marital affair. She was still apparently married, the letters were hardly ever dated.

> **Dear Gil,**
>
> **Please try to understand why I couldn't go with you to New York. I know how disappointed and hurt you are. But we just can't go on like this. We have almost gone too far as it is.**

There is so much more to both of our lives than our love or infatuation of whatever it is that draws us together. Our legal mates, our responsibility to our children, our religions, just to mention a few things.

My husband is showing his better side, at long last. So the least I can do is give him a chance. Please forgive the note—my darling, I miss you, and I love you so much. But we will not find happiness on the ruins of other people's lives. Think it over. Your wife is not well, and if she found out about me, you would feel terrible if she got worse.

(But I can only guess from this letter that she did indeed go to New York)

Dearly Aloved:

New word: you are so very "high class" that you deserve more than just a B.

Aren't you glad I came on Tuesday? I am. I feel like myself again. It was terrible thinking you didn't love me. Lucky that my heart's so stubborn, because my head was completely against the trip.

Yesterday I had quite a talk with Otto. Also, we got together on our financial problems—at last. He knows I will not stand for any more crap.

I got home about 1:30 a.m.—took a taxi from 69th Street. The paper bag broke just when I got into the house. Anne and Bob were in the living room, so we all had some of the peaches—so good! I took a hot bath (my knee was really stiff

from the spill I took running for the bus)—Holy Cow! I must be out of my mind! I sincerely hope you do not affect many ladies like this.

Your "Gal"

Gil to Mommy, a rare letter, because all his letters but this one were hidden in Mommy's trunk of her car and at some point, discovered and seized by Otto. No date or location given, but a reference to the lovers' tryst in New York

Hiyah, pal, How is the circumlubrilator rejuvenating while the moon beameth so beautifully over the horizon this fine boralizing night? Just can't help talking like this, being alone and missing you something awful while driving around talking to myself with nowhere to go.

I am just wondering what you are doing with yourself while we are not together. We will just have to do something about this long-distance separation. What can you suggest? Nutrilite—or the making of us being together or somewhat attached, with no separation point?

The part of the third honeymoon outing was enjoyed to no end, except for the parting. You must have really had a ball in New York, even without me [after they parted], **being confused in the large city, and thinking of the wonderful time we had together.**

You are just wonderful. I cannot really explain why you are so nice; and how you follow with me in such a smiling wonderful and pleasant fashion. I am also sure you must be doing a lot of thinking as to what to do soon, and how to do it, and maybe the

possibility of working together in Penn Towers Apts. around Sept 1st, if I take the deal— what do you really think about this deal, and would you like it?

It is so funny in the way that you have changed your way of living, and the wonderful trance that I must have you in, and our loving mood being enjoyed as one person, etc.; but you manage to keep going along anyway, one way or another.

Who knows when you will solve your domestic situation, and if you really want to do this or not, and whether you really want us together, as we feel. I do not know your answer, since you really must decide.

You are a terrific inspiration to me, and after leaving you (which is awful) I seem to get lucky in my business affairs and do pretty well the next day— which happened again today. I also hope I am lucky for you too.

You are just a grand wonderful person, and I think the world of you, for which you must know and feel by now, and trust you feel the same fantastic way. We are certainly good for each other, and keep our spirits really moving.

Excuse the writing, but I am trying to write you as promised in my Olds with no tablet, board, or desk. But am finally in private under the beautiful moon and carrying on this fine chore, which is much overdue. Incidentally, the fog was terrible all the way down to Atlantic City, after leaving you [in New York?], but it was worth it just to be together.

So long for now. You know something, I love you.
With all my fondness,
Love, etc.
Butch
Keep fighting and keep thinking—it helps.

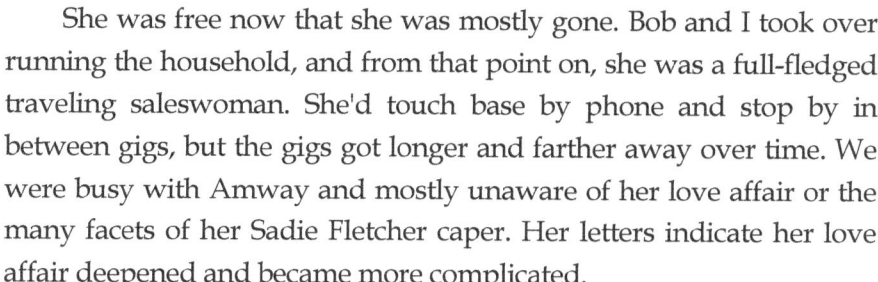

She was free now that she was mostly gone. Bob and I took over running the household, and from that point on, she was a full-fledged traveling saleswoman. She'd touch base by phone and stop by in between gigs, but the gigs got longer and farther away over time. We were busy with Amway and mostly unaware of her love affair or the many facets of her Sadie Fletcher caper. Her letters indicate her love affair deepened and became more complicated.

An undated and unsent letter to her lover's wife Elaine, never intended to be sent to her but as a spoof to Gil:

Dear Elaine:

It's funny, there's so little I know about you, and I think about you so much. You may not realize it, but the kind of person you are and what you do will affect my life and, I believe, what I am and what I do will certainly affect you.

You see, I am having an affair with your husband. Except for our first meeting, which was quite proper, we have met only because we both very much wanted to see each other just to see and speak to each other, if only for a few moments—which took a lot of planning and finagling for both of us.

My life before Gil was, as far as men and marriage, an open book—no secrets—no temptations, really. I've had too many other interests, and I've always been strictly virtuous. I'm not bragging; it was never difficult for me to be so.

You may wonder what he sees in me. I'm not sexy, or brilliant, or gorgeous or an expert on men. It's just that I love him—with my whole heart. He is an unusual and splendid human being; and if only I have him in small stretches of time and in shadowy places, the warmth and love we share is sweet and livelier than most people ever know in all of their lives.

For me, he is the only guy in the whole world. When we are together, I know what it means for two people to become as one. It came into being because no such beauty and love existed in either your marriage or mine. I was lonely and so in need of love and appreciation, and so was Gil. We never said this to each other, but I know it's true.

I was ready for divorce many times. I started proceedings again but stopped until January at my husband's request.

Of course, I don't know how you feel. I remember how I felt when my first husband asked me for a divorce (our third child was only three months old). My whole world was shattered. My bitterness at this woman for depriving my children of their father made me quite capable of murder. The miserable unhappiness the children and I lived through at that time I would never wish on anyone. But I found myself, and I became a stronger person because of it.

So, the world goes on—you have Gil, but he loves me. Otto has me, but I love Gil. I'm sorry for you and

Otto, but this is nothing to the happiness it gives me
to love Gil and to be loved in return by him.

You are his wife—if that is what you want.

*Here is the first instance I knew my mother was a poet. A love poem from
Dorothy to Gil, no date:*

When you left at dawn without me, I was sad . . .
But here are some things I really want to know:
Do you live part of the time
On a rainbow?
Now . . . As you cast from water's edge toward the
sea,
Are all your wishes fishes,
 Or are some of them for me?
Do you feel the passion of the deep rolling waves
That end in foam-rimmed kisses in the sand,
And is there a suddenly aching loneliness
That is local to your hand?
As you squint at the grey-white flock of gulls against
the blue,
Do you absolutely know that they are flying two by
two?
Don't you know the whole world is waiting?
I do.
And tonight I'm glad I will be waiting, waiting for
you.

WITH NO DATES AS REFERENCE, I cannot be sure of the span of time in the relationship. But the love affair seems to have been negatively colored possibly by a bad turn of events in Shelly's affair with Richie, or possibly because Gil was becoming sick with kidney disease and having severe business losses, resulting in a worsening turn of events on both fronts. I can only read between the lines. This little missive to him expresses the pure joy she feels in having him in her life:

Dear G.,

When I was a little girl, I remember on one marvelous Saturday playing in the woods climbing rocks and trees and going to a friend's house to see newborn kittens and running all the way home—just because I felt like running. No one was home, and I had a bowl of bread and milk. It was so good, I thanked God from my heart for the miracle of green grass, brown cows, and waving fields of grain.

That's what it is like to love you: wholesome and good and nourishing and necessary. Of course, it's much, much more than that. It's sometimes—

like last night—flying and floating and rockets and sunsets and deep rolling waves and the sea and sand and flowers and roller coasters . . . and falling like a leaf back to earth. One flesh. And then we become our separate unique selves again. But mostly you are bread and milk, and I love you. I just love you! D.

Her concerns about their relationship continue to grow, even as she contemplates spending a week at her favorite place in the world, Avalon, that Gil has offered to pay for, to do something nice for her and her children, and so they could see more of each other.

Dorothy to Gil "Dear Sir:

Having been 82 (eighty-two) full hours since your last communication to me, a few casually disturbing thoughts are beginning to form nasty little bubbles in the pink and grey matter of my brain . . . such as:

- He really loves Shelly—not me? (She stopped last night to help me escape, but I didn't go. Otto is still on good behavior, so I've no excuse for leaving.
- But Shelly went to A. C. today and DIDN'T EVEN CRY when I told her I couldn't go along—highly suspicious.
- Has Lilyass Lillian Reis got him at last? [She was the famous hostess and dancer at the 500 Club] If so, I'm lost. She is far more glamorous and fascinating than me, besides being rich $$$.
- Elaine has locked him in the apartment and disconnected the phone.
- He's busy—this I can understand, but not very much.
- He has called and called, with no answer. I must THINK POSITIVE!

Golly, it isn't easy when your love is a traveling man in A. C. with temptation and worse on every side, including LILLIAN REIS doing the twist on the bar in a sexy Roaring Twenties outfit. Why couldn't you have been a clam digger or a chicken farmer? Well, I guess I wouldn't have gone for you then, anyway. Stay the way you are; but be careful— desperate women are a menace.

Really, my love, I hope you are entirely healthy in all departments. Still miss you a little.

Mrs. Fech"

No date, but my mother is now in Avalon her with her three younger kids, when she and Gil plotted to spend as much time together as possible with each other. Shelly seems to have spent the week nearby at the shore, too. Gil may have rented this cottage from a friend so that there was a telephone available—since there was not one in our home, because of Otto continually ripping it out of the wall. To be able to talk to each other on the phone was a rarity. When they arranged to meet, it was usually arranged by telegram or through Shelly receiving a call for Mommy to get in touch, which she usually did at the phone booth of the A & P supermarket.

No date, except Tuesday 1 p.m.
"My Beloved:

Was I ever happy to get your wonderful letter. I absolutely knew you had written to me but didn't know if you would send it to Shelly's or Richie's [shore] address. By yesterday, after not hearing from you, I was feeling low—and thinking of the most depressing possibilities.

I read an article on a very interesting type of

paranoid insanity that usually affects people in their forties; females . . . They imagine someone—a doctor, an old friend, a celebrity—is madly in love with them. They build this up sky-high; the slightest thing becomes significant. In one case a patient developed this crush on her doctor. The doctor realized she was nuts and put her in the loony bin where she was happy as a clam, certain he had put her there in order to have her all to himself forever.

The ladies (those pre-menopausal, forties-types) are always sure the object of their affection is determined at some future time to properly marry them, while the males so afflicted are sure their love object desires only to be their Number One mistress!

How do you like that? I figure we have a double case of this ailment; and I hope we can get locked up together! Oh, how lovely to be slightly paranoid with love manifestations. Hot dog! Rutty and nutty! (Excuse, please; for I couldn't resist.)

Really, darling, I have no business writing any more, but THAT COMPULSION has me! So you see, in this particular loony disease you are allowed to make up reasons for everything—for writing now, when in less than two hours I will be talking to you on the phone.

Darling, I love you with all my heart and mind. Please love me, too—Dot XXXX"

I don't really know how the week went, but less than perfectly, for sure. They overcame obstacles, apparently, to have several "dune dates" late at night after the children were asleep (she loved sunbathing nude in the sand dunes, swimming naked in the sea early in the morning, and probably thought the dunes were a perfect love nest — hard to imagine.

The "Avalon letters" from that week seemed to indicate that things were changing. Maybe Gil was already sick; there were also references to his business going bad with a possible partner or large client who gambled away a large sum of money owed to Gil.

I also believe Shelly, at a low point that week, had just been dumped by Richie and was feeling bitter about being forced to face her marital situation. Here is part of another letter from Mommy to Gil:

> **. . . It's not these Avalon waves that cause me to think of severing my home ties and depart for the tide lands. It's you. . . . It's so incredible that a complete stranger should have become, so swiftly, a major necessity in my life. . . .**
>
> **Even though my love affair with you has been frustrating lately, my old love affair with Avalon has been marvelous. . . .**
>
> **I'm really disturbed about why you think I will go home and patch things up with Ott, and that underneath I still love him. Either that is what you hope is true so you can easily break off with me to avoid a possible scandal and mess, or— because my reference to his good behavior and my delay of definite action make you wonder if I really want him. Or maybe seeing more of me with my family has made you feel it is all too much [*to tear apart*]. These are dark stones in my heart— and perhaps yours, too.**

And so, Gil, I stick my neck way out; and this, though I love you, has nothing to do with you—I felt this long before I knew you: I do not love Otto. I married him for the sake of my kids. After I wanted to call off the wedding because of my doubts, friends, relatives, our minister, all thought the match was right. I had understandable nervousness because of how my first marriage ended. I have only said the words "I love you" three times to him—only once since we've been married—and I would have given a lot if I could have been able to say it and mean it. For that is the reason he is so unhappy. He needs love so much, and yet he is so nasty he'll never get it. I feel so sorry for him and responsible, but truly it would be a great relief if I could never see or hear him again. And I've felt that way for years. The kids do not miss him either; his absence is always a cause for rejoicing . . . Sleeping with him is a kind of prostitution.

I know this, Gil: I can't go on cheating or living this way. I have been so close to telling him that I love someone else and to stop trying to win me back—and this could be dangerous.

My darling, if you have or do decide it is best for you to go no further, let me know directly and with NO EASY TAPERING OFF. I am much better equipped for that than a long period of longing and uncertainty. I am so afraid Otto will smother me for good. I'm near enough to getting free of him—if I don't weaken. And if you string me along, he will overcome me. If it is over, I have no regrets—for it has been one of the nicest bonuses life has handed me—so, so beautiful.

Well, Gil, this is what I've been thinking when I couldn't sleep. If Shelly read this (she can't; I'm way down the beach sitting on an old sandcastle), she would say I have no pride. But I do—in loving you . . .

Dorothy to Gil. Tuesday, August 20, after Avalon week

Dear Gil:

We got home *[from the week in Avalon]* **about ten p.m. Sunday.** Your remark about my complete change of personality was deserved. I was not myself. Shelly gave me a very bad time. I was shocked at her reaction. There is much more to this than I knew, and I doubt you did, either. Ever since we've been home, I've stayed right with her—sat in her car until 3 a.m. this morning. At last I have her over this bitterness.

Just before you called, she had talked at length to Richie and then (bitterly) said this to me:

"You'll see . . . Gil will phone, and he'll be cool and too busy to see you for the next few weeks. They (you and Richie) are probably together right now, after planning the best way to handle unloading us. It's all over, Dottie. It's fine when it's convenient and fun—but the game is over. So what? I have several (other men) choices. One thing: WE must not see THEM again—because it won't be fun anymore."

Then you called, and I felt sick and empty—awful. She said I had no business letting myself fall in love with you—that I should just have fun but don't believe anything. On and on; the whole week was like this.

The poor kids, instead of having a mother [at the shore] that was loving and fun, I was just trying to get rid of them. I consciously tried to do things alone with each kid, but I had trouble getting away from Shelly.

I never knew Shelly to be like this before. She had some real crazy things she wanted to do. I spent most of my time thwarting her plans, for her own good, but she was unpleasant.

Gil, I love Shelly as my sister, and these things I say are not in judgment. She loves Max [husband] deeply—more than she does Richie—but for years Max has been unable to show her any warmth and affections or fun. He is only cold and critical, and now doesn't speak. He is unable to express affection except to their young children. I want her to make a real effort to help Max, but all she wants to do is run away.

Holy cow! You planned such a beautiful time for ME and the children and really knocked yourself out. I love you. I'm sorry things have turned sour, but it's not the end of the world. I will not allow myself to believe you no longer love me until I see you— no matter what.

Still love you, Dottie"

BY NOVEMBER OF 1966, IT seemed, from what I could determine as I read her letters, Gil had been spirited out of her life by a very negative turn of events, after which he apparently had some difficult losses in his business, and an illness related to failing kidneys. These events, I estimate, had gone on for most of a year. Through the last several months of that year, her letters indicate she was aware that he was quite ill, but his communications to her were completely cut off. He died, separated from her till the end of his life, around February of 1967.

Nov. 11, 1967, handwritten note, written, probably right before he died

Oh, Gil, it's so wonderful to love you—and so terrible. After we talked on the phone in September, I never felt so low in my life. I went to the *[wedding of her co-worker and friend Ceil's daughter]* **reception at the Brigantine—couldn't stand all the gaiety, etc., so I took a walk on the beach. I walked down to where I could look across to Captain Starn's and prayed and prayed and felt so desperate. I thought I would never see you again. You'd sounded so hopeless and heartbroken to me:**

" . . . No spirit at all . . . 'They' have me a prisoner . . .'They' want to move to Philadelphia . . . my business is all washed up . . . this is the way life is . . . I'll 'try' to write . . . I can't even write checks . . .'They' have 'lost' my glasses . . . I'll let you know when I go up to see the doctor; you can meet me . . . She *[his wife who is now apparently keeping him sequestered in their A. C. apartment]* doesn't give me the mail . . . It will take time . . . I only eat fruit and vegetables . . . doctor says it will be a long time until I'll be allowed to drive. "

I sense a conspiracy against you, and it feels like you are in a prison somehow. Darling, if only you had had more children like I do. Ott could never overcome me because the children wouldn't let him. When I had the stroke *[in 1963, I believe]* and you came to the hospital right under his nose, it was the best thing that could have happened for me.

Sunday after the Brigantine wedding (how about that Brigantine Hotel? It's really nice—nobody ever had so much happiness in that motley hotel as we did, including Father Divine. I can't wait to commit adultery with you again. Ye Gods, remember when you served me the Chinese dinner and I wouldn't even let you kiss me? I regret I was such a goody.) . . .

. . . Anyway, Sunday after the wedding I then went to the Mayfair House *[the apartment where Gil lived with his wife and son]* and stayed at the bar awhile, and then I went up and stood outside your door—

hoping to hear your dear voice. For fifteen minutes I waited, hearing Elaine [Gil's wife] speak low. I tried to project my love to you through the door, but it seemed futile.

My friend I was staying with thought I had gone out of my mind for doing that. Then I stopped at your shop. God! I cried all the way home; what you must have gone through [possibly a bankruptcy of the business].

I know that you know how much I love you. But I also know the first thing in your life is your business. Instead of praying that you love me, I pray that you regain your health and your business; then you'll be able to love me. I can wait; you are more than worth some waiting for.

My health is fine, but all summer and into the fall I was terribly depressed. I couldn't shake the awful feeling that I would never see you again. July was the worst. I couldn't even work—too upset—thought I was going to have a nervous breakdown. I took off a week from work; couldn't think.

Well, I had a horrible dream about you: I could see you, but you couldn't see or hear me. And there were small people brutally beating you, about three or four little figures. You were so much bigger, you could have easily shaken them off; but you just seemed to give up. They were killing you. But they were like creatures from Mars and maybe didn't know what they were doing. I was frantic. And you couldn't hear me. Linda heard me moaning and crying in my sleep. I stayed in bed all day, with these shaking spells. I had Linda call my two appointments and cancel. By evening I felt better and later went to Letty's *[Hedgerow Theater friend and customer celebrating her 75th birthday]* party. It was so nice, and she was so happy. When I kissed her Happy Birthday, she whispered, "Did you hear from Gil yet?" When I said no, she said, "Tuesday is Valentine's Day—don't give up."

On the way home I cut over West Avenue past the cemetery. I had had three glasses of wine and was feeling a little high. Oh, Gil, you would have loved that party, so many interesting people—actors and writers, artists, sculptors—all kinds of talented nuts . . .

Well, anyway, I was driving very slowly because it was about midnight and I felt really spooky. As I drifted past the cemetery where your father and grandmother are buried, I noticed the gates were open. Do they always leave Jewish cemetery gates open at night? I was so amazed I backed the car up. I sat there and had the damnedest desire to drive through that place. I think I would have done it, but a police car came along, and I felt so silly... "Intoxicated woman locked up for reckless driving in cemetery..." Some headline that would make. I went home worried about whether I was getting mentally unbalanced.

On Tuesday I went to the doctor, still depressed. I was sort of worried I had had a slight stroke or heart attack after my nightmare. He said I'm fine,

but probably starting the change. Told me to stay in bed for a few days; I did, read and slept the whole damned week away.

No Valentine—or phone call—or telegram-- arrived. What the hell, honey? If you want to keep me in the mood to spend our glorious old age together you shouldn't forget Valentine's Day. I hope you like yours—I'm sending your favorite poems I wrote to you . . .

February 14, 1967: I believe Gil had already died, but she may not have known for sure yet, because he was shut off from everything in his apartment. The letter she wrote to his sister Eleanor, dated February 15, 1967, finally revealed many of the details of the love affair, his illness and death. But there are some time-line aspects I have not been able to sort out. Below is her Valentine gift to him, the poem.

Beloved,
When we are very close and know one another in
the live warm joy of contact
It alarms my heart
To be so exquisitely sensitive and aware
Of your touch
The feel of your crisp hair
The strong curve of your neck
Oh, my love, you are so much
A man
And yet . . . there, where my finger
Traces rings,
I know
Will grow your angel wings
My palms become my lips
And caress along your spine

To find
The secret hollow of your hips
Oh. I love the way you feel and smell and taste
Your gentle tenderness as you have your
Way with me.
Your patience, And then at last
Your fiery haste
As from your heart flames
Names of love
Your lips impart on mine
And in my ear
And on my breast.
Surely, beyond our mortal
Deserving we are blest
For in this trance comes the
Magnificent throb of beauty
When our very souls entwine
And dance
As we discover
In Love's one splendid hour
The square root of happiness
Raised to the millionth power.

(Gil, it's funny, I'm not good at math, but I'm glad
I remembered that square root part. It's a perfect
ending for my poem to you.

While my mother did not have the use of Google searches at this time, she sure did have the World Book and made ample use of it for references she needed to elucidate her epistles.

In this handwritten letter Mommy still may not have known for sure he is dead. She went to all their places where they would normally meet between the DeVille Diner in New Jersey to a furniture store in Wilmington. Not finding him at any of the places, in desperation she stops along a major highway outside of Wilmington for a "reading" at a fortune teller. I include this sad letter because it is also hilarious and reveals her constant ability to find humor in the most difficult situations. The letter begins with another poem.

My Dearest Love,

I can no longer bear to be
Beyond your warmth
Beyond your touch
Beyond the sound, the sweet sound, of your beloved voice.
For it has happened
Even in the full exciting stream of life I stop, I catch my breath, I know
My heart is homesick
And I must go
To you again.
For you are more to me
Than family
Or friend
Or money
Or even home
You are the urgent need of my flesh and heart
Our love is the circle we can never depart
However far we go.

Today I went to the De Ville Diner, as I wrote you I would. I checked with the cashier; no message, no you. I could not stand to sit inside, not wanting to get in conversation with anyone. Besides the times we've met there, I used to meet each morning with Tim and Ray and Ceil when we worked that area. So I got in my car. I checked the entire parking lot for your "Beautiful Blue." Not there. Then I parked and waited three quarters of an hour. In all that rain, no one could even tell I was crying.

I called Atlantic City person-to-person, and the operator said, "Gilbert Kline cannot be reached at GR 3-8679." I didn't call *[his home]* then; no use upsetting Elaine. In September you said "they" wanted to move to Philadelphia so you would be nearer to the hospital. Oh, Darling, I hope you haven't had a setback.

Well, I was too upset to work. I thought if you were well, you might be working in Kyle's *[retail furniture store]*; so I drove to Wilmington. I didn't see your car and didn't even go in the store to inquire. I was too afraid of what they might tell me, and I didn't think you would want me to ask them about you.

I decided on a crazy impulse to drive back by way of 202 and stop at the Reader and Advisor, Madam Maria. The place seemed so very familiar—and well it should: I found out after I entered it was our original sample home when I was working selling Caddie Homes . . . This doll had even bought the furniture from the model, too. You should see how she embellished it: on the wall where the big picture window is, there was one long sectional couch covered in Kelly green stretch slipcovers, separated by a large drum, like DuPont uses to ship dry chemicals in. This was covered with a handwoven Indian blanket with green and yellow and orange stripes. On this piece of magnificence was a huge lamp like South Philadelphia mooches *[salespersons' code word for sucker who will buy anything]* put in their picture windows when they move to South Jersey. This one was a real doozie: cream-colored silk shade with three inches of fringe. The base was a glorious ceramic camel. On the opposite wall were one Lawson sofa in moss green brocade, marble tables with ornate brass legs, more outlandish lamps. The side wall was a brick fireplace with a raised hearth and the mantle running the entire length of the wall, twelve feet long. On the mantle was a collection of "gifts from grateful clients:" mostly ceramic cats, dogs, kangaroos, bears, etc. Even two whiskey poodles, those crocheted bottle cover things right out of "Sadie Fletcherland." On the wall were two Atlantic City-boardwalk-type pastel portraits of a male and female Indian. Stuck in the frame of one was a pencil drawing on plain paper of a Cadillac ('67). I would not have been surprised if there had been a dozen assorted colored balloons on the fireplace and a chance to throw darts to win one of the gifts on the mantle while waiting for Madame Marie. Fake maroon and gold Oriental rugs and about $100 bucks' worth of plastic flower arrangements: one orange tree and one apple tree with ten life-sized plastic apples on it. Along the wall by the foyer there was a walnut carved coffin, open at one end for the glorious color T.V., featuring at the time a cowboy drama.

Next to that was a black leather modern lounge chair.

Madame Maria had taken and put away my coat and said I would have to wait a bit, as she had a client (sucker) in the "reading room." I sat on the green brocade sofa and felt like a guy who . . . on an impulsive action winds up in a "house of joy," with the action about to begin when he realizes he has lost the appetite for the quick fix; and he wants to simply walk out. Well, there I was; and the spook had my coat with her in the damned inner sanctum. Eight minutes before I had been free as a bird, but not now.

Then this boy comes in from the kitchen or bathroom or someplace and sits himself down on the Kelly-green sofa next to the camel lamp. His bones measure about 5'10", but there are about 250 pounds of flesh hanging on those bones. He is plainly bored, . . . seeming to have had enough of cowboy movies for the moment. To my further distaste, I know he's figuring out what sum "Madame" will be able to get out of me, added to the take from Sucker #1. Well, $3.00 is my limit, son.

I figure Mme. Marie could be his mother or older sister—she's about 38 or 40 years old. It turns out not to be true. I figure he could be 15 to 18 years old. He looked like a stupid Mario Lanza. My sense that this was a bad decision was growing. I only ducked in to get out of facing my growing fears for you. To spend 20 more minutes waiting while at the mercy of my thoughts in the obscene vibrations of this trashy place could finish me off. It was time to distract myself by trying to find something good in this lump of a human being.

"Who in this house is the ARTIST?"

"The pichurs?" He said, "she had some guy do them."

"No, I mean the line drawing of the Cadillac."

"Yeah – I do that – you like that?"

"Well, I'm a counselor of students for "Famous Artists. I'd like to see some more of your work."

"Yeah – I do this stuff – I like to draw cars."

He gets up and walks lightly to the dining room and opens and shuts drawers; he comes back with four or five drawings of Caddies. As he walks, I see he does indeed have muscles, and I see he is both proud and embarrassed about his drawings. I asked what year he is at in school. He says he is a drop-out – didn't finish. I think maybe he's 18 or 19 now. So I tell him Abe Lincoln was a dropout, and so was Norman Rockwell (I find myself moving into my pitch.) "Lots of guys were. You have talent, and that's nice; but it's much better to develop it."

He's all attention now. I asked if his mother knows he has the talent. "She's dead."

"Is Mme. Marie your sister?"

"No, she is my wife."

Well, he tells me she thinks he's good at drawing too; but she wishes he could draw people and not just Caddies all the time.

So now I'm really launching into my pitch, and I get my sales case from the car. I give him the "Dr. Max test:" three pages of multiple-choice picture selections (a trained clam could pass this entry test) that show sense of picture composition, design, etc. While he is absorbed in the first part, I pace back and forth to get a closer look at a mysterious item sitting on the floor that looked like a black Jack-in-the-Box. On the second pace, I see that the item is actually an accordion. The house is a mirror image of the one I worked in. On the kitchen table I see what looks like the skinny end of a guitar. Behind the house is a red Volkswagen in a large parking lot, rather than a yard.

He finishes the first part of the test. I sit beside him now to mark his test and evaluate him... His wife, Mme. Marie, comes out of the back room. It is the smallest bedroom of the model, and we had used it for our second office. There is now no sign of the previous client, and I hear the VW start up and drive off. I figure there must be a door, a secret exit, from the large closet out to the back hall and the parking lot.

Oh yes—I also found out what the boy does for a living: he does blacktop on driveways. That explains why there's 4 acres of parking space around this cozy cottage.

Mme. washed her hands with Dove soap and came and sat next to her young husband. "What's this all about?"

"Oh, nuthin. I was just showing her my cars." She sighed and looked disgusted.

With that I realized I could not sell him on himself and his talent; I couldn't sell her on him and his talent, and I suddenly didn't want to hear any of my future from such a spooky and negative character. I got up and wordlessly went into the inner sanctum, retrieved my coat, and ducked out through that secret exit, breathing in the fresh air.

So, my future—and yours—remains untold. I wish I could talk with you. I went home with a heavy heart, full of fears still.

Please let me hear from you, my darling . . .

Days and Nights of constant weeping rain,
Have dissolved and washed away
The crust that our time apart
Has formed around my broken heart,
And now the pain begins anew
The awful pain of needing you.
Don't wait too long, my love, to hold
Me so that we touch at every point,
My naked heart can't heal until
You once again annoint
Me with your love.
Don't wait too long.

THE ENDING OF HER LONG and sad letter to Gil's sister reveals her decision to divorce our father and stepfather. And then Otto found Gil's letters in her car trunk and she lost "the aces in her divorce deck of cards" after all the years of his verbal and sometimes physical abuse because he had the letters to prove her love affair he had suspected her of.

> . . . Now Elaine was going to sue me for stealing Gil's love.

> Otto had gotten his parents so well brainwashed about me (long before I knew Gil), but they found out the truth after I made him leave. He lived with them for two years, and his father said to me, 'if my son paid me a million dollars, I would not let him live with us again.'

> Otto hired a private detective who saw how much I worked, because I was working six days a week to pay for the divorce. Gil was also sure Elaine had him watched.

> The last meeting I had with Gil was in July of 1965. He called at the office and said Elaine would be away and to meet him on Saturday in Sea Isle City.

I had a full day of work planned and after picking up my people in South Philadelphia at 9 a.m., we worked all day in the hot sun.

I drove down and met Gil at 4:30 in Sea Isle, and we had dinner there. He was jittery and nervous. I was a little tired too. It was the only time we were ever together that he wasn't happy and relaxed. Normally, to be alone was so very precious. But that time he said Elaine phoned constantly whenever she left the apartment; that he was breaking up with his partner; and he'd lost his Ocean City business that he liked so much. A close friend Gil had some financial dealing with had committed suicide by jumping out the window at the Mayfair *[where Gil and Elaine lived]*. This had shaken him up badly. Kyle's Furniture store in Wilmington wanted him at $500 a week, but he didn't want to work for somebody else. I think he hoped for some good deal to turn up. He seemed so desperate. He said 'they,' meaning Elaine and [former boyhood best friend who turned on him and colluded with Elaine] Stanley 'had him by the balls.'

He did not stay all night *[at Mr. Kane's love nest, I guess]* as he so much wanted to—he was too afraid she was having Richie's apartment checked. The next morning he came back to the apartment. He looked tired and said someone had stopped in, so it was good he'd been home; also, Elaine had called twice. He asked me to drive him to Philadelphia so we could stay together longer. I remember it was terribly hot. I often drove back with him to the shore from Philadelphia and then took a bus back home late at night. I was so delighted to think of having his company, but I said he was foolish, that he needed his rest rather than a hot ride up to Philly only to turn around and ride back on a bus. It seemed like she really had him buffaloed. I was afraid he might crack up.

I urged him to take Kyle's deal and move up to Wilmington instead of trying to be in so many places at once. I could work in Wilmington, and if we could at least be together now and then, it would be better than four times a year. He said I couldn't count on him for anything until he got out of the woods.

. . . He did drive up with me. When I left him off at Broad and Market, I was so frustrated. I had said, 'I love you—your body and mind mean as much to me as my own, and these things are killing you. There must be some way you can gather your forces.'

Well, from then on, I was miserable. I had to drag myself to work. I was so unhappy inside. You can't sell when you feel so rotten . . .

I was working in Wilmington at this point. I stopped at Kyle's store *[where Gil had apparently decided he needed to work to bring in some cash and possibly get some distance from Elaine]*, but I had missed him. I left word for him to contact me; I had a lady who wanted drapes (which I did). I was purposely working my own sales in the new developments so I could also catch some business for him. There was no way he could call me in those days. But no letters either. Nothing.

I wrote possibly three times; once when I couldn't work because of a blizzard. My daughter Anne was so worried about the way I was driving myself and how depressed I was.

My goal was to get out of debt in fourteen months, God willing; and I would be in the clear. I had had to borrow money when I had the stroke and was unable to work for six months. My home is paid for and is mine, but I have $250 per month in loans and all the monthly expenses. Gil knew I wanted to be square; we had talked about selling my house for working capital, or else living in it . . .

I saw him once more. But I was very careful to make sure he did not see me, at the burial of your grandmother Anna Cohen in Mt. Sharon cemetery. I knew in my heart I would never see him again. Since I had heard nothing and had tried to contact him at Kyle's, his place on Main Street in Pleasantville, and through Richie, I had to realize it was possible he did not want me. Perhaps Elaine had changed; maybe his health was better, and I would hear from him when he was satisfied with his financial position again.

During June and July of 1966 I was terribly depressed—especially in July as I was helping Anne prepare for her wedding on August 13, 1966. I felt like the world was coming to an end

Shelly took me to New York to visit her folks . . . I wasn't good company. I resented Shelly terribly.

She always wanted me to date friends. I couldn't have cared less. Next, she invited a professor friend of Richie to a steak dinner our company had. I had Anne and Bob come so I could go home with them to avoid getting stuck with him. Shelly thought Gil had found someone else or was more interested in keeping the 'status quo.' In other words, I was a damned fool not to wise up.

When we got home from visiting her family, I threw myself into Anne and Bob's wedding—and it was really so very nice. I sent Gil a formal invitation to his Pleasantville address with a very loving note. Elaine probably got it.

After the wedding, I was again dreadfully depressed. Then I tried unsuccessfully to reach Gil at the end of August. I called the Atlantic City Hospital and found a Mr. Kline WAS there, but that Mr. Kline had died in November. Later, my friend Paul had quite a talk with me. He said I should call, and the hell with Elaine. So I did, and I reached him. Gil sounded terrible, said his kidneys were failing. I used a fake name, of course, but Elaine listened; and she knew it was me.

I went to Atlantic City in September and called Gil from there on Saturday afternoon, knowing Elaine goes grocery shopping then; so we were able to talk. Skipping over his kidney failure, he wanted to know all about the wedding, each of the kids, my job, etc. I asked him if he was in a wheelchair. No, he said, but he couldn't understand what was happening to him; complete collapse. Elaine had made life unbearable for him because I had called. Well, I understand that. When I was still paralyzed in the hospital, Otto would say over and over, 'This is what you get for f-ing with that Jew,' and everyone on the floor could hear his ranting.

I wanted to visit him; he said, 'no way, they might be back at any minute,' I asked him if he were going to die. No, but it will take time [to recover], he answered.

'Please don't give up, Gil, I will pray for you.'

He didn't answer at first then he said, 'I have loved you so much, it was so beautiful.'

I said, 'Please don't way 'was,' you have always told me to keep fighting.'

'I'll get word to you somehow. I have to go up to the doctor's; we can meet then.'

During that phone call I was right there in Atlantic City. After I talked with Gil I left and walked the beach and prayed with all my heart.

After that period, I started to read the obituaries every night. My horrible fear was that someone who had condemned him would deliver the news he was dead—someone like Otto or Richie or Shelly.

Up until December I worked South Philly—terrible hours; I often fell asleep with my clothes on. Working hard I could make $100-$300 a week. I wanted to pay off debts.

I was in Lankenau Hospital twice the week before Christmas to see Shelly when she had a hysterectomy. I wanted to ask if Gilbert Kline was a patient there. 'I've got to get a grip on myself,' as I walked around and looked at the portraits of the former doctors, but I couldn't shake this feeling . . . All the way home I made myself listen to Jack McKinney on the radio to distract myself.

I threw myself into my job, happier in my work than I've been in years. I began to set another deadline for Gil: February 14, Valentine's Day. I knew if he was alive, I would hear from him then. I'd stay home and not use the phone.

On Monday *[Feb. 13]* I had appointments—no good. Tuesday was my deadline. On Tuesday waited for the telephone and mail, Gilbert's last chance unless he was dead. So, feeling like a Shakespearean character, I decided I had better check the obits.

Just as I read 'Gilbert S. Kline, . . . ' the phone rang. It was a Nutrilite customer at the Presidential Apartments. I took the order and dialed Mr. Wilson to order what I needed to fill it. I decided to drink my coffee before reading that rotten obit. Then I finally read it all. It made me furious, the phony stuff about him. One of the most beautiful, splendid human beings God ever made to end up as such a nothing. My impulse was to hurry to the funeral home so I could see him before Elaine got there—then I knew Gil wouldn't want me to see him all pale and cold.

E. ANNE POUNDS

I don't remember much that I did that day. I went to the store, made dinner, had two appointments, sold one . . . I was so mad at myself for not calling or writing to you long ago, Eleanor. You could have helped if I had made myself known to you.

The last year and a half was horrible, but what we had together was the most beautiful thing one could dream of."

And I never knew of her pain—or her joy—kept to herself until I read the letters.

MY MOTHER CALLED HERSELF A pill pusher in her Nutrilite business—but her doctor was a genuine pill pusher, starting with the diet pills in the 1960s and progressing to the leading edge of the opioid epidemic and moving out oxycodone on a large-scale basis in a cash business. But long before that, he cashed in on the hormone therapy trend when it was all the rage. He may have contributed to my mother's early death, but we will never know.

With Mommy's passionate allegiance to all things "natural," selecting an osteopath as her family doctor around 1962 seemed another natural choice for her--at 46 years old. Gil was possibly about 40, I estimate. She was just on the edge of "the change" and head over heels in love; she wanted to keep all her juices flowing. The new help for women came in the form of hormone replacement therapy (HRT) As I reconstruct it with no records except my memory and the found letter below, she received hormone injections for at least eight years, maybe more, probably beginning around 1962.

"Well, Doc Wert has put me on horse piss," my mother declared with a big guffaw one night. "Soon I'll be full of piss *and* vinegar!" And she gave a big long whinny. She already was indeed full of vinegar, since she regularly drank it and rubbed it on after a bath, alternating with the corn oil rubdowns. Unable to resist her usual joke, she came out with:

"What's the difference between a vitamin and a hormone? You can't make a vitamin, but you can make a whore moan. Just don't pay her."

She snorted with laughter at her own joke. (Dirty jokes were often ones told at women's expense, and often by women on themselves.) Warming up:

"What's the definition of horticulture?" She was obviously benefiting from these magical elixirs Wert was now giving her in the form of injections. "You can lead a whore to culture, but you can't make her think."

She was becoming more energetic, but no less distracted. The hormone injections became an important part of her life, and Dr. Wert was seemingly on the cutting edge of HRT therapy, with a big practice in bi- weekly injections of the "horse piss." He also created quite a business dispensing diet pills; and later the booming cash business in oxycodone he ran for years, finally being arrested in 2013 at age eighty.

We, her children, privately worried that Doc Wert was doing his own experiments in mad-scientist fashion, using women as guinea pigs for his own gain. He had been charging her a lot of money over several years for these increasingly regular "pick-me-ups", possibly initiated by the start of her love affair.

Almost a year after Gil died, now at fifty-one, Mommy apparently settled back into her home and family. With Gil gone and the Sadie Fletcher Caper wound down., she wrote this long letter to Dr. Wert.

Nov. 11, 1967
Dr. Dr. Wert:

Rather than call you when you are busy, I'll write my "complaints"—and you can read this and then call me at your convenience.

The past two months my earnings have been less than half of what I normally should earn—mostly due to my not being on the ball and following thru with my plans. I do not want to lose my job. I really

like it... And when I'm my usual self I'm quite good at it. (I sell the Young People's Art Course for Famous Artists Schools and call on families by appointment when a teenager has gotten a good mark in an art talent contest and has a real interest in art.)

As you know, *[I have not felt my usual healthy self recently]* I have had slight headaches a few days, and a great deal of fatigue. I feel like a bear who wants to hibernate until next Spring!

I did hibernate after my beloved Gil died so tragically last February. My normal gusto for life returned in due time; and my problem now, I think, is mostly physical. This past week I've spent three days in bed dozing and reading, all the time planning to get going in the next half hour and then sleeping until it's too late to do anything—then saying, "what the hell . . . tomorrow I'll get an early start. The two days I worked (one evening and one morning) I was lucky and earned $160.00—the first sales in over two weeks, when I pushed myself to see the regular number of prospects. Yesterday I had my day all lined up and was looking forward to it. I got dressed, drove Linda to work at 7 a.m., and then Nancy and Danny to school. I had a good breakfast and fixed my hair and makeup. I lay down fully dressed because it was a bit too early to make my calls. I then slept all day and got up a few times for food, etc. I made a few phone calls, slept some more and at 3:30 a.m. got undressed and slept until 10:50 a.m. the next day. I still felt like staying in bed, even after a bath and cold rinse!

(Our mother was not the kind of person who could have identified or admitted to herself or out loud that she was in a deep depression since Gil's death, but her letter seems to indicate that she was mired down in lassitude as badly as she was when her first husband left her without resources.)

On all these dreary days I took the green and yellow diet pill. *[Her too, then!]* Except for my back when I got up or down, I have no pain—I am not depressed, just BLAH. Also, I am having hot flashes—not severe, maybe eight or ten a day. I don't perspire much. Just slightly. At first, I thought my thermostat wasn't working and the whole house was overheated. I even told a couple of nice people in whose homes I was pitching the art to that it was pleasantly warm outside, and it would be nice to open a window or two. I didn't say it was HOT in their home—because I am polite, but it WAS. And at my house I've been nagging everyone to take iron tablets and wear sweaters. I have the house at a comfortable 65 degrees. I think my kids are anemic.

My mother died suddenly at my age of a coronary thrombosis. (I expect to live a long time—and HOPE to outlive Otto—I'd always outlived him in terms of having the time of my life! But I hope to out-distance him, too.) Since both of his parents are long livers, and both of mine were short livers, he has the advantage there. But I have a lot of other advantages—I don't drink or smoke to excess, and I just naturally have a ball most of the time (except lately).

Since most of my spare time the last 20 years has been spent talking with people and trying to channel the conversation to end up with me getting some of their money, I haven't had any time to sit and drink tea with my contemporaries and discuss the problems women face while bravely going through The Change. I thought it was sort of a luxury only wives of good husbands (who SUPPORT them) could indulge in.

(Going off the rails here, in her usual fashion. Note: I realize the portion of the letter is so very politically incorrect. I include it to reflect the freedom White people had in those times.)

About eight years ago I did get quite an earful on the subject of The Change while I was delivering some Nutrilite to Joe Walcott at 119 Venango Street in Philadelphia. He is a Negro and was a prizefighter who once got a broken neck and then got into labor relations (not the famous "Jersey Joe Walcott," however.) Though I had sent him two Nutrilites every month for years through the mail, I had never met this Joe Walcott personally. But this day he had called me; and I said I would bring it in person to his home for once—which by the way was a really beautiful home. *[this was in the heart of Kensington, where we'd never been]*

When I got there, he wasn't home yet; and a Negro woman named Margaret Thomas let me in and showed me into his elegant living room. She has an apartment on the third floor and is a "pract-nikt-able" nurse, she told me. During her pract-nikt-able nurse training she learned a lot of secrets about Life. She mentioned she also had a brother who wanted to get Nutrilite. Well, it was revealed that she thought Nutrilite was sort of a powerful sexual stimulant for a man who has "slowed down." I tried to set her straight.

Well, Joe Walcott was a long time in coming home, and this Margaret surely told me some fascinating "true-to-life" stories while I waited.

And since my Nutrilite powers really didn't fall in that category, she got on the subject of "us women." Just the night before she and her friend Grace had gone to a viewing of a mutual friend who had just "passed." On their way home Margaret and Grace were discussing the friend, who was their age—early fifties, also now my age. And Grace said,

"She never even got OLD—just up and passes! But she sure looked nice! I'm almost HER age and I feel as good as I did when I was 16!"

Both of these dark ladies were currently without husbands. "Nonsense!" says Margaret. "You NOT 16—you past 50!!"

"Yeh, but I FEEL 16—and I'm much more inerested in gettin' LAID than laid out! Practickly any half-decent man that has plenty of stamina would have hisself working weekends with me!"

"Shame on you, Grace . . . you may FEEL 16, but you 50. And you glands is 50, so you gotta get a grip on yousself! You is speriensing the MAN-PAUSE. And this is just a HOT FLASH—it's when you gets HOT for a MAN and you starts flashing, and you got to PAUSE. You is changing Life and you can't go messing with no MAN. You jes' gotta PAUSE."

Well, Lenny, I still don't have any good husband supporting me, so I can't keep up this relaxing and reclining schedule without landing on relief or getting hooked up with Otto again—who would like that.

I sure hope you have some fast-acting Lydia T. Pinkham's-type stuff to get me over this hibernating/warm flushing stage I'm stuck in. Hope you can read this. I wrote it in bed.

Besides the things I've already complained about, I weigh 160 lbs., up from 154; and I sometimes have spells of violent hiccups when I eat.

Sincerely, Dorothy Fech

This may have been the point at which, after her plea for an energy increase, that Dr. Wert increased the frequency of the hormone injections.[3]

---

[3] "Lansdowne Doc Gets Two Years" 11/15/13

Media Courthouse—A prominent Delaware County doctor who was arrested in May for running a "pill mill" out of his Lansdowne office pleaded guilty Thursday in two counts of prescribing a controlled substance to a drug-dependent person. Dr. Lenwood Boyer Wert, 80 [. . .] was also ordered to surrender $418,247, as well as a shotgun, four rifles and two handguns seized by law enforcement during a raid on his home and office [. . .] The octogenarian [. . .] had been charged with more than 1,000 criminal counts following his May 14 arrest, including 536 counts of selling or giving a controlled substance to a dependent person and 542 counts of administering a controlled substance by a practitioner. [. . .] Wert ran a "cash only" practice, where patients could pay an initial $150 and a $100 fee for each subsequent visit. Anyone trying to use insurance was turned away, the affidavit said

SHE WAS WANDERING FARTHER AWAY over time on her sales trips for Windsor [*which she was also still doing, along with Famous Artists and of course, Nutrilite*], and we had gotten used to it. We were losing her, and it wasn't a subject any of us needed to discuss. In some sense I was happy for her that she was having adventures at last, after the loss of her dear Gil.

Danny had found himself a beginning job at the local steel factory, He was busy getting into regular trouble for minor things that on several occasions involved an overnight in jail — drinking or being caught with a stash of marijuana. One morning, he told us recently, Mommy woke him up after one of those stints and handed him a paper, saying "Sign this!" Hungover and fuzzy, he wanted to know what he was signing.

"It's an insurance policy I've taken out on you. Since you're not going to live past twenty-five, you're going to be my ship finally coming in. Sign here." She was a bit tired of his antics and her need to drive to some little county jail to bail him out; and she thought she may as well capitalize on his bad habits. (She bailed out J.G. and me as well.)

Nancy was in community college with a dream to go to fashion design school and working part-time for a record promoter who was making money in wheelbarrow loads and paying her handsomely. He may have been the payola king, for all I know. I was a starry-eyed newlywed and young entrepreneur with Bob in our new Amway business; and J.G. was working at the local auto repair shop and had been informally adopted by the woman next-door to the garage who kept them in sandwiches, coffee and beer and unmitigated love for "the guys," one of whom was her own son.

Having proved her abilities to close a book and make a good profit, Mommy had been offered a big chance by Windsor to travel south and cover some of the communities surrounding New Orleans. It sounded exotic and fun to her. Gil was gone; and (now divorced) Otto was ensconced in his little apartment near the trolley and the bar and really trying to stop drinking. She discussed the trip with us—we knew she would go. Maybe it was what she needed to shake off her doldrums. She soon packed up, headed for Lake Charles, Lafayette, and some smaller towns like Broussard and New Iberia, Louisiana, where she was charged with selling these smaller chambers of commerce on the idea of a book.

The Cajun man wanted 'Jolie blonde' to stay

When she made the sale, the second step was to sell the ads to businesses and work on the layout. Then close the book and do it again next town over. She seemed to succeed regularly, because she was gone for a long period.

On the way down, she got listening to her 8-track player. She only had two I can remember—Chet Atkins on guitar and Janis Joplin imploring the Lord to buy her a Mercedes Benz. She got to bouncing around in her best car yet, her Mercury sedan, into the music totally, as she told it later. Crossing the Pee Dee River in North Carolina, picking up her speed without quite noticing that she was traveling way over the speed limit, she sailed right past a cop chasing another speeder, albeit a slower speeder than our mother.

By the time she was pulled over by still another cop who picked up the call, several more police cars arrived at the scene. She was clocked at one hundred ten miles per hour. Since our mother usually drove at about twenty-five miles per hour., taking in all the sights and commenting to any passenger-victims so they could enjoy the scenery with her, it was the first time she had ever been stopped for speeding.

She had on her usual uniform of red Murray Space Shoes and her skipper blue jumpsuit, which just happened to match her blue eyes. And she was quite good at being charming to total strangers, even policemen, apparently. She instantly took on her Sadie Fletcher persona and, while she may have been worried about how much this would cost her, she must have enjoyed the challenge in a sporting way. We were not witness to this amazing scene—all of this was reported in detail later to us.

The usual discussion one would expect with my mother ensued; she didn't have her registration, and her license was expired. Before long she found herself in the little town jail.

"Hot dog! Holy Hannah! My kids are never going to believe me! I have to document this. Would you mind if I got my camera and took a few shots of you fellows and maybe if one of you would take me behind bars?"

My mother was not the organized type who recorded events on camera; we have a very scant collection of family photos from our childhoods. The only reason she had a camera at all was because she needed one in her work of doing these chamber books.

She brought the camera in and soon had everyone in the jail posing for her. She again got permission to go to the car and brought back her special peanut butter ball candies, talking to them about nutrition and Nutrilite as they enjoyed eating them. She even had a short nap on the cot in her cell while they did something to check her identity.

Within a few hours she was able to write a check for some small amount to get released. Now the cops were all charmed to within an inch of their lives and falling over themselves to get in another photo she took. She showed the clerk how to operate the camera and had her take one more shot, this time with her writing the check and smiling, the group of men in blue all around her. She was almost ready to get on her way again. She asked for the address so she could send the copies of the photos. "Just promise you won't post them on the "Wanted" board, she asked.

"Sirs, before I leave, do I get my one phone call," she asked. "I don't want my kids to worry about what happened to me, because I've been delayed for a few hours."

They set her down at the clerk's desk with the phone and gave her the moment of privacy she requested (claiming embarrassment about telling her family).

The phone rang at 4030 Berry Avenue.

"You're not going to believe this, she said, "but I'm in jail. They're just about to release me. They got me for speeding and passing an officer of the law doing a hundred and ten. It's fine, though; we're getting along famously. And my fine was only twenty-five dollars, because I've shot so many photos of them and promised to send them copies as mementos of the good time we've had. I'm getting off on good behavior." Dropping her voice to a whisper,

"They don't know that I didn't have any film in the camera. But they're happy as clams, and they loved my peanut butter balls. We've had a wonderful afternoon, and I'm on my way again."

So she entered triumphantly into the town of Lake Charles, with a solid adventure already under her belt—and ready for the next one, which came very soon, appearing in the form of a genuine Cajun man named "Sport." I have a photo of her taken by him, wearing a bathing suit looking very pretty. They apparently had at least a brief romance; I do know he wanted her to move to Lake Charles and operate his dance hall/bar/bowling alley with him. He was pure Cajun, illiterate, and full of fun and back-country colloquialisms.

In Acadiana, they seemed to have gone dancing every night. Sport taught her zydeco jitterbug, the Cajun waltz, and introduced her personally to Cajun music

She fell in love, possibly with Sport, but for sure with the Cajun culture. When she returned home, she brought with her the priceless Hackberry Ramblers' record so we could learn all the dances and songs. The Cajuns called her "Jolie Blonde," from a famous Cajun song. We'd put the record on and begin to *"laissez les bons temps rouler,"* let the good times roll, and dance around the living room, her teaching us the fast-beat zydeco dances.

She wrote Sport a few letters, and he would answer as often as he could find some literate friend to write one for him. She decided not to take him up on his offer, though he would have had an instant moneymaker with her hostessing the club. He sent this letter, a subtle marriage proposal:

Dear Yankee Blonde:

I'm sorry I've taken so long in answering your two very sweet letters. But I finally found a letter writer, and I'll try to bring you up to date.

"Lady" has a colt, my cows are doing fine and are having calfs [*sp.*] **and eating all the time. Also added six pigs and a few chickens. Also got a ratcoon** [*sp.*]**, ducks and quail.**

All that's missing on my farm is the haystack, pardner!!!

I can't tell you how much I enjoyed being with you in New Orleans in your sparkly sweater, dancing all night—well, almost all night. I'll have memories in my OLD AGE!!

I haven't found that redhead to marry, but I still have you! But after all these years of bachelorhood, I don't believe a woman could stand living with me. But we could try. I'm officially retired, doing absolutely nothing I don't feel like doing. My house is empty, and my bed is lonely and cold. Come back! If it wasn't so cold up north, I might consider coming up and forming a pardnership—you working and me spending!

I've given up the dance hall, closed the pool hall, and just being free as a bird, collecting my check each month and looking for someone to spend it on.

Well, Pardner, that's about it for this trip. Keep all your lines tight and your cargo well stored and write often.

Love, Sport

ONE DAY MOMMY INVITED BOB and me to an evening at Ginger's, where we had never been, to meet a man she was dating. He was from South Philadelphia, and she introduced him as The Ham King, explaining that he "controlled" all the ham that went in and out of Philadelphia. She later told us he was reputed to be a Mafioso made man. It was a strange night. The Ham King made the most delicious anchovies marinated in milk and garlic and served on crostini. We had our first ever martinis as he played to perfection the classic theme from "Godfather" on his mandolin. The movie had not been made yet, but I still felt its heavy implications somehow. He tried very hard to have her warm up to him, but I believe she may have been scared to consider the life and all that it entailed — and that was before the Sopranos!

After this discarded attempt at romance, Ginger asked Mommy along as her fellow chaperone for her two daughters' class trip to Italy, all expenses paid — an offer she couldn't turn down and her big chance to experience European travel. Before then I don't remember our mother going anywhere on an airplane — no one in our family had experienced air travel, not even J. G. when he went into the Army Reserves. We were all jealous of the trip and the daughters; Nancy really felt the pain of Mommy's attraction to those darling daughters. They were the same age as her, and her direct competition.

"Why can't she take me?" she moaned aloud. She was young enough to feel neglected, and rightfully so— she *was* neglected, as was Danny. She has described her impending sense of loss that her

Mommy in her traveling outfit

dream of fashion design school might not happen. At least she *had* a dream to go to college.

The trip was a success. Mommy had a wonderful time, reveling in gelato and charming Italian men as only she could. On her arrival back home, she had a presentation ceremony of gifts for us daughters. Maybe she felt guilty about being with someone else's daughters, but the reality was that the trip would not have happened if she had had to cover the expenses.

"I have something for each of you," she said, as she brought out tiny blue boxes lined in white satin. The boxes revealed small glass pendants. "It's Venetian glass," and she told us the wonders of the Murano glass process and the history going all the way back to Marco Polo. Next came the beautiful

One of Mommy's random rummage sale gifts

kid gloves, thin as writing paper. I still wear mine today.

Most gifts Mommy gave came from a thrift shop and were hastily wrapped in tinfoil just before presentation, clearly nothing but afterthoughts. At Christmas time she could go through a whole roll of tinfoil, pulling together such things as a hobnailed glass ashtray (I'm looking at it

right now), that agate tea strainer with a small chip from the rummage
sale (I still have it and use it), a designer sweater in reasonably good
condition but never new, a pair of faux glazed ceramic ducks from the
Ming dynasty era (such luxury—a pair!), or a small collection of
samples from her new Edith Rehnborg line of cosmetics Nutrilite had
just introduced: tiny lipsticks in adult-only bright red, and little tubes
of Dermajeune night cream (for mature skin) packaged with cotton
wadding. Here, a deviation from the Reynolds Wrap, presented in a
plastic Nutrilite box with scenes from last year's Christmas cards glued
on to the ingredients panels, lovingly obscuring the label. She would
work all night finding her gifts around the house and wrapping them
as artfully as possible with no preplanned gift or wrapping paper
purchase.

These Italian elegant gifts thrilled us, because we knew she had
picked them out for each of us with real thought. And yet the gifts
caused a lump in the throat: they were small compensation for these
prolonged absences with someone else's girls. On balance, we had
some sense of happiness for yet another of her exotic experiences. She
was drifting away from us. For some reason, I did not feel resentment
at her distractions. It may have been because I suffered from the same
wandering instinct myself.

I believe it was Ginger who again afforded her another gift, this
time a trip to Hawaii. The high point of the trip was documented by a
photo of her with THE King of Hawaii, King Kamehameha himself!
She looks so proud in the photo, wearing that self-satisfied grin. Every
time she showed off the photo, she'd put on her closed-mouth
beaming smile and say, "I got lei'd several times on my trip to Hawaii.
Each lei was better than the one before." And she'd pass another
photo of her wearing a lei. Recently I wanted to learn more about the
King, so I went to Wikipedia — our and everybody else's World Books
being long disappeared. I discovered that there are *many* descendants,
or maybe-descendants, who claim the title of King Kamehameha!

When I told Nancy this recently, she said, "I'll bet she met him at one of those touristy luaus. There's probably one at every luau."

But Mommy was *sure* she had met and dined with THE King.

Mommy meets the real King Kamehameha (he tells her)

She came back from the exotic experience somewhat worried, though. She kept feeling a sense of "heat" in her left breast and felt uneasy about it, saying her breast also felt like it did when she was nursing babies. She went to Dr. Wert, who examined her and said, "You're fine, I feel nothing."

She went to another doctor, who ordered a diagnostic test called a thermogram. In 1971 it was the definitive diagnostic for breast cancer — at least she believed it was. It's possible she was sent for a thermogram by Dr. Wert. The thermogram showed nothing of concern. But she kept feeling this "heat." Over several weeks or months, her senses told her to press on and landed her a doctor who ordered a biopsy at Jefferson Hospital. I was there when she had the consultation following the biopsy.

"You have a very aggressive sarcoma that has advanced to the point that we can offer you only palliative care," said the rather disinterested doctor. Disbelieving, we needed an explanation — an interpretation of that ugly word that we already knew the meaning of.

I can still feel the chill emanating from him as he coolly told her, "We have nothing of a curative nature. We can start your radiation treatments right away, to slow up its progression." I came back with her a week later for her first treatment. I was sick with fear for her as they marked her up with indelible purple lines on her back and front. The purple lines transferred from the heat of the Niagara massage pad and are still there, indelible.

The radiation treatment was the essence of everything she had railed against for years, and the conflict smacked her in the face. It was her "us against them" mentality going back to when the FDA came after Nutrilite for claiming cures.

"The A.M.A. and organized medicine are in cahoots. They WANT people sick, because that's where the money is. Think about it: cancer is big money — it's so big they can't afford to find a cure, and if they did, they'd bury it."

She had given us plenty of evidence over the years that the natural organic way was far superior to orthodox medicine, drug companies and the A.M.A. There they were, the Enemy, now providing her with a very small temporary stay of "palliative care." Those chilling words again.

Now, during the treatment, I felt so sick at heart as I watched the process. I, too. had been conditioned to believe the radiation would kill her before the cancer could. She frenetically began searching other options that aligned with her principles and beliefs. She bought books, still on my shelf today: *Questioning Chemotherapy, The Essiac Report, The Gerson Diet,* and more. She was back in her own home that week, but we saw little of her except to bring her meals; she was mostly in bed and absorbed in research.

THE IMAGES OF THAT GOLDEN day in September, a day of pleasure and pain of our rare time together, will never leave me.

It was Mommy's first time at Ben and Gilda's farm, our now-best friends, where Bob and I seemed to spend half of our lives. Here, in a place where we felt love and nurturing, I wanted her to be bathed in that warmth on this temporary stay of execution. It would be an unusual event, for her to "just be," before she left for Mexico for her alternative treatments, no distractions on her part.

The damson plums had produced their first bumper crop and were piled up in the mudroom on the washer and dryer as we gathered dusty jars and lids Gilda and Ben had found at yard sales and flea markets. We scrubbed, boiled and sterilized them.

Gilda was especially kind that day, her acerbic holier-than-thou demeanor set aside. With her new-found wealth from Uncle Jim's "found money" inheritance and the recent security and status conferred upon the Philadelphia schoolteachers as new members of the AFL-CIO Teamsters Union, she had become increasingly confident and smug, a bit more tough and judgmental in her new status.[4] Now a newly certified Master Gardener, a producer of organic crops and a high school English teacher of the toughest kids the inner city had, she enjoyed the power of it all.

Gilda had told me many times that she was an education snob. Both very bright, she and Ben were fun to have intellectual jousting sessions with. Gilda and I had kind of an ongoing competition on who was the smarter, and the challenges led to weeks-long discussions at times backed up by good documentation on our respective points. She considered it mandatory for me to finish my degree, but once I saw

my way to becoming an entrepreneur, being a business owner seemed a quicker way to get to my highest value, freedom. I knew I didn't want to be "owned" by a boss who had control of what I did, even for eight hours a day, and I had learned that even a degree can't necessarily remove that hold an employer has on an employee.

She took jabs at me and my decision regularly. Usually quick to remind me of how

Mommy at age fifty-six, four months before she died

weak our position was in our new roles as business owners: no pension, no benefits, and no summers off. But that day her kindness was remarkable. I felt ill at ease with it, waiting for the next blow, which didn't come. She was soft, sparing me just for this occasion.

The year was 1972, and hippiedom hung all about us, still. Quite new to homesteading and both having grown up in the city of Philadelphia, Gilda and Ben were undertaking all kinds of bucolic experiments. Gilda's and my close friendship had continued after we met and married our respective new spouses. She and I baked bread together. We worked the garden together, learning from her ninety-year-old neighbor. We made pasta, hanging spaghetti all over the kitchen on broomstick handles. We canned and froze spaghetti sauce from our tomato crops. The men produced some really fine Concord grape and Muscatel wine. We made cheese out of their goats' milk. We picked Gilda's crops of blueberries, raspberries and climbed rickety ladders together to pick their sour cherries. We made pies, jams, preserves, even a delicious liquor from goat's milk and lemons called *bain coeur*. Ben set up a basement still, where he and Bob could intently observe bourbon dripping out of the still. Ben grew marijuana in amongst the corn, "good shit," it turned out to be.

Today it was the first harvest of plums, and Mommy was entering *my* world, a reverse from the usual. It was a day of suspended animation for each of us. Never really quite present with her children in ordinary circumstances, on this day I felt honored she was with me. Pensive, she didn't utter hopelessness out loud; her language expressed renewed confidence in her decision. Not sure how much time she had to turn around the disease, her Taurus-the-Bull persona said, "no second-guessing, my only choice." Hope had said goodbye to Philadelphia's finest hospitals and packed its bags to move across the border to the tawdry town of Tijuana, Mexico, where she would take a treatment based on natural healing.

We three women were like wax on a hot day, able to be molded into the shapes needed for the moment.

Both Gilda and my mother were wistful and softened, qualities I'd rarely seen in either of them before.

That big kettle of lush damson plum jam gave us a splendid focal point to avoid the obvious subject. Gilda thought Mommy was stone-crazy for choosing the "natural route" to save her life, but today her opinionated voice was quiet. I was concerned but indoctrinated enough on "orthodox medicine" to more than half believe that the cancer business in the USA *was* indeed big business and that a cure would never be found because it was too profitable for the medical world to abandon.

I can taste the tang of damson plums and relive the sensuous licking of the wooden spoon as we dripped some into a glass of cold water to see if it had jelled yet. "Mmmm," we'd say, over and over, tasting it as we stirred and dripped. The tang of that jam we clung to as if it were a life force… "Mmmm…."

How many times did we say that? I can roll the sweetness around on my mind's tongue right now, as tears spring to my eyes. Several times I saw my mother lay her hand on her left breast, to check if the heat had gone away yet. Each time she did, I found a twin pain in my left breast, right over my breaking heart.

Ladle in the hot jam . . . wet paper towel to clean spills off the rim. Take the tongs and pick up a lid; screw the lid on.

"Not tight. We tighten them after they cool. Turn them upside down on the towel, and as they cool, they'll clamp down and seal. If the lid pops up, it didn't seal, and we'll put it in the basement fridge where we keep the eggs and goat's milk."

Gilda barked her instructions throughout the day, eager to show off her knowledge. Her ever-present Master Gardener voice, enhanced by her authority from *Mother Earth News* and *Organic Gardening* studies pervaded her new farm woman persona, her of the straw hat and egg collecting wire basket. And yet I felt her kindness and empathy under her veneer of bossiness.

Mommy and I talked about her plan. She would fly out to Borrego Springs, California, and someone, hopefully my long-departed father's sister, Aunt Toni, would put her up at the small motel she and her husband operated, and Toni would transport her across the border for her treatments. Once very close sisters-in-law, they hadn't seen or spoken to each other in the years since my father left; but somehow Mommy had found a way to contact her. Aunt Toni was ready to spring to her side and help. Mommy gave the impression that it would be a quick treatment and recovery, and then back home.

She had already started on the Gerson Diet. Technically, any taste of damson plum jam was *verboten* — *NO* sugar at all was the protocol. Sugar feeds cancer, it said. She was always willing to dance around the rules — but just a little today; this was serious business.

She ate mostly almonds. And peach pits, which is what Laetrile, the key medicine that would cure her, was made of. Actually, not peach, but apricot pits. A lover of those summer peaches, she was sure they were close to apricots in levels of something called "amygdalin," which the body converts to cyanide. Yes, cyanide was going to save her life, according to her latest guru, Dr. Ernest Krebs. He called the substance B-17, or Laetrile. The F.D.A. had banned it in the USA in 1971, but it was available in injectable form in Mexico.

So she looked for peaches ripe enough that the pit would have split open. Even apple seeds, she said, had a touch of the life-saving amygdalin in them. They added hope to her breakfast routine when she munched on them along with the apple. Black coffee was important, not actually as a drink, but as an enema. We did not discuss this, except to learn that it helped to cleanse the toxins from the body.

The jars were filled, several dozens of them. Gilda made a ratatouille with her first-ever harvest of eggplants and tomatoes. Ben produced a bottle of red wine, claiming he knew nothing about wine as he poured the fine Bordeaux. Gilda took a serrated knife through her crusty French bread. I knew she had achieved that crust by baking it on red clay tiles in her ancient oven, something we'd practiced many times.

Every piece of the day was a celebration of organic homestead farming. But we all knew it was something other than a celebration. It was a sweet goodbye, a launch into the wild blue yonder, the unknown dimension. The air was heavy despite the wine and the gaiety of the harvest. We forced that gaiety as if there was a guillotine waiting in the mudroom just beyond that cozy kitchen. I don't remember eating or the taste of the food. I only remember how hard it was to swallow.

———————————————

4 Ben's Uncle Jim was an ancient bachelor who had stayed on in the city after the rest of the family migrated to the city's edge. He existed in a small rented room, living an impoverished life and mending his socks and underwear and handkerchiefs to save every penny he could. A somber fellow, he had survived the Holocaust camps, and didn't talk; he just ate as much as he could at the holiday meals around Ben and Gilda's table. The entertainment of the evening was watching Jim put away the vittles.

One day Ben got the inevitable word that Uncle Jim had died. Ben and Gilda as surviving relatives had the job of disposing of the few articles that made up his mean existence. But surprise: In his pockets, beneath his mended greyed underpants and paper-thin handkerchiefs, under the lasts of his worn leather shoes, sewn in the lining of his few suits, under the paper that lined the bureau drawers, they discovered CASH! Every social security check he'd ever received, in exact amounts, were found, even the coins. It was as if he had secretly received those sums while still in the death camps and hidden them away from the Nazis. The sum came to a total of something like $400,000 by the time they were done combing through this one-room hovel. I'm not sure what they ever told the IRS, but the find certainly improved the quality of their lives.

M Y MOTHER'S MEDICAL EMERGENCY SITUATION called for every assistance we could muster as she prepared to leave for Mexico. We, her children, were sick with fear to think of losing her. With Mommy working on the nutritional solutions to her dire diagnosis, we sought help from her friend Alice Brant, who went into high gear on the spiritual end. It was critical, she said, to get her to a healing service at her church in Philadelphia. From her descriptions, it was a huge church just filled to overflowing with the Holy Spirit. Every week hundreds were healed; and she assured us it was the best possible place for her to be. All kinds of healings happened, and she assured us God would know what healing she needed. Bob and I had finally gotten religion, getting more involved in his family church first in agreeing to serve on a search committee for a new "more spiritual" minister, then in a small home worship group that eventually led to our group regularly doing field trips on Saturday nights to visit a charismatic Pentecostal church in the nearby rural town of Parkesburg, PA.

While our group never succeeded in converting our congregation—or ourselves—to charismatic worship, we were fascinated with the apparent joy these worshipers found in their services. The Amway business also was something Bob and I had adopted as a near religion, and between these two large influences in our lives, we were edging into becoming True Believers. Now we were completely open to Alice's prescription for what might be an instant healing, no Mexico trip needed.

As people can suspend belief when reading a good book or watching a movie, they can also suspend *dis*belief, which is what I was in the process of doing. The facts of her illness presented a very bad movie, according to the experts' prognosis.

Yet I wanted our mother to LIVE, and I opened myself wide to whatever God wanted to provide for her (as long as it was a healing — you know how that goes). I knew that as splendid a person as she was, he would not pass her by. I began having private conversations with God, explaining how we, her children, had never really had enough time with her for one reason or another and telling Him that it was not time for her to die. I remember speaking to God and letting him know that her children had not yet gotten a full dose of her when she was alive and kicking, and we still had hopes of capturing her interest before she disappeared permanently.

There will always be this Great Mystery of Life about whom God passes by and who catches his attention. But I, as a recent convert, had begun to think it was a good time to be a Believer. I didn't want to presume to know God's plan, but physical healing was right up there at the top of my prayers. I'd have been happy for healing of any type, but I had my specifics.

I had never heard her "proclaim" aloud that Jesus was her personal Lord and Savior; but on the other hand, she was a rather private person and not given to shouting such things out. She had never denied Him, and there was plenty of evidence she had a strong spiritual underpinning. Yet she had just never gone around raising her hands and saying "holy roller" stuff" out loud. A dignified Lutheran, to sum it up.

So, there we found ourselves, in the Philadelphia Church of Charismatic Worship. The sanctuary was vast, soaring and filled with fully robed choir, pipe organ booming away, and a full complement of ecstatic worshipers. It felt more like a cathedral than the churches I had been exposed to. It was even *better* than the Parkesburg church! People were falling all over the place, screaming out, "Thank you, JeSUS!," and tongues and prophesies were happening right and left. I can't recall the sermon or order of worship, just the wild goings-on of a fully unleashed charismatic assembly of apostates. It was Spirit-filled to the max; I felt my mother's chances were good.

The minister was Reverend James Poole, a handsome devil of a guy. His wife and young daughters occupied the first row where they could gaze up adoringly at him. His obedient wife wore a high-necked Victorian sort of dress with lace (the kind of refined attire you would have seen in a B cowboy movie from 1950 worn by a fine young widow lady traveling across the country by stagecoach. The scene: She leans out from behind the stagecoach curtain to lock eyes on the handsome sheriff who's been rounding up the cattle rustlers and who recently lost his wife in childbirth). Next to the pastor's wife were their three blonde daughters, dressed for a Victorian child's birthday party in the mansion garden, in ankle-length dresses with big bows tied at their backs and wide-brimmed hats perched on their golden locks.

Everything was right in this holy place, and we felt a confident degree of assurance: right place; right time. Alice was guiding us, of course; and I felt sure she would get us "connected" with the healing Spirit all around us.

I thought I had conditioned myself carefully after the Parkesburg forays, but I felt unsure how to proceed — with emotions so fully invested in the mission. Anxiety high, I remember not knowing whether we should offer my mother as a kind of sacrifice; or whether she had to come of her own free will up to the front of the massive church, or quite how we got the attention of the most healing-equipped person in the place. At a loss, I didn't want the event to go by without her experiencing healing, hopefully on the spot and with some dramatic sense in her that it had happened. This was it!

And then something big did happen. Someone laid hands on her. Maybe Alice orchestrated it. Alice spoke in tongues, tears flowing down her face copiously as an endless stream of words beginning with "shl" sounds poured out. Someone interpreted, with biblical references. It all sounded and felt good. Mommy seemed impassively open and enthusiastically going with the flow, as they say. It was her kind of "what the hell; might as well" stoicism that she had about much of her life events.

The three key solid things had happened: hands, tongues, prophesy. She did not actually get slain in the Spirit, nor did she have any visible changes to her person. This inserted a tiny sliver of doubt, not admitted aloud by Bob or me to each other. We believed.

We left the church feeling that a good thing had happened. Alice was praising Jesus and thanking the Holy Spirit. She was sure she had gotten through. Now she wouldn't have to go.

And yet my mother packed for Mexico. I could not argue with her. She still felt the heat, the evidence more powerful than the hoped-for healing.

IT WAS SUDDENLY LATE SEPTEMBER, and Mommy was leaving the next day. Taking our mother to the airport previously had not been a happy experience for either her Italy or Hawaii adventures, without any of us along. Now this, the worst leave-taking of all. By land or in the air, she had taken to leaving us behind more frequently and telling her rollicking tales later on. Uncertainty prevailed; we were not sure we'd hear great stories this time.

Would she be healed? It seemed such a sure thing, after our big Pentecostal experience. Would she survive? What if she liked California and decided to stay after she got well? That was a real possibility. Would she write or call? She often forgot. What if she died? The Jefferson doctors had already pronounced her as good as dead within six months.

And then she was gone—on a one-way flight, with no return date set. She would be back when she was well.

Lisette Diamond called Nancy the very next day and screamed into the phone, "Your mother's going to die there! You listen to me! She'll die!" Nancy was upset by the call—she wasn't prepared to accept that her mother could die. Why she chose Nancy is a mystery. At seventeen years old, Nancy was just finishing high school and working a job with the record promoter while trying to navigate her way into fashion design school without help or funds from the usual sources — a caring parent, that is. Advocating for the betterment of her children and their future was never our mother's (nor either of our fathers') strong suit.

Lisette, now a little calmer, then called Linda but again declared in a matter-of-fact tone: "She'll die there." Lisette didn't know the intense stubbornness of our mother. We had no input or ability to change her thinking. To her, it was stay here and die or go to Mexico and live.

Time went by with increasing unease as we heard almost nothing to indicate progress. We got a few short phone calls in which she raved about the care Aunt Toni and Uncle Warren were lavishing on her, as she was now staying with them in their small motel in the desert.

We celebrated a quiet Thanksgiving without her as we prayed fervent prayers around the Thanksgiving table, prayers of thanks for the healing taking place in our again-absent mother. We prayed our gratitude for Aunt Toni. It had been over 25 years since Toni had disappeared from our lives, and now it was as if she had always been there when we received her letter:

Hi, Everyone,

Thank you so much for the get-well card and the Thank-U-Gram, although it wasn't necessary—I'd do anything for your mom.

She was feeling much better today, she sunned herself by the pool and relaxed, and I could see that a lot of tension has been relieved.

Don't worry that Dot isn't writing, she's in good hands and probably feels (although I don't know for sure) that until she has really great news for you, they don't get written. "I'm going to write the kids today"—but somehow the days just flit by so quickly. Dot feels really great for about two hours after she gets up—she briskly walks up to

Christmas Circle where our very tiny village is, observes what everyone is up to, and reports back to us. We have oatmeal and juice and bread and almonds, and then Dot rests for a while.

. . . I will close so you can get this right away. The tape of the sermon came today, and the batteries. Now if the card and the microphone get here we'll be in good shape. The fall leaves and the bittersweet were inspirational! Dot enjoyed all of it.

Love,

Aunt Toni"

From Mommy:

Dear Anne:

I've read your precious letter over and over. Man, you're really turned on!

Last night I listened to the *[sermon]* tapes—Wow! I fell asleep during your 4 a.m. reading. Toni wrote down all the Bible references. I'm doing my homework. We got a kick out of Bob's tour of his booze factory *[Ben's bourbon still]*, and I loved the $1.00 record and the story of Tom Edison!!

Thanks for all the presents; they look so pretty— loved the leaves and Toni made a lovely arrangement of the bittersweet. *[Drawing of the arrangement]*. She has pumpkins and lemons, avocados and the bittersweet in a ceramic crock.

The lipstick is just perfect, love the soap. I doodled on the sketch pad—haven't used the pastels yet. But I will when I feel up to it. It is so good to listen to James Poole's *[Pentecostal]* church. I've played that over again this a.m. Toni made whole wheat bread yesterday. It's really good.

I wrote to my doctor *[her Mexican "doctor"]*, giving him a report on me AND

Toni—I hope we can both see him soon. Toni's X-rays show kidney stones and a mass—she is supposed to go back to the hospital for more tests to see if it's cancer. She wants to get the other test—so we will both be going back to Mexico. I think biopsies are dangerous. I'm really crippled from mine.

Anne—I keep praying and believing—I think I'm getting better—but I feel so lousy. It's hard to tell—as the cancer breaks down, you've got to feel half sick.

I'll write more later—I want Warren to take this so it goes out of the desert today. Please send two XXII! Toni wants to sell it, so also include a Nutrilite kit— application or basic stuff: "Food and your Family," Program book, etc. She gave me $15.00.

My shingles are gone. That is, the scabs are. I take Darvon three to four times a day; still have a lot of pain from both afflictions.

It is just beautiful here—temperature is about 80 degrees in daytime—lovely to sit by the pool. As soon as the sun goes down it gets quite cool.

Write again and call Sunday. I love you all so much. It's really so great I can be here with Toni and Warren. I would just give up and come home and die otherwise. I know I am going to get well. It's just a matter of time—or getting that wonderful healing.

Love to all, Mommy

Toni told us the treatments had progressed to radiation of her breasts, a treatment from which she had fled at Jefferson, and 25,000 IU's of vitamin A injected into her each day. She said, "progress is slow but encouraging." Neither of them really told us whether the cancer was progressing or regressing — the subject was being avoided by all.

That day, the day after Thanksgiving, we three sisters were headed to the Reading clothing outlets to find her a colorful long robe with a zipper up the front to make it easy to maneuver. Toni had made her some muu-muus, the fashion of the day, out of colorful cotton fabric. We had begun to get clues about her state of illness from her needs for easy attire, but our faith was still overriding this creeping new knowledge.

We picnicked at Reading's famous red pagoda, feasting on post-Thanksgiving sandwiches of turkey, stuffing, cranberry sauce and lots of mayonnaise on soft white bread. This sandwich — it makes all the suffering through the work of the previous day worth it all. As we ate, we each kept our feelings of hope, love and loss to ourselves, chattering lightly and finding topics to entertain us. To admit aloud to each other the pain we felt would be to pierce our shields of protection over her.

I can still see us holding up our choices across the aisles to each other, searching out the perfect garment to send to her. We chose a soft nylon red, white and blue long color-blocked robe with a zipper. It was the era of patriotic colors in wardrobe choices, and it seemed so spot-on.

We had a solid comfort food dinner at the restaurant in the old West Reading Hotel after our shopping day. Linda broke the festive mood we were working hard to keep up. My junior by four years, she again surpassed me in maturity and commitment, as she had when Mommy had her stroke nine years earlier. She declared over our dinner that she was going to Mexico to bring her home to have Christmas with us. Her announcement was itself a tacit acknowledgement that the illness was advancing and that it was unlikely our mother could return home as she had left every other time, jaunty and ready for another adventure. We had each begun to privately worry that without intervention she might not make it home at all.

SOMEHOW, WE GOT TOGETHER MONEY and figured out how to get Linda on a plane to San Diego and then Borrego Springs, where Aunt Toni would pick her up and help her assess honestly the situation and deal with crossing the border and getting our mother packed up and homeward bound. We really had no idea what condition Mommy was in when Linda left, because the optimism projected across the miles left us in states of both hope and fear. Mommy had just assured us she was going through a physical battle, something approaching an exorcism, where the Devil is forced to release his possession of your body and soul but raises hell on the way out. We held on to hope, aware of her tenacity in tough situations.

Just about the time we were shopping for her robe, I wrote her a passionate letter telling her to hang on and just keep believing, as I did; and she would be healed—for sure.

Sunday, November 26, 1972

Hi, dear Mom, my thoughts have been with you so much these last few days—and all day today. Bob and I spent the day over J.G. and Cheryl's— had dinner with them. You won't be able to tell much from the tape, but Joey is quite a talker now [. . .report on her two toddler grandsons].

Tonight God made some wonderful things happen. I was really chicken to approach Pop on AA, but I had really prayed about it, and I definitely felt God wants to work on Pop through me—and through you, too. And my result was more positive than I had ever hoped. We had a nice talk about what it would mean to him if he stopped drinking, and he responded by admitting he would really like to stop—knows he should; and he would like some time to think about it. I told him that if he needed someone to talk to, I would be his friend, and that I would do all I could to help him stop. He was happy and surprised.

And then I was talking with Mike Z., who needs a parts man at his job at Videon Motors. Result is an appointment for an interview with Danny. I called Danny, and he was really elated; told me "thanks a million, Anne." Praise God for his help! I am so happy tonight.

(Danny was an eighteen-year-old lost soul at this point, out of school, jobless and getting heavily into alcohol himself. He has been a recovering alcoholic and a leader in the A.A. movement for more than twenty-five years today.)

And now to you: Rest in the Lord, trust in the Lord, KNOW that he is with you always. "Fear not, for I am with you always," Jesus tells us. Always, always, always. Just trust him enough, Mom. Give yourself up to him and let him do the worrying! I'm afraid that God just is not satisfied yet with where you are spiritually. I don't believe he will be satisfied till you are in the palm of his loving hand and/or at his feet in surrender. I think he wants

you to have spiritual healing before physical healing. He tells us that our bodily condition is not so important as the condition of our hearts and souls, which he wants us to fill with love and complete surrender. The only condition he makes for all his promises to us is BELIEF! You must trust and believe his promises, Mom. *[I go on at great length giving her careful instructions on what I wholeheartedly believed would save her life.]*

God bless you, my sweet Mom! You'll hear more from us soon and often. We'll do tapes, so you have our voices.

Love, Anne

The greatest thing we have to fear is fear itself. You'll see, it won't be so bad.

(What won't be so bad? It already was as bad as it gets, as Linda would soon discover.)

We did not hear from Linda for days, just as we did not hear from Mommy for long stretches—as if they were on planet Mars. Linda was busy working through the difficulties of getting Mommy out of the swamp of illness and home in time for Christmas. The hospital didn't want to release her, or the money being paid to them. Two weeks in, Linda called to briefly say what flight they'd be on, arriving December 18th. She spared all the details—long distance from California was expensive. So we'd have Mommy home for the holidays!

The things we didn't know until many years later was what happened when Linda got there. Aunt Toni wanted to give her a tour of the area and go to a festival. Mommy was now in Mexico full time and staying in the hospital. With treatments intensifying, it became necessary for her to be an in-patient, the doctors said. Linda hadn't seen her yet and became distressed at Aunt Toni's desire to distract her. "I want to see my mother! That's why I came. I don't want to go to festivals!"

Reluctantly, Aunt Toni lent Linda her VW Bug and instructed her on crossing the border to get to the "hospital." Later Linda knew why Aunt Toni was avoiding the subject.

She arrived to find conditions in the facility worse than imaginable, with Mommy quite sick and undergoing horrific treatments daily. Yet she was expressing an urgent desire to bring Christmas gifts home to everyone — a first. With her history of tinfoil-wrapped oddities, she wanted her gifts to be perfect this time. She had a plan of exactly what she wanted to give each of us, and some specific ideas of where to obtain each gift. She sent Linda into the Tijuana markets with her list. For me she instructed her to get a blue agate pin. She also had her find a small crystal figure of a nun, a reminder of those nun sisters who were lovingly caring for her. It's on my windowsill right now. I know now Linda must have been sure she was carrying out her last wishes.

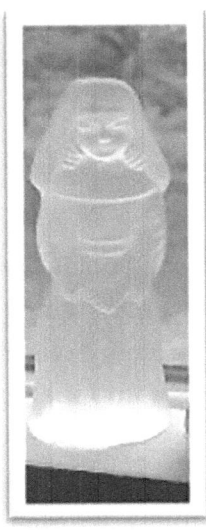

My reminder of the nuns who cared for my mother

Linda told me later that on each of the several days she went out to shop for her gifts she saw a beautiful rainbow. She began to feel sure it was a sign that all would be well, despite what she was confronted with. Our religious faiths had come in direct confrontation with the evidence.

The facility Linda found could not be called a hospital. Because she couldn't talk about it, she never told me how bad it really was until many years later, but she confirmed to herself that her initial goal was accurate: to get her out of there while she was still alive! The injected daily massive doses of Vitamin A had been enough to be toxic. Linda also watched them inflict on her daily doses of high radiation with outdated equipment, and she covered her ears to block out Mommy's screams of pain at the apparent overdose. When she told me, I thought of Ben's rabbits screaming at the moment of their death. I had never heard my mother scream in all the violent nights with Otto. The so-called doctor told her the radiation was needed to save her.

It took Linda three weeks of working to convince Mommy that this was not the right place to heal. As a shy young woman in her early twenties, Linda had to become quite forceful to make it clear to the hospital people that this revenue stream was about to dry up. Linda observed people dying in the rooms all around her. The "administrators" were not forthcoming to the patients on this matter. Linda had also had to emotionally deal with the potential legal issues of getting our mother's body out of a foreign country if she died before it was too late.

I don't remember if we were all there to greet them the day they arrived at Philadelphia International Airport. I really don't remember much except my pain. I saw Linda pushing a wheelchair with someone we didn't know. It was our mother. I rejected the vision before me. I thought of the empty shell of a locust at the end of summer, all that noise gone. Just four months ago she was beautiful, and we were canning damson plum preserves. This didn't line up with my Pentecostal prayers, my fervent belief that everything we had put in place would supersede the illness. Up to that very moment, I KNEW she was not going to die—until I saw the ghost of Dorothy Elizabeth Wise Field Fech—devoid of all that had sparkled and glowed and radiated from her.

She lasted four days. The cancer had spread to her right breast and her lungs. Her chest looked like charred wood, any remnant of what had been flesh now gone. The Mexican hospital had burned her chest to ash. Her lungs rattled with every breath, and she was too weak to walk. Somehow, we granted her wish to have a bath in her beloved claw-foot tub. It was a bath she badly needed after the neglect of the butcher shop in Mexico, but I was so afraid to touch her and worried about whether we'd be able to get her up and back into bed. She was so gone.

We realized she needed real medical care, but now, finally, she didn't want to leave the beautiful bedroom we'd hoped would lure her back home. The poignancy and irony we didn't consider at the moment. We were just scared, struggling with our new reality.

Our mother did agree to go to the real hospital this time, where we assured her they could help her. She was going away once again, in an ambulance this time, with none of us allowed to accompany her.

They did all they could to help her. Her lungs were destroyed by the cancer or the radiation. They tapped the lungs every few hours to remove the fluid and make it easier for her to breathe. Our realization had come home that this was now going to be our last goodbye.

As she visibly faded away from us, she roused herself and chuckled slightly. She wanted to say something, and she was gathering the strength to do so. What? One more joke? One more story? Maybe a last private joke that she was going to share with us. I so wanted to hear her zany humor and know she was with us still.

Just a hint of a wry smile. "I accept Jesus as my Lord and Savior," she said. And then she was gone. She always was a stubborn woman, and she had saved that until she really needed it, saved it for the last.

She never wore the red, white and blue robe we were going to give her for Christmas in just a few days. I wore it until it was in shreds. It became my mourning cloth.

W E SIBLINGS SAW HER THAT one last time at the funeral home for a private goodbye, dressed up in her pretty black velvet gown and Murray Space Shoes. I remember wishing the embalmers knew how funny she was — they wouldn't have made her expression so solemn. She should have been beaming that smile that hinted at something funny she was about to share. But then they never met Sadie Fletcher. They never saw her modeling her newest design of "going away gowns" in the casket when she was almost ravished by her pretend employer. Maybe they should have positioned her hands in mid-air with one of her long blonde hairs between them, poised to place the hair on my stepfather's daily sandwich. If only they'd known her.

The memorial service was awful; cleaning out the messy house was awful; putting up our homeplace for sale, now poor Nancy's current home, was awful. I remember wailing, inconsolable at this loss, unbelieving this time she was gone from us for good. Nancy and Linda moved in with Bob and me, and I remember they gave me a lot of comfort as we held each other together,

Then, seemingly suddenly one day, ten years had gone by; and a lot had happened to change our lives. All of us had married and started families. And yet the loss in our lives was still so deep.

One afternoon Linda was listening on public radio to a program about all the people who never pick up the ashes of their loved ones.

We were some of those people, unable to even think about that little box of ashes being all that was left of her huge presence.

"Hello, my name is Linda Steward, and I am calling to see if my mother's ashes are still there." Her voice broke into kind of a stutter to cover the tears as she got the last words out. She made the call, once again the strong one. She waited, shivering in trepidation, while the ghostly voice at Videon Funeral Home disappeared to check the records.

"Here she is, and she's been waiting patiently for you to call," he cracked, surely one of the few jokes undertakers are permitted. Mommy had been filed away on a shelf in their "archives."

It had to have been a difficult task even after all these years, but Linda took it on, bringing her small daughter Troy with her for strength. Linda walked out of the funeral home with the cheap square cardboard box and gingerly set it on the back seat of her Datsun B-210. At the next traffic light Linda's mind wandered, and she almost ran through the light without stopping. She slammed down hard on the brakes, jamming to a stop.

"Guess whose mother just fell onto the floor?" six-year-old Troy said. With that, they both broke into hysterical laughter, with tears rolling down their faces. Tears of renewed sorrow for Linda and tension relief for Troy.

"**L**et's go, let's go, let's GO!" I clapped my hands with each utterance, like a high school gym teacher dragging her kids onto a muddy field in a March rain for practice.

We weren't on the field, and it wasn't practice. It was a sunny July morning in 1992, and we were again struggling with a reality. We five and our children and spouses were on our annual summer week together at the vintage Victorian house we'd rented for the last ten years or so. It was a Stone Harbor classic with seven bedrooms and numerous other sleeping places and a huge wraparound veranda with rockers, where whoever was the chefette of the day — the men sat, the women cooked — served the rest of us cocktails and appetizers. Each of the women prepared and served a lavish meal for one of the nights. The men fished and crabbed and fixed broken boat engines and went to Fred's bar to catch the Phillies game and drink hearty. The women hit the beach early in the morning with all the kids, toys and lunch. It was a week of partying, cooking, fishing and crabbing, and packing myriad peanut butter and jelly sandwiches for the beach trek.

I was rounding up the crew very early on that morning, all of us hung over and groggy, working on the rationale that maybe if we started at dawn, we could finally do what we'd avoided for those ten years.

Mommy's ashes had accompanied us to the shore each year since Linda had acquired her from Videon's. This might be the year. The night before we had sat around the living room and discussed how we were finally going to say goodbye to Mommy. Plan A was going out on brother Danny and his wife Meg's boat to scatter the ashes, but since we didn't seem to be able to go without some drinks in us, it was rejected as a bad plan. We needed a Plan B.

As we bandied about various ideas, Nancy became sad and upset. "I don't want to let her go yet. Bring her out!" Often at our fun evening gatherings in the double living room—it was quite rare for the adults to go out because we had youngsters, so we had dance parties and a continuation of cocktails in the house—someone would indeed say, "Mommy would love this—bring her out!" And Linda would bring that cardboard box out so Mommy could join the party—in a manner of speaking. This night, another rollicking night, passed again without a solid plan in place. We kept celebrating our own version of The Day of the Dead, partying with our mother to the best of our abilities.

It wasn't just the partying. We were constantly entertaining, too busy with getting a great bunch of people fed and housed and greeting or saying goodbye to the freeloaders. To call them such may be not quite a fair assessment; they usually brought too many peaches, tomatoes, four dozen ears of corn, and a dozen fresh cinnamon buns that disappeared within a minute between twenty to twenty-five human piranhas. The result was we usually had several bushels of Jersey "tomadas" which had to be processed, peaches going bad with fruit flies multiplying like . . . fruit flies. This oversupply of produce resulted in a constant need to make peach cobbler, a Mommy favorite, and dozens of ears of corn that we wished we didn't have to shuck but which MUST BE eaten before they turned to starch.) The time to scatter those ashes had never been quite right for all these reasons.

Now the time had come; this was the year. The next night, more sober in several ways, we again invited Mommy to the party as we tried to warm up to the idea of our final goodbye. Meg, Danny's wife, helped us out.

"I have something for each of us," Meg said, as she produced lovely little colored glass perfume bottles with

A tiny perfume vial holds her ashes

ornate stoppers and 24-karat gold trim.

She held on to the dramatic moment as we gazed at them with questions. "What are these for?" someone asked.

Still in her role, Meg got a long piece of waxed paper from the kitchen. She took the cardboard box from Linda and opened it—for the first time in ten years. We were peering with trepidation, finally, at those grey fragments—what had been Mommy's flesh and bones. It was eerie and sad, and it was hard to speak. Yet we still didn't get Meg's plan.

"The vials are for each of you to be able to keep some of her," she told us.

Gulp! Now we understood. Meg had quietly observed how reluctant Nancy and we each were about the finality of scattering the ashes, so she had found these little treasures at a flea market and bought one for each of us.

I felt the lump in my throat and the tears spring to my eyes. Meg graciously helped each of us make a little funnel out of waxed paper and pour some of the ashes into the tiny bottles.

As we spooned some ashes and bone bits into our chosen vials, we bestowed each of Mommy's traits onto the person who needed them most. J.G. got Love and Patience. Linda, the most serious one, got Humor. I got Forgiveness and Kindness. Nancy got Peace. Danny got Good Judgment and Self-Love.

We found a proper container on the mantel, an antique stoneware crock in which we usually had a big bouquet of blue hydrangeas, the giant shrubs that surrounded the old house. We cleaned it out and solemnly emptied the cardboard box into the vase and gave it to Linda as the protectorate for all these years to have the honor of transporting it.

The next early morning, we all piled into our various vehicles, agreeing to meet on Mommy's Beach, the 21st Street beach in Avalon, still early for any stops at the bar, so no excuses. There were twenty of us, counting spouses and our children. It was calm on the beach, still early, but not quite as early as we had planned. We wanted to get there just at sunrise for our private ceremony, but the early bird beach goers were already setting up their camps, and the joggers were out. We had come this far, so we gave up privacy and got into it.

It was the era of amateur mix tapes on cassettes, which fueled our dance parties — we each prepared and brought a mix tape for one of our party nights. And now, Nancy had prepared her own cassette tape with Mommy's favorite songs on it. She carried our giant boom box to play the music. As we began our ceremony, out poured our mother's music: Willie Nelson songs, Mommy's Zydeco and Cajun music by the Hackberry Ramblers, and one of her favorites by Janis Joplin:

> *"Oh Lord, won't you buy me a Mercedes Benz?*
> *My friends all drive Porsches, I must make amends.*
> *Worked hard all my lifetime, no help from my friends, So Lord, won't you buy me a Mercedes Benz?"*[5]

The words went on, asking the Lord to buy her a round, don't let her down, and they seemed to speak to her disappointment that she had never found a man to support her. Her second husband didn't count any more than the first one. What might these lyrics have meant to Mommy? She never really did get to the promise she made so often to us, that one that started "when the money starts rolling in." The plaintive words to the song seemed like a plea to God to just give her some damned money and fun without having to work so hard for it.

Each us had a chance to say something about Mommy if we wanted to, and then we passed the vase from one person to another, as we waded in the water and sprinkled a little of the ashes, each being careful not to empty her too quickly. We laughed and joked, as she would have, always finding a way to make difficult situations infused with humor. Even so, it was like she had died all over again.

The previous night I had hurriedly written an essay to read as part of our "memorial service." I read my essay, which I called "The Dolphins." We were all crying now, as the youngest child emptied the last of the vase into the ripples at the edge of the beach.

The Dolphins

  She was my mother, but she belonged to the sea. She had given birth to me, but I couldn't catch hold of her for long. Running after life, tasting, experiencing, laughing, she taught us to find joy in the ordinary, and laughter in the disappointing, even in the tragic.

  A champion distance swimmer in her youth, water was her medium. When she read Water Babies to her children, we felt we could almost claim her as our own, as she shared her swirling fascination with the sea and its creatures. Water—she loved to be with it, around it, in it, swimming long, lazy strokes. At the seashore in Avalon she would often rise before the dawn and sneak away to the beach alone, becoming one with the ocean. This was the time, she told us, that she danced with the water fairies, who only appeared as the sun came up and whose rainbow colors could only be glimpsed in those last little waves as they curled and left puffs of rainbow foam on the beach.

  As a child, I had looked intently for hours at the succession of those last little breaking waves, always seeking those water fairies. But I had never seen anything more than tiny coquina clams in the backwash and little sand crabs tumbling helplessly until they could dig in again. Never a fragment of a water fairy.

  And so one morning I sneaked out behind my mother, down to her beloved beach in Avalon. I was hoping to be able to catch her playing with the nymphs, helping them gather the sea foam to make saltwater taffy—so she told us. Hiding behind the lifeboat dory, I watched her lean over and catch a handful of bubbles at water's edge.

As the sun cast its first pink glow on the sea, my child's mind believed I had glimpsed gossamer rainbow wings dancing on the waves, but I couldn't be sure. I wanted to run to her so she could help me find the fairies, but I stayed hidden, spellbound.

At 5:00 a.m. the beach was still empty; she was alone, except for her young voyeur. I watched her shrug off her blue swimsuit and fling it back above the tide line ("buck bathing," she called it and would do it at every chance). She tiptoed into the water, stepping carefully to avoid any fairies underfoot. I watched as she arced her body and dove into the surf, disappearing in a wave as always. I looked for her to emerge, feeling danger in her aloneness and loss at my separation.

But she did not emerge. Instead, a dolphin broke the surface of the water, and soon it was joined by seven other dolphins swimming and playing, rolling in the surf. They were close enough to the beach that I could see their smiles as they disappeared and reappeared.

While their cheerful expressions momentarily removed my fear, I wondered if the ocean had swallowed up my mother. And then I saw her emerge far down the beach as the dolphins disappeared from sight. I stayed hidden, gulping with relief, yet feeling like an interloper to a very private experience.

Later, in the still-early morning we had our breakfast meal. I kept my secret.

She's been gone for many years, but I can always find her at the beach when the dolphins play, at sunrise.

The vase was empty. She was finally and completely gone. Astonished, we watched a dolphin break the surface about ten yards out from the shallows we stood in. We were smiling through our tears as the sadness dissipated.

And so we finally gave her up to the sea, where she perhaps always belonged.

---

5 *Mercedes Benz lyrics © Universal Music Publishing Group*

About the Author

BECOMING A BUSINESS OWNER IN her early twenties qualified Anne Pounds for what she calls ". . . a different version of an MFA: a self-awarded doctorate in people quirks," having been schooled by her mother to dig deep until she finds that fascinating something in every living soul.

After years of keeping journals and notes while she pursued a career in building a sales organization, marketing and business writing, the stories are bubbling over the pot into an umami sauce that hits all the flavor notes — sometimes sweet, savory, meaty, and sometimes sour, salty, or occasionally bitter.

Anne tells more stories from her years of sailing with her husband/business partner Bob in her forthcoming book, ORDINARY SAILORS.

She has also authored a book set in Kennett Square and Unionville, PA, to be published later this year about a multi-cultural community where rich and poor are juxtaposed and interdependent. It is a story of the difficulties of an unplanned love, the harrowing lives of immigrants, climate crisis, and how one overshadowed woman found her strength and self-reliance while handling others' problems. And yes, there's some stolen money.

Anne lives in Chadds Ford, PA, with her husband and son, and all her siblings as close neighbors. In addition to writing, Anne enjoys birding, gardening, cooking and entertaining, and watercolor painting. And she continues to enjoy being a businesswoman!

www.ingramcontent.com/pod-product-compliance
Lightning Source LLC
Chambersburg PA
CBHW020429130626
46549CB00001B/48